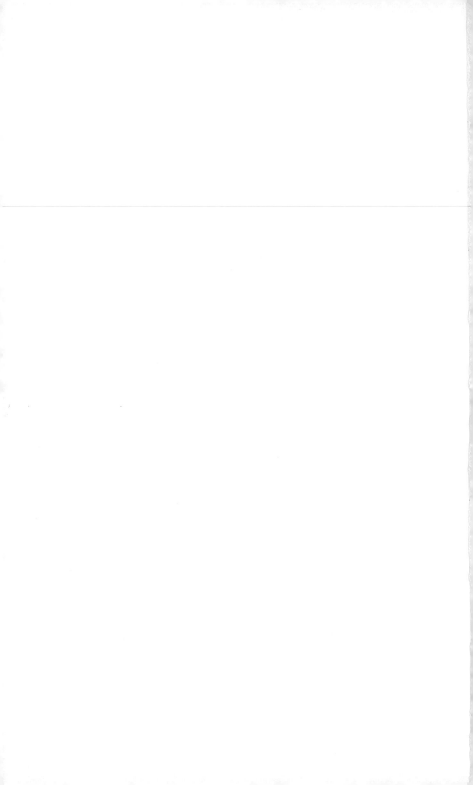

I Never Knew That
ABOUT
IRELAND

Christopher Winn

I Never Knew That
ABOUT
IRELAND

ILLUSTRATIONS BY
Mai Osawa

Thomas Dunne Books
St. Martin's Press ❧ New York

THOMAS DUNNE BOOKS.
An imprint of St. Martin's Press.

www.thomasdunnebooks.com
www.stmartins.com

Library of Congress Cataloging-in-Publication Data

Winn, Chris, 1958–
    I never knew that about Ireland / Christopher Winn ; illustrations by Mai
Osawa—1st U.S. ed.
        p. cm.
    ISBN 978-0-312-36880-7 (hardcover)
    1. Ireland—Description and travel. 2. Northern Ireland—Description and
travel. 3. Ireland—History. 4. Northern Ireland—History. I. Title.
DA978.2 .W56 2007
941.5—dc22

                                                                      2006100670

ISBN 978-1-250-06524-7 (Barnes and Noble Edition)

St. Martin's Press books may be purchased for educational, business, or pro-
motional use. For information on bulk purchases, please contact the Macmillan
Corporate and Premium Sales Department at 1-800-221-7945, extension 5442, or
write to specialmarkets@macmillan.com.

First published in Great Britain by Ebury Publishing, a division of Random House

First Barnes and Noble Edition: January 2015

10 9 8 7 6 5 4 3 2 1

For Eben and Themy, whose generosity
and infectious love of Ireland were so inspiring

Contents

Tearaght Island Lighthouse

Preface

Ireland is like nowhere else. Ireland is magnificent, mischievous, moody and misunderstood. It is Europe's Farthest West, the edge of the known world, a step too far for the Romans, a land wreathed in mist and mystery. In the Dark Ages when Europe was stumbling around in ignorance, Ireland burned bright as a centre of learning and civilisation. From Ireland came forth saints and scholars to spread their wisdom and their knowledge. Celts and Kings, Druids and Wise Men have left their memories carved in stone, on crosses and decorated arches – treasures that in any other land would be scrubbed clean of history, fenced off, subsumed by car parks and gift shops. In Ireland they are just there, left as they were meant to be, majestic, haunting, rooted in their landscape.

Ireland has a landscape to rival anywhere, from Europe's highest cliffs and wildest shores to the languid, lacustrine plains of the heartlands. The beauty of her scenery and the power of her legends has produced some of the world's great literature, poetry and music. And all is touched by a turbulent history, with a tinge of melancholy, a frisson of menace, an undercurrent of defiance.

But Ireland is also a modern country, forward-looking, energetic, alive with ideas and inspiration, drawing upon a legacy of innovation and inventiveness second to none. It is this combination that makes Ireland so intriguing, so alluring and so addictive.

This book tries to reflect that splendid, subtle complexity with tales of old and new, of tradition and discovery, nature and science, characters, philosophers, rogues and romantics. Like Ireland itself, there is something here for everyone.

One warning. In Ireland, nothing is straightforward. Every name has two or three different spellings and myriad pronunciations. Every story has several endings and every legend a different setting. Where I have been forced to choose I have decided simply on the option that I, personally, like the best. If this offends I can only apologise and blame Ireland – frustrating, friendly, infuriating, unforgettable and forever fascinating, Ireland.

ULSTER

CONNACHT

Donegal

Derry

Antrim

Tyrone

Belfast

Fermanagh

Armagh

Down

Monaghan

Sligo

Leitrim

Cavan

Louth

Mayo

Roscommon

Longford

Meath

Westmeath

Galway

Offaly

Dublin

Kildare

Laois

Wicklow

Clare

Carlow

LEINSTER

Limerick

Tipperary

Kilkenny

Wexford

Kerry

Waterford

Cork

MUNSTER

The Provinces and Counties
of
IRELAND

I *Never Knew That About Ireland* is divided into the four ancient
provinces or kingdoms of CONNACHT, LEINSTER, MUNSTER
and ULSTER, and the counties within them. The Irish rejoice in
both their provinces and their counties. The provinces are the
backdrop to history and legend, to battles between Kings and
High Kings, warriors and saints, new ideas and new religions.

The name Connacht is derived from *Connachta* – the
dominant tribal grouping in the north and west of the island
during the early centuries AD. Leinster means land of the
Laighin, one of the earliest Celtic tribes to arrive in Ireland, who
settled in the south and east. The suffix '*ster*' is Norman French
for 'land'. Hence Munster comes from the land of *Mumhain*, a
derivation of the pre-Christian goddess Muma, and Ulster is the
land of *Ulaidh*.

There were once five provinces, the fifth province being
Meath, meaning *midh* or 'middle', which consisted of the
modern counties of Meath and Westmeath with part of Offaly.
COUNTY OFFALY was known for a while as KING'S COUNTY in
honour of King Philip of Spain who was married to Queen
Mary of England – whose own QUEEN'S COUNTY is now
COUNTY LAOIS (or LEIX).

The counties are where people come from, where they
belong, where their loyalties and identities lie. Each is distinctive, with its own character, architecture and landscape. They all
have their own stories to tell.

Connacht

COUNTY GALWAY

COUNTY TOWN: GALWAY

Gaillimh – 'stony river'

Tuam Protestant Cathedral – rebuilt in 1878 and incorporating the widest Romanesque arch in Ireland (12th-century)

Galway City

Well Executed

GALWAY, capital of County Galway and THE BIGGEST CITY IN CONNACHT, is a seaport and tourist resort with a salty, maritime tang.

GALWAY RACES, held in July, are a great Irish occasion, and in September Galway hosts one of Ireland's premier oyster festivals. The city has a Spanish feel to it, with many of the older houses built around an inner courtyard, Spanish style – a reminder of the days when the city's chief trading partner was Spain.

LYNCH'S CASTLE, at the junction of Shop Street and Upper Abbeygate, is an interesting early 16th-century tower house, now occupied by a bank, and is THE OLDEST BUILDING IN EVERYDAY COMMERCIAL USE IN IRELAND.

In Market Street, beside the cathedral of St Nicholas, is LYNCH'S WINDOW, which commemorates a legend that has worked its way into the English language. In 1493, the Mayor of Galway, JAMES LYNCH FITZSTEPHEN, was compelled to execute his own son, WALTER, on this very spot. Walter's sweetheart had been mischievously flirting with a handsome Spaniard, who was staying in the Mayor's house as an honoured guest, and young Walter was driven by jealousy to run the fellow through. The Mayor had no choice but to condemn his son to death and, since no one would come forward to perform the execution, Walter's father had to do it himself. This story is thought by many to have given rise to the expression 'LYNCH LAW' or 'LYNCHING', meaning *law administered by a private person, resulting in summary execution*. It has also, over time, come to mean *mob law*.

Whilst on the subject of execution, the man who beheaded KING CHARLES I is thought to have been a Galway man, known only as GUNNING. It was proving difficult to find an Englishman prepared to execute the English King, so Oliver Cromwell sent out into Scotland, Ireland and Wales for volunteers. Two men from Galway, Gunning and DEAN, came forward, and on 30 January 1649, Gunning found himself standing on the scaffolding outside the Banqueting House at Whitehall in London, axe in hand and wearing a black mask so as to

Lynch's Window

remain unrecognisable. He stood poised while Charles uttered his last words, 'I GO FROM A CORRUPTIBLE TO AN INCORRUPTIBLE CROWN . . .', then the King knelt down and placed his head upon the block. Gunning struck and an awful groan went up from the crowd.

On his return to Ireland, a grateful Parliament granted Gunning property in the centre of Galway, where the appropriately named KING'S HEAD pub now stands in the High Street. There is a plaque noting the story on a wall in the bar.

Another possible candidate for the King's executioner was the Mayor of Galway, COLONEL PETER STUBBERS, one of Cromwell's generals. Whoever it was that wielded that axe, he came from Galway.

Galway's CATHEDRAL OF ST NICHOLAS is one of the largest medieval cathedrals in Ireland, and possesses an unusual triple nave and three-gabled west end. CHRISTOPHER COLUMBUS worshipped here in 1492

before sailing west to discover America.

Close to the cathedral is IRELAND'S SMALLEST MUSEUM, the NORA BARNACLE HOUSE MUSEUM. This was the home of writer JAMES JOYCE's wife and inspiration, NORA BARNACLE, and contains exhibits, letters and photographs of their life together.

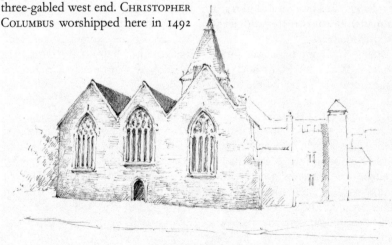

Cathedral of St Nicholas

Ballynahinch Castle

Humanity Dick

Fighting for the Animals

CONNEMARA is wild and moody country in western Galway and one of the most beautiful parts of Ireland. The chief town is CLIFDEN, founded in 1812 by a local landowner in an attempt to tame the wilderness and provide work.

Most of Connemara was once owned by RICHARD MARTIN (1754–1834), whose family held some of the biggest estates in all Ireland. His home, the 18th-century BALLYNAHINCH CASTLE, stands above a small lough some 8 miles (13 km) to the east. As a young man Martin had a reputation as something of a hothead, earning the nickname of 'HAIRTRIGGER DICK'. Most of his duels were fought over the maltreatment of animals – in 1783 he was seriously wounded in a pistol duel

with 'FIGHTING FITZGERALD', a Mayo landlord who had shot dead a dog. Martin believed that all animals had feelings and awareness and that abusing them was akin to abusing humans so, in 1822, he put through Parliament THE WORLD'S FIRST ANIMAL RIGHTS BILL. Two years later he founded the SOCIETY FOR THE PREVENTION OF CRUELTY TO ANIMALS, which became the RSPCA. In recognition of this he was renamed 'HUMANITY DICK'. He died broke, but much admired, in France.

A later owner of Ballynahinch Castle, from 1927 to 1933, was HH THE MAHARAJAH JAM SAHIB OF NAWANAGAR (1872–1933), known as 'RANJI'. One of the world's most brilliant batsmen, he played in fifteen Test Matches for England. Later in life he did much good work for the LEAGUE OF NATIONS.

Derrigimlagh Bog

Pioneering Stuff

A little to the south of Clifden, off the coast road and down a rutted lane that peters out into bleak, brown DERRIGIMLAGH BOG, there are some concrete blocks and a length of rusty chain – the sparse remains of THE WORLD'S FIRST PERMANENT TRANS-ATLANTIC RADIO STATION. Here, on the shores of a small lough, almost as far west as it is possible to go in Europe, the radio pioneer GUGLIELMO MARCONI built a huge complex to house capacitors, receivers and accommodation for 150 staff. Having proved that radio waves could travel beyond the horizon by sending a message to Newfoundland from Poldhu in Cornwall, Marconi moved here to Galway, where there was no land mass to interfere with the signals from his directional aerials. The station opened in 1907, and for nine years forwarded messages across the Atlantic from London and Dublin. It must have been an extraordinary

place, with sparks and flashes like lightning bolts, hums and crackles that could be seen and heard for miles across the barren landscape.

There are few clues left to indicate that this remote bogland was once at the forefront of technology – the station was burned down in the Troubles and the introduction of new, more powerful transmitters meant that radio stations did not need to be located so far west. Marconi moved back to England, although it was apposite that his first proper radio station should have been established in Ireland – his mother was Irish, ANNE JAMESON of the celebrated whiskey family.

Close to the remains of the Marconi radio station, a white, beehive-shaped cairn marks the spot where, at 8.40 am on 15 June 1919, JOHN ALCOCK and ARTHUR WHITTEN BROWN nose-dived into DERRIGIMLAGH BOG after completing THE FIRST NON-STOP FLIGHT ACROSS THE ATLANTIC. They had set off the previous evening from ST

Alcock and Brown's Vickers Vimy biplane

JOHN'S in NEWFOUNDLAND in a converted VICKERS VIMY bomber biplane, powered by twin Rolls-Royce engines and with a cruising speed of 90 mph, and completed the 1,900-mile (3,000-km) journey in 16 hours and 12 minutes.

The flight had been hazardous – their transmitter froze not long after take-off, and for long periods they had to fly at no more than 300 FEET (90 m) above the ocean to keep ice from forming. Several times Brown had to climb out on to the wings to chip the ice away. On spotting the aerials of the Marconi radio station, they came in to land, in somewhat spectacular style, on what they thought was firm ground but turned out to be soft bog. It was all worth it – they had joined the immortals, won £10,000 in prize money from the *Daily Mail* and were both knighted. They had also brought with them a mailbag containing letters for delivery in England – THE FIRST TRANSATLANTIC AIRMAIL. Alcock

tragically died in an air crash later that year while Brown lived until 1948. Their airplane is housed in the Science Museum in London.

As you gaze across this empty, sea-swept bog today it seems inconceivable that two of the most influential events of the 20th century occurred right here, putting Derrigimlagh Bog at the vanguard of the modern world.

Coole

'our shadows rove the garden's gravels still'
W.B. YEATS

A couple of miles north of Gort, there is a tumbledown stone gateway leading to a dark avenue that winds out of sight through deep woods. As you enter, the trees seem to close in and muffle out the rest of the world, time stops and a drowsiness descends. A shaft of light appears up ahead, you step through a hidden gap

Coole Park

Autograph tree

in the pink stone wall and, suddenly, sunlight blazes and there, laid out before you, is a secret garden paradise of spreading green lawns, shady bowers, riotous flowerbeds and noble trees. To one side is a glorious copper beech that speaks of romance, and if you fight your way under its branches to the trunk, you will see why. Carved into the bark are the initials of some of Ireland's greatest writers, artists and thinkers, a living memorial to the days when WILLIAM BUTLER YEATS, GEORGE BERNARD SHAW, JOHN MILLINGTON SYNGE and SEAN O'CASEY all wandered along these walkways and dreamed of wit, great thoughts and poetry. You can feel their spirit still.

This is the magical walled garden of COOLE PARK, beloved home of AUGUSTA, LADY GREGORY (1852–1932) from 1880 until her death. She was a friend of many of the great figures of the Irish literary revival and they were often drawn here to stay. Lady Gregory recalls George Bernard Shaw singing and playing the piano and the poet JOHN MASEFIELD, shy and in awe of Yeats, giving impromptu readings at tea. Along with Yeats, EDWARD MARTYN and GEORGE MOORE (*see* Mayo, page 20), in 1899 she founded the Irish Literary Theatre, which in 1904 became Dublin's ABBEY THEATRE.

The house was pulled down in 1941, and all that is left are the foundations roofed with grass, a fate predicted by Yeats:

> *When all those rooms and passages are gone,*
> *When nettles wave upon a shapeless mound*
> *And saplings root among the broken stone . . .*

Amongst those who have initialled the autograph tree are:

GEORGE BERNARD SHAW *Playwright*
JOHN MASEFIELD *Poet*
AUGUSTUS JOHN *Painter*
DOUGLAS HYDE *Playwright and First President of Ireland*
WILLIAM BUTLER YEATS *Poet*
SEAN O'CASEY *Playwright*
JOHN MILLINGTON SYNGE *Playwright*
GEORGE RUSSELL (Æ) *Writer*
GEORGE MOORE *Writer*

Edward Martyn (1859–1923) lived at nearby Tullira Castle and was a descendant of Richard 'Humanity Dick' Martin (see Ballynahinch Castle). In 1905, along with Arthur Griffith, he co-founded Sinn Fein, a political party dedicated to the creation of a united republican Ireland, and became its first president. Sinn Fein means 'we ourselves'.

Thoor Ballylee

A Poet's Retreat

William Butler Yeats so loved Coole that, in 1916, he bought himself a retreat just down the road – Thoor Ballylee a remote 16th-century riverside tower where 'under my window ledge the waters race'. He would bring his family here whenever they could escape from

Dublin, and his 1928 collection *The Tower* contains a number of poems inspired by Thoor Ballylee.

On a wall of the tower are the words:

I, the poet William Butler Yeats,
With old mill boards and sea green slates,
And smithy work from the Gort forge,
Restored this tower for my wife George;
And may these characters remain
When all is ruin once again.

Thoor Ballylee did indeed become a ruin again after Yeats died, but it has since been restored and opened as a museum. Today you can climb the spiral staircase and gaze from the battlements at the hilly woodland views that so moved the great poet.

Clonfert

Romanesque Glory

Hidden away down quiet country lanes in eastern Galway, close to the Shannon and the Grand Canal, is the tiny clutch of buildings that is Clonfert. Clonfert means 'Meadow of the Grave', and even in this country of so many unexpected treasures, the glorious surprise of St Brendan's Cathedral, rising out of that meadow, still has the power to astonish and awe. St Brendan, who many people believe discovered America over 900 years before Columbus, was buried here in AD 578, outside what is now the great west door and the supreme

SWANSONG OF NATIVE IRISH ROMAN-ESQUE ARCHITECTURE. It is a huge, delicately carved portal that dates from 1166 (just three years before the Anglo-Norman invasion), unmatched in Ireland if not the whole of Europe, six arches deep and crowned with a tall triangular tympanum.

The present cathedral, which incorporates this wonderful door-way, dates from the 13th and 14th centuries and is built on the site of a monastery founded by St Brendan in AD 558. A beautifully carved mermaid decorates the chancel arch inside – no doubt in tribute to the maritime heritage of the cathedral's founder.

St Brendan was born in Co. Kerry around AD 483. He became known as THE NAVIGATOR as a result of his many sea voyages around the British Isles. He sailed up and down the west coast of Ireland, visited Iona in Scotland and went to St Malo on the Brittany coast. Wrapped in the mists of legend is his seven-year voyage in search of the fabled LAND OF PROMISE beyond the western horizon. According to *Navigatio Sancti Brendani*, a medieval manuscript written in about 1050, St Brendan and several companions, guided by his Celtic cross, sailed as far as Iceland, Greenland and even America. They celebrated Easter on the back of a whale, fought off a huge sea horse, met Judas Iscariot clinging on to a rock, and experienced many other adventures on the way.

Is it possible that St Brendan could have reached America? In 1977 the explorer TIM SEVERIN built a replica of the type of boat that St Brendan would have used, made from ash wood and ox-hides, and succeeded in making the journey safely from Galway to Newfoundland . . .

St Brendan has the honour of having an Irish cream liqueur named after him, produced in Co. Derry, Ulster.

Buried in woods to the north of the cathedral is an avenue of ancient yew trees, over 1,000 years old, laid out in a cruciform shape. One arm of the walk leads to the BISHOP'S PALACE, a long mid-17th-century house that was once the Irish home of SIR OSWALD MOSLEY Bt. (1896–1980), founder of the BRITISH UNION OF FASCISTS. Mosley's second wife was DIANA, one of the famed

MITFORD SISTERS, who had previously been married to BRYAN GUINNESS, of the Irish brewing dynasty.

The house was mysteriously burned down in 1954 and is now a poignant, ivy-covered ruin that somehow seems to complement the mystic aura of this ancient and bewitching place.

Well, I never knew this
ABOUT
COUNTY GALWAY

LOUGH CORRIB IS THE SECOND LARGEST LAKE IN IRELAND OR BRITAIN, after Lough Neagh (*see* Ulster, page 209).

On INCHAGOILL island in LOUGH CORRIB, beside the little church of TEMPLEPATRICK, stands a stone bearing THE OLDEST LATIN INSCRIPTION IN ALL IRELAND: *Lie Luguaedon Macci Meneuh* (Stone of Luguaedon, son of Meneuh). It dates back to AD 500 and is probably translated from an earlier Ogham stone inscription.

Incorporated into the 19th-century Protestant cathedral in TUAM are the remnants of a 12th-century barrel-vaulted chancel from a previous church, which includes THE WIDEST ROMANESQUE ARCH IN IRELAND.

ANNA LYNCH, grandmother of South American revolutionary CHE GUEVARA (1928–67), was born in Co. Galway. Her son, ERNESTO GUEVARA LYNCH, Che's father, said, in 1969: 'The first thing to note is that in my son's veins flowed the blood of Irish rebels.'

The ARAN ISLANDS, lying across the mouth of Galway Bay, are famed across the world for the pure white, distinctively patterned ARAN SWEATERS which have been made here for generations. The women of the islands still wear traditional red petticoats, thought to be THE ONLY GENUINE NATIONAL PEASANT COSTUME IN WESTERN EUROPE. The playwright JOHN MILLINGTON SYNGE set his play *Riders to the Sea* (1907) on the Aran island of INISHMAAN, and in 1934 the American director ROBERT FLAHERTY filmed *Man of Aran* here, using island folk as the cast.

On a lonely, windswept peninsula jutting out into Galway Bay, at ORANMORE, stands one of Ireland's most romantic ruins, ARDFRY HOUSE. Built around 1770 on the site of a castle, the house has had a colourful history. In 1784, during the wedding of the 1ST LORD WALLSCOURT to a daughter of the EARL OF LOUTH, there was uproar when the Earl stepped into a particularly fruity offering left in the drawing room by a

Ardfry House

dog belonging to one of the guests, who had insisted on feeding the animal 'ripe peaches and apricots'. The Earl stormed around the house in a rage, leaving ruination and filth wherever he trod, much to the consternation of the unfortunate wedding party. The 3RD LORD WALLSCOURT was a man of enormous strength and temper who found it restful to walk about the house in the nude. His wife, the celebrated beauty BESSIE LOCK, insisted that he wore a cowbell somewhere about his person in order to warn the maids of his approach! Ardfry House was used as an atmospheric location in the 1973 JOHN HUSTON film *The Mackintosh Man*, starring PAUL NEWMAN. The house is presently undergoing renovation.

Mary Anne Phelan, mother of actor MARTIN SHEEN who plays President 'Jed' Bartlett in the American TV series *The West Wing*, was a native of Co. Galway.

COUNTY LEITRIM

COUNTY TOWN: CARRICK-ON-SHANNON

Liath Druim – 'grey ridge'

Parke's Castle – restored 17th-century fortified manor house beside Lough Gill

Dromahair

Ireland's Helen . . .

DROMAHAIR is a pretty, unassuming village on the River Bonet, east of Lough Gill. The 17th-century OLD HALL on the river bank occupies the site of BREFFNI CASTLE, ancient home of the O'ROURKES. Here, 850 years ago, there took place an incident that changed the history of Ireland for ever – a legendary tale of love and betrayal that set in train a series of events that would prove as dire for Ireland as the abduction of Helen was for Troy.

In 1152, TIERNAN O'ROURKE, Prince of Breffni, set out from Breffni Castle to make a pilgrimage to the holy island of St Patrick in Lough Derg. He left behind his beautiful young wife DEVORGILLA, safe, as he thought, within the castle walls. But when he returned she was gone, along with all her cattle and furniture, taken by a band of horsemen. Did she go willingly or was she abducted?

From the descriptions given by his terrified servants, Tiernan recognised the leader of the horsemen as his arch-enemy DIARMAIT MACMURROUGH, King of Leinster. Tiernan went straight to the High King, TURLOUGH O'CONOR, and demanded revenge.

Together, they raised an army and attacked MacMurrough's capital at FERNS and recovered Devorgilla. MacMurrough fled to England and sought help from the English King HENRY II, pleading for a force of armed men to assist him in recovering his kingdom. This was just the excuse the English King had been looking for to intervene in Ireland. In 1170, Henry allowed the EARL OF PEMBROKE, RICHARD DE CLARE (known as STRONGBOW), to go to Ireland with an army to fight for MacMurrough, in return for Mac-Murrough's promise to acknowledge Henry as his overlord. This was the early stirring of the Norman invasion of Ireland that was to have such devastating consequences for all.

Was Devorgilla a knowing player in the tumultuous politics of Ireland? Was she an unfaithful temptress? Or just a helpless victim? No one knows.

The Loughs of Leitrim

Lough Melvin
Old Trouts

Unchanged, unpolluted and undisturbed since the last Ice Age, Lough Melvin is home to three kinds of rare brown trout that do not cross-breed and have evolved there naturally – the *ferox*, the *sonaghen* and the *gillaroo* – the latter two UNIQUE TO LOUGH MELVIN.

On a small wooded island in the middle of the lough are the ruins of ROSSCLOGHER CASTLE, which

features in the adventures of a Spanish Armada captain, FRANCISCO DE CUELLAR. His ship, like so many others, was wrecked on the coast of Sligo in 1588. Although suffering from a broken leg, De Cuellar managed to make his way inland to find refuge with the MACCLANCYS of Rossclogher. He remained there for three months, successfully defending the castle against the Lord Deputy, SIR WILLIAM FITZWILLIAM, who was attempting to round up and dispose of all the shipwrecked Spaniards he could find. De Cuellar eventually made it back to Spain, where he published his story.

Glencar Lough
'The cataract that smokes upon the mountainside.'
W.B. YEATS

At the eastern end of this beautiful small lough, compared favourably by some to the Lakes of Killarney, are

the spectacular GLENCAR WATER-FALLS, the greatest of which tumbles 50 feet (15 m) into a deep brown pool to flow into the lough. This was one of William Butler Yeats's favourite spots, and can be reached by a path from the road.

Lough Allen
The Buckle of Leitrim

Leitrim's largest lough, LOUGH ALLEN covers the whole centre of Leitrim, from north to south, where the county narrows into a waist. It is the first of the great loughs on the River Shannon and is the point where the youthful stream turns into a mature river. IRELAND'S BIGGEST IRON ORE DEPOSITS were found to the east of Lough Allen, and the remains of some 19th-century blast furnaces can be found at CREEVYLEA.

CREEVYLEA ABBEY, a Franciscan friary founded in 1508, was the LAST FRIARY TO BE BUILT IN IRELAND BEFORE THE DISSOLUTION OF THE MONASTERIES BY HENRY VIII.

Well, I never knew this
ABOUT
COUNTY LEITRIM

County Leitrim has THE SHORTEST COASTLINE OF ANY MARITIME IRISH COUNTY, stretching just 2½ miles (4 km) between the counties of Donegal and Sligo, on Donegal Bay.

The GREAT DOON OF DRUMSNA runs for 5 miles (8 km) across Co. Leitrim from near CARRICK ON SHANNON to the river at DRUMSNA village. It is thought to be part of the BLACK PIGS DYKE, a series of defensive ditches and embankments built in the 1ST CENTURY BC to protect the lands and livestock of ULSTER from the marauding tribes of the southern kingdoms. It is called Black Pigs Dyke from the legend that it was dug out by a great black boar using its tusks. The dyke appears sporadically in many border counties, sometimes up to 9 ft (2.75 m) high, and follows uncannily close to the route of the modern boundary between Northern Ireland and the Republic. It is also said that the dyke marks the boundary of dialects where the harder northern accent softens into the mellower Irish brogue.

The family of legendary Hollywood tough guy JAMES CAGNEY (1899–1986) came from Co. Leitrim. Cagney's father, James Francis Cagney, was descended from the Leitrim family of O'Caignes, and Cagney's maternal grandmother was born in Co. Leitrim. James Cagney never actually said '*You dirty rat . . .*' in any of his films.

The Costello Memorial Chapel in Bridge Street, Carrick on Shannon, is the second-smallest chapel in the world. Built in 1877 as a resting place for the remains of businessman Edward Costello and his wife, the chapel measures just 16 ft (5 m) by 12 ft (3.6 m).

Surgeon-Major Thomas Heazle Parke (1857–93), the first Irishman to cross Africa, and co-discoverer, with Henry Morton Stanley, of the Mountains of the Moon (Ruwenzori), was a native of Carrick-on-Shannon.

Thomas and Rose McGoohan, the parents of actor Patrick McGoohan, known to television audiences as Danger Man and The Prisoner, emigrated to America from the family farm in Co. Leitrim in the 1920s.

County Leitrim can boast Ireland's earliest salmon river – 17 times in the past 20 years the first salmon caught by rod has been taken from the River Drowes at Tullaghan near Lough Melvin.

COUNTY MAYO

Mhaigh Eo – 'plain of the yew tree'

Ashford Castle – the first castle in Ireland to appear in Technicolor film

Croagh Patrick

Holy Mountain

CROAGH PATRICK, also known as THE REEK, is IRELAND'S HOLY MOUNTAIN. It is 2,510 ft (765 m) high and its distinctive conical shape dominates the coastline south of Clew Bay. The summit is in fact a plateau, where there is a small dry-stone oratory dating back to the 5th or 6th century. The views are breathtaking and it is easy to see why this place has been a place of worship since before Christianity.

In AD 441, Ireland's patron ST PATRICK climbed to the top of the mountain and fasted there for the 40 days of Lent. During this time he is said to have driven all the snakes and poisonous things of Ireland into the sea – and it is undeniably true that there are no snakes in Ireland to this day. (No moles, polecats or weasels either.)

A relic of this episode can be seen in the National Museum of Ireland in Dublin – THE BLACK BELL OF

ST PATRICK. The saint rang his bell and hurled it over the precipice, from where it was returned to him by angels – and each time he flung it *'thousands of toads, adders and noisome things went down, tumbling neck and heels one after the other . . .'* (Thomas Otway). The bell was originally white but was burned and blackened by the fiery encounter and is THE OLDEST KNOWN EXAMPLE OF IRISH METAL WORK (*c.*406).

Every year, before dawn on Reek Sunday, the last Sunday in July, thousands of pilgrims, many of them barefoot, make the two-hour climb to the top of Croagh Patrick to receive Communion. In hardier times some pilgrims would make the journey on their hands and knees. Before the 12th century, people would come here in Lent, like St Patrick, but in 1113 there was a terrible storm and a large number of pilgrims were killed by lightning on the mountaintop. The time of pilgrimage was then changed to the more benign summer months.

Moore Hall

A House of History

On a tiny peninsula by the eastern shore of beautiful Lough Carra, 10 miles (16 km) south of Castlebar, stands all that is left of MOORE HALL, ancestral home of the writer and friend of Yeats, GEORGE MOORE (1852–1933). Although the house is now a burnt-out ruin the place is alive with history and atmosphere.

Moore Hall was built in 1795 by wine merchant George Moore, a Catholic who had amassed a fortune

Moore Hall

in trade with Spain. In 1798, his son John was made PRESIDENT OF THE REPUBLIC OF CONNACHT by GENERAL HUMBERT, who had landed at KILLALA BAY with a force of French soldiers to help the rebellion of the UNITED IRISHMEN. Moore held the position for only one week before being arrested by the English and sentenced to transportation, but he died at Waterford en route to New Geneva. In 1961 John Moore's body was exhumed and brought back to be buried at Castlebar with full honours, due to his new-found recognition as IRELAND'S FIRST PRESIDENT.

A later George Moore won the Chester Gold Cup with his horse *Coranna* and was able to use the winnings to help alleviate suffering during the Great Famine. No one from the Moore estate was evicted or died during the Famine.

The writer George Moore was a friend of W.B. Yeats and John Millington Synge and played an important role in founding the Abbey Theatre. His initials are on the autograph tree at Coole (*see* Co. Galway, page 5). In his lifetime his novels were bestsellers, considered by many to be scandalous – his first novel, *A Modern Lover*, published in 1883, was widely banned. Moore Hall and the surrounding area feature strongly in many of his books.

When George Moore died in 1933 he was buried on an island in Lough Carra. His ashes were ferried across the lake in a boat rowed by his friend, poet, politician and wit OLIVER ST JOHN GOGARTY, whose name is commemorated in one of Dublin's most popular pubs and who was the inspiration for BUCK MULLIGAN in James Joyce's novel *Ulysses*. The strenuous task forced Gogarty to strip off his silk hat and frock-coat. 'I presume you will retain your braces,' remarked Moore's sister, who was sitting primly in the stern, clasping the urn.

Moore Hall was torched in the Troubles in 1923, but the grounds are open to the public. RENVYLE, Gogarty's house at Letterfrack in Co. Galway, was also burned down in 1923, but was rebuilt and is now a hotel.

The Two Graces

The Pirate Queen and the Princess

In the 16th century, lovely CLARE ISLAND, sitting in a commanding position at the mouth of Clew Bay, was the stronghold of the dashing pirate queen GRACE O'MALLEY. Grace was born into a seafaring family in 1530 and, from a very young age, was determined to sail with her father on his adventures. At first her father refused to allow it, saying that the sea was no place for a girl, so Grace dressed herself in boy's clothing and cut off all her hair, forcing him to relent. This is how she acquired her nickname GRANUAILE – GRACE THE BALD.

At the age of 16 she married a local chieftain, DONAL O'FLAHERTY, and she bore him three children. This did not quell her buccaneering spirit, and when Donal was banned from trading in Galway because of his reputation as a troublemaker, Grace sailed out into Clew Bay and intercepted merchant ships heading for port, either raiding them or negotiating safe passage with them. Her bravery and sailing skills soon ensured that she controlled the shipping along most of the west coast of Ireland, and she became very rich. She was said to keep all her ships tied up to a hawser that was passed through a hole in the castle wall and tied to her bedpost.

There are examples of castles owned by Grace O'Malley all over Co. Mayo. One was a castle on an island in LOUGH CORRIB, captured from the JOYCES by her husband Donal and named THE COCK'S CASTLE, in tribute to his nickname, Donal the Cock, given to him because of his courage in battle. When Donal was later killed, the Joyces tried to recapture the castle, but Grace defended it so stoutly they were forced to withdraw. From that time on it became known as THE HEN'S CASTLE.

Favourite of Grace's castles was ROCKFLEET, superbly sited on the northern shore of Clew Bay. This was the property of her second husband, RICHARD BURKE, whom she married in 1566. They made an agreement that either party could terminate the marriage after one year, and when the year was up, Grace barricaded herself into Rockfleet, slammed the door in Burke's face and

Rockfleet Castle

sent him packing, making the castle her own.

In 1584, SIR RICHARD BINGHAM became Governor of Connacht and confiscated all Grace's lands and possessions, determined to bring her to heel. Grace went to England to petition QUEEN ELIZABETH I, offering to attack the Queen's enemies off the coast of Ireland in return for getting her lands back. She was THE ONLY GAELIC WOMAN EVER TO BE RECEIVED AT COURT and she must have impressed Elizabeth because the Queen agreed to all her demands – 'the wild grandeur of her mien erect and high, before the English Queen she dauntless stood'.

Grace returned to Mayo, where she died in 1603. She is buried in the small Cistercian abbey on Clare Island under an inscription of her family's motto – *Terra Marique Potens* – Invincible on land or sea.

Facing Clare Island across Clew Bay is the little town of Newport.

Grace Kelly's Cottage

About two miles (3 km) inland lies tiny DRIMULA, beside a little lake called the LEG O'MUTTON. At this lonely spot you will find the remains of a small stone cottage, its thatched roof gone, grass growing from its walls, the chimney askew and about to tumble – the humble ancestral home of one of the world's richest and most glamorous women, film star GRACE KELLY, later PRINCESS GRACE OF MONACO. Here, her great-grand-father JOHN KELLY was born into poverty, and from here he emigrated to America in 1870.

In 1961 Grace visited the cottage with her new husband PRINCE RAINIER and had tea with the owner, MRS ELLEN MULCHRONE. In 1973 the Princess went back and bought the property along with the adjoining land for £7,800, returning many times and mingling with the shoppers in nearby Newport. Her last visit was in 1979, when she revealed plans to turn her cottage into a holiday home. She was much loved by the local people and they were devastated when she died in a car crash three years later in 1982, aged 53. Grace's

son PRINCE ALBERT inherited the property and he dropped by to see it, unexpectedly, in 1987. Since then no one has been back and the 18th-century cottage has fallen into ruins.

Knock

Visions

KNOCK must be one of the tiniest places in the world to have its own international airport – you can fly to this village, slumbering on the quiet plains of Mayo, direct from London and many parts of Europe or even New York! What happened to make this sleepy place in the wild west of Ireland attract such attention?

It all began on a rainy evening in August 1879. Two village ladies, MARY McLOUGHLIN and MARY BEIRNE, were walking past the parish church at about 8 pm when they thought they noticed something moving under the gable at the south end of the building. On closer inspection this turned out to be three luminous figures, one instantly recognisable as the VIRGIN MARY, dressed in a cloak and flanked by ST JOSEPH and ST JOHN THE EVANGELIST. As twilight fell the figures grew all the more visible and a crowd began to gather. There also appeared an altar with a lamb standing on it, and a cross, and a number of hovering angels. Although the apparitions were quite bright they cast no shadows, and the ground beneath stayed dry despite the pouring rain.

The visions, which were quite silent, lasted for over two hours, and were seen by at least 15 people. There was talk of miracle cures in the days afterwards.

The apparitions at Knock were thoroughly investigated and it was proved that they could not have been created with either luminous paint or magic lanterns or with any other technology available in those times. Eventually, the Church accepted that these visions were reliable and Knock became a recognised Marian shrine. Official Church support was confirmed in 1979 with a visit from POPE JOHN PAUL II to celebrate the centenary of the Apparition. MOTHER TERESA also made a pilgrimage here in 1993.

Today, over a million and a half visitors come to Knock every year.

The gable where the apparitions appeared has been covered over to make a chapel, while a modern basilica has been built beside the church to house a shrine to Our Lady. All along the main street there are opportunities to purchase bottles of 'holy water', fluorescent green models of the Virgin Mary complete with pump-action tears, onyx crosses and other trinkets, should you so wish.

Despite its popularity, the simple piety of Knock manages to overcome all this glitter and the village remains a place of special atmosphere and a sense of deep peace.

Well, I never knew this
ABOUT
County Mayo

Musical Bridge, Bellacorrick

At Bellacorrick, west of Ballina, there is a MUSICAL BRIDGE – if you roll a pebble along the stone parapet, a melodic note can be heard. There is a popular pub close by.

In 1920, THE LARGEST PIKE EVER TAKEN BY A ROD (53 lb/24 kg) was caught in Lough Conn.

The tiny island of Inishglora, off the Mullet Peninsula, was home to the Swans of Lir for their last 300 years (*see* Co. Westmeath, page 120). There is also a legend that bodies buried here are preserved so that their hair and nails continue to grow – it is said to be something in the soil.

The Neolithic Ceide Fields, on the bleak north Mayo coast, have been preserved in bogland for over 5,000 years and are THE OLDEST KNOWN FIELD SYSTEMS IN THE WORLD as well as being Europe's LARGEST STONE AGE ENCLOSURE.

THE HIGHEST CLIFFS IN EUROPE, dropping 2,192 feet (650 metres) into the Atlantic, are on Achill Island, which is Ireland's LARGEST OFF-SHORE ISLAND, 14 miles long and 12 miles wide (22 km by 19 km).

Ballintubber Abbey was founded in 1216 and is THE ONLY ROYAL ABBEY IN IRELAND TO HAVE BEEN CONTINU-OUSLY USED SINCE IT WAS BUILT.

Killary Harbour is Ireland's ONLY FJORD. The village of Leenane on the south shore was the principal location for the filming of the 1991 movie *The Field*, starring Richard Harris and Tom Berenger. Pub scenes were shot at Gaynor's, one of the bars in the tiny village street. The dramatic fight scene was filmed at the picturesque Aasleagh Falls, upstream on the Erriff river.

In 1951, Hollywood stars John Wayne and Maureen O'Hara descended on the village of Cong, to film JOHN FORD's *The Quiet Man*. They stayed just outside the village at ASHFORD CASTLE, a vast Victorian baronial pile built by ARTHUR GUINNESS of brewery fame in the 1870s. The castle appears in the opening shot of the film and guests can take a ride in the jaunting car driven by the stars. As Maureen O'Hara commented, THIS WAS THE FIRST TIME THAT IRELAND HAD EVER APPEARED ON FILM IN TECHNICOLOR.

Two miles (3 km) to the east of Cong is MOYTURA HOUSE, built in 1865 by OSCAR WILDE's FATHER, SIR WILLIAM WILDE. The family spent many happy holidays here.

A few miles north of Cong is LOUGH MASK HOUSE the residence of CAPTAIN CHARLES BOYCOTT (1832–97), land agent for the Ulster landowner LORD ERNE. In 1880 his tenants demanded a substantial cut in their rents, which Boycott refused. THE IRISH LAND LEAGUE, led by CHARLES PARNELL, persuaded all the tenants, workers and tradesmen in the area to stop their dealings with him. The household servants downed tools, no one would work on the land, shops refused to serve him and even his mail wasn't delivered. Despite the fact that a group of Ulstermen marched down from Cavan and Monaghan to help Boycott gather in his crops, Parnell's tactics were very effective and were soon widely adopted elsewhere. *The London Times* picked up on the name of Boycott as meaning to 'ostracise'

or 'refuse to deal with' and the English language acquired a new word.

The NATIONAL FAMINE MONUMENT near Croagh Patrick depicts a coffin ship and was sculpted by JOHN BEHAN. It was unveiled in 1997 by Irish President MARY ROBINSON to commemorate 150 years since the Great Famine and is THE LARGEST BRONZE SCULPTURE IN IRELAND.

A small white cottage in Providence Road, FOXFORD, was the birthplace, in 1777, of ADMIRAL WILLIAM BROWN, known as the 'FATHER OF THE ARGENTINIAN NAVY'. When he was nine, his family emigrated to America and, after a sporadic maritime career, Brown found his way to BUENOS AIRES, capital of Argentina. He became a government privateer during the war with Spain (1812–14) and succeeded in driving the Spanish fleet from the River Plate, paving the way for Argentina's independence and becoming a hero in that country. The Admiral visited Foxford in 1847 with his daughter and was shocked by the effects of the Famine. He died in 1857 and is buried in Buenos Aires. The central square in Buenos Aires is named PLAZA DE MAYO in his and his Irish county's honour. He is commemorated in his native Foxford by a bronze bust.

THE WORLD'S FIRST GUIDED MISSILE SYSTEM was invented by LOUIS BRENNAN, born in CASTLEBAR in 1852. He devised a torpedo with two propellers each connected to a separate reel of wire 2 miles (3.2 km) long. The torpedo was launched from a runway on land and then steered via the wires by an engineer on shore who could follow its progress by watching a small mast that protruded from the water. Travelling about 10 feet (3 m) below the surface with a range of 2 miles and a top speed of 25 mph (40 km/h), this was THE FIRST WEAPON EVER BUILT THAT COULD BE DIRECTED ALL THE WAY TO ITS TARGET. The system was adopted for coastal defence all around Britain. Only one launch station was built in Ireland, at FORT CAMDEN near CROSSHAVEN, for the defence of CORK HARBOUR. The guide rails for launching it are still there. Brennan also invented a gyroscopic monorail and a gyroscopic helicopter with which he achieved THE WORLD'S FIRST CONTROLLED UNMANNED HELICOPTER FLIGHT some time around 1920. He died in 1932 after being knocked down by a car in Switzerland. He was a founder member of the NATIONAL ACADEMY OF IRELAND.

Louis Brennan's Gyroscopic Monorail

COUNTY
ROSCOMMON

COUNTY TOWN: ROSCOMMON

Ros Comain – 'St Coman's wood'

Roscommon Jail

Roscommon Town

Head Girl

ROSCOMMON TOWN, the capital of its county, is a pleasant, bustling market town with a huge Norman castle, built in 1269 by THE LORD JUSTICE OF IRELAND, ROBERT D'UFFORD. Despite being one of the biggest and strongest castles in Britain or Ireland

it was sacked 11 years later by HUGH O'CONOR, KING OF CONNACHT (*see* Clonalis House) and had to be rebuilt.

Main Street is dominated by the looming bulk of ROSCOMMON JAIL, infamous as the haunt of the fearsome executioner and hangwoman 'LADY BETTY'. Betty was an educated woman from Kerry who was left destitute when her husband died. She and her only son made their way to

Roscommon, where they survived by squatting in a derelict cottage and begging in the streets. Eventually her son disappeared and Betty was left, alone and embittered.

Many years later a finely dressed man called at her meagre home seeking shelter for the night. She took him in and then, at the dead of night, stabbed him through the heart, intending to rob him of his possessions. Imagine her horror, as she was rifling through his things, when she discovered that the victim was her son, come back for her having made his fortune. Betty gave herself up and was sentenced to be hanged. On the very day that she was to meet her end, the official executioner took ill and Betty volunteered to take his place and execute the other prisoners, in return for her own pardon. She proved so good at the job that when the hangman died shortly afterwards, Betty was made

official executioner, with a salary and lodgings in the jail.

It was a busy time, with the Rebellion of 1798 providing plenty of victims, and Betty relished her work. Parents would invoke her name to ensure the good behaviour of their naughty children, and the taverns of Roscommon rang with lurid tales of her bloodthirsty rituals and cackling laughter as she sent another poor soul to his doom. 'Lady Betty' died in 1807 and her name is still spoken in whispers in Roscommon Town.

Strokestown

Famine

The first thing you notice about the little country town of STROKESTOWN is the elegant, tree-lined main street, one of the widest in Ireland. It was laid out by a local squire who wanted

Strokesdown Park

to create an avenue similar to Vienna's RINGSTRASSE. At the end of the street is an impressive Georgian Gothic arch, marking the entrance to STROKESTOWN PARK, a splendid 18th-century house with a tragic history.

The house, which incorporates a 17th-century tower, was built in the 1730s for THOMAS MAHON, an Irish MP whose grandfather had been granted 30,000 acres (12,000 ha) of Co. Roscommon by Charles II.

When MAJOR DENIS MAHON inherited the estate over 100 years later, at the time of THE GREAT FAMINE, it was deeply in debt, divided

> *Ireland's Great Famine lasted from 1845 until 1851 and was due to a parasitic fungus that caused potatoes to rot in the ground and become inedible. It is thought that the blight was imported into Belgium in 1843 in a shipment of potatoes from North America that had been infected from Mexico. The fungus then spread throughout Europe, arriving in Ireland in 1845. Potatoes were the staple diet of Ireland's livestock as well as many of the country's poorer families, and when the crop failed, one quarter of Ireland's population – almost two million people – either died or were forced to emigrate, most of them to America. Many landlords were sympathetic and did all in their power to alleviate the suffering; others used the situation to clear their estates of unprofitable tenants.*

into blighted plots too small to sustain the tenants, who had no way of paying off their rent arrears. Major Mahon's agent, his cousin JOHN ROSS MAHON, decided that the only way to clear the debts was to evict the tenants and put the land to tillage farming. He advised Major Mahon that it would be cheaper to send the tenants to America than to turn them over to the workhouse, where he would have to pay for their keep. At a cost of £24,000 the Major chartered a number of ships and in May and June of 1847 some 900 men, women and children were sent to Liverpool to be shipped to America. Ships such as these became known as 'coffin ships', as the appalling conditions and overcrowding on board caused the deaths of many hundreds of the emigrants.

In November 1847 Major Mahon was returning from Roscommon when he was waylaid by two men and shot dead. The men were later hanged for his murder and extra police and a troop of Dragoons were brought in to maintain order at Strokestown, so that John Ross Mahon could continue with the policy of eviction.

Strokestown stayed in the Mahon family until 1979, when it was taken over and refurbished by a local firm. In 1994 the Irish President MARY ROBINSON opened the FAMINE MUSEUM in the stable yard, which tells the story of tenants and landlords, good and bad, during those dreadful years.

In the gardens of STROKESTOWN PARK IS THE LONGEST HERBACEOUS BORDER IN THE BRITISH ISLES.

Clonalis House

Seat of Kings

Just outside CASTLEREA, embowered in trees and surrounded by the lands that the O'Conors have owned for over 1,500 years, is CLONALIS HOUSE, ancestral home of the proud dynasty of O'CONORS, KINGS OF CONNACHT, and LAST OF THE HIGH KINGS OF IRELAND. It is a huge, cement-rendered, Victorian Italianate pile, built in 1880 by Frederick Pepys Cockerell. The ruins of an earlier, late 17th-century home, incorporating the remains of a medieval castle, can still be seen across the grounds. This house was abandoned because it lay in a low-lying position close to the

River Suck that became regarded as unhealthy. It was wrecked by a storm in 1961.

On the grass in front of the present house is the O'CONOR INAUGURATION STONE, dating from 90 BC. Similar to the Stone of Scone, now in Edinburgh Castle, upon which Scottish and English monarchs were crowned, the O'Conor stone was brought here from the prehistoric earthworks at RATHCROGHAN, their ancient royal seat a few miles away.

In 1911, DENIS O'CONOR DON became THE FIRST MEMBER OF AN IRISH GAELIC FAMILY TO ATTEND THE CORONATION OF AN ENGLISH MONARCH (George V). The banner he carried for the occasion hangs above the stairs in the cavernous front hall of the house.

Nearby, there is a portrait of red-headed HUGH O'CONOR, the founder of ARIZONA'S OLDEST CITY, TUCSON. He was known as 'EL

Clonalis House

CAPITÁN COLORADO' – THE RED
CAPTAIN – because of his flaming
red hair. As a brilliant military commander working for the Spanish
Crown, and one-time interim
Governor of Texas, Don Hugo was
directed to set up a network of
presidios or fortresses along the
northern borders of Spain's territo-
ries in America. These were needed
to protect the settlers and trade
routes from the native Apache
Indians. In 1776 he chose a site close
to the centre of what is now
downtown Tucson and established
SPAIN'S MOST NORTHERLY OUTPOST IN
THE NEW WORLD.

Clonalis is renowned for its
unrivalled archive of over 100,000
documents recording Irish history,
but perhaps its most prized possession is kept in the billiard room – the
harp of TURLOUGH O'CAROLAN,
LAST OF THE IRISH BARDS.

> *Carolan, the last of the Irish bards,*
> *slept on a rath, and ever after the fairy*
> *tunes ran in his head, and made him*
> *the great man he was.*
> – W.B. YEATS, from *Fairy and Folk Tales*
> *of the Irish Peasantry*

TURLOUGH O'CAROLAN (1670–1738)
was born near Nobber in
Co. Meath, the son of a farmer and
blacksmith. He became blind from
an attack of smallpox at the age of
17, but by then his talent as a
musician and poet had attracted the
attention of his father's employer,
MRS MACDERMOTT ROE of Alderford
House, near Ballyfarnon. She gave
him some money, a horse and a harp

and sent him off on his travels as an
itinerant harpist or bard. For the next
30 years he wandered throughout
Ireland staying with rich and poor
and repaying their hospitality with
songs and compositions. In 1720 he
married MARY MAGUIRE, by whom
he had seven children. He never
really recovered from her death in
1733, and in his last days he went
home to his friend and patron
Mrs MacDermott Roe. He died on
25 March 1738 and, as befitted a
lover of whiskey, women and song,
his wake lasted for four riotous
days. He is buried in the old church
of KILRONAN near Keadue in
Co. Roscommon, next to the
MacDermott vaults. For years his
skull was displayed in a niche in the
church, draped with a black ribbon.

Turlough O'Carolan was, and will
always remain, a hugely important
figure in Irish music, and is sometimes referred to as IRELAND'S
NATIONAL COMPOSER. His image
appeared on THE OLD IRISH
50-POUND NOTE.

Well, I never knew this
ABOUT

COUNTY ROSCOMMON

SIR WILLIAM WILDE, born in CASTLEREA in 1815, is best known as the father of writer and wit OSCAR WILDE, but he was a man of many talents and achievements in his own right.

An eminent doctor, he specialised in eye and ear illnesses, developing medicines and instruments at his own clinic in Dublin and making a number of discoveries about genetic inheritance. He was also a fine arche-ologist and natural historian, and wrote several books on Irish folklore and 19th-century Irish history, along with medical studies on the conse-quences of the Famine. In later life he was broken by a libel court case, following allegations of sexual assault against a Mary Travers – strangely presaging the fate that awaited his son Oscar. William Wilde died in 1876 and is buried in Dublin.

Where the Mountains o' Mourne
sweep down to the sea . . .

The author of these wistful lines, WILLIAM PERCY FRENCH (1854–1920), was a native of Co. Roscom-mon, born in his family's ancestral home at CLOONYQUIN, near Elphin. Best remembered as a writer of immortal Irish songs full of humour and affection ('*Come Back, Paddy Reilly*', '*Phil the Fluter's Ball*'), French was also a poet, entertainer and painter of considerable talent. His watercolours are highly sought after today.

The FIRST PRESIDENT OF IRELAND, DOUGLAS HYDE (1860–1949), was born in the Rectory at FRENCHPARK, where his father Arthur was the Church of Ireland Rector. Douglas became fascinated by the Irish lan-guage as spoken by the older people in Co. Roscommon. In 1893 he co-founded the GAELIC LEAGUE in an attempt to halt the decline in the use of Irish and became its first president. He resigned in 1915 when he thought the organisation had become too political. He worked with Yeats and Lady Gregory on the Gaelic revival and his initials are on the autograph tree at Coole (*see* Co. Galway). Pro-Irish, but non-political, Douglas Hyde was the per-fect choice to be elected as the first President of the Republic of Ireland

Douglas Hyde Museum

after the declaration of the new constitution in 1937. He is buried in the churchyard of his father's old church, 1 mile north of Frenchpark on the N5. The church is now a museum dedicated to his life and work.

William Augustus Byrne, born at Araghty, Co. Roscommon in 1863, was regarded as THE FINEST VETERINARY SURGEON OF HIS TIME. Much of his life was spent in private practice in Co. Roscommon, although he travelled widely throughout Ireland, working at race-meetings and other sporting occasions where animals were involved. His wife Aleen Isabel Cust was THE FIRST WOMAN EVER IN IRELAND OR BRITAIN TO QUALIFY AS A VET. William Byrne died in 1910, aged only 46, and is buried in the churchyard at Araghty.

Five miles north-east of Roscommon Town, in the grounds of Holywell House, are the remains of St Brigid's well. In the early years of the 18th century, two little girls, sisters Mary and Elizabeth, would ride over here every day from their father's house at Castle Coote, and bathe in the crystal-clear waters of the well. There must have been something in the water, for they grew up to be the 'beautiful Miss Gunnings', the loveliest women in all of Europe, 'two nymphs adorned with every grace'. Mary married the Earl of Coventry and Elizabeth wed the Duke of Hamilton, by whom she had two sons. She then married the Duke of Argyll and gave birth to two more sons, ending up THE MOTHER OF FOUR DUKES.

Maureen O'Sullivan (1911–98), who played Jane opposite Johnny Weissmuller's Tarzan in the Tarzan films of the 1930s and 40s, was born in Boyle, Co. Roscommon. Edgar Rice Burroughs, the creator of Tarzan, called her 'my perfect Jane'.

Albert Reynolds, Taoiseach of Ireland from 1992 to 1994, was born at Rooskey, Co. Roscommon, in 1932.

COUNTY SLIGO

COUNTY TOWN: SLIGO

Sligeach – 'a shelly place'

West door, Cathedral of the Immaculate Conception, Sligo, built in 1874

Drumcliff

*Under bare Ben Bulben's head
In Drumcliff churchyard Yeats is laid.*
W.B. YEATS, 'Under Ben Bulben'

In 1948 WILLIAM BUTLER YEATS, one of the greatest poets in the English language, was finally laid to rest as he had wanted, just outside the west door of the church at DRUMCLIFF where his grandfather had been the Rector. Yeats had died nine years earlier at Roquebrune in France, and been interred there, but his greatest wish was to be buried here, surrounded by the glorious Sligo countryside he had learned to love as a boy, 'under bare Bulben's head'.

Ben Bulben

Places associated with Yeats can be found throughout Co. Sligo, unofficially known as YEATS COUNTRY. 'Sligo has always been my home,' he used to say and certainly, as a schoolboy in London 'where I was nobody', he yearned to be in Sligo 'where I was somebody'. Yeats, with his  brother Jack, was often sent to stay here with his grandparents, while their father was struggling to make his living as an artist. He absorbed not just the dramatic landscapes and evocative scenery but the folklore, the tales and songs and poems of a misty, magical lost Ireland. His poetry, particularly his early works such as 'The Lake Isle of Innisfree' and 'The Stolen Child', drew strongly on these romantic influences.

Inscribed on his simple tombstone

are the last words from his very last poem, 'Under Ben Bulben':

> *Cast a cold eye*
> *On life, on death,*
> *Horseman, pass by!*

The horseman is a ghostly rider from Sligo legends who carries the souls of the wicked off to Hell.

Across the road from the church is the stump of a round tower, said to be a relic of ST COLUMBA'S MONASTERY and a reminder that near here, in AD 561, the BATTLE OF THE BOOKS was fought. Columba borrowed a psalter from ST FINIAN of Moville Abbey in Co. Down, and made a copy of it. Finian demanded that Columba hand the copy over to him but Columba refused and the matter was taken to the court of the HIGH KING DIARMUID at Tara. Diarmuid ruled in favour of Finian, saying, *'Le gach bain a bainin, le gach leabhar a leabhrán'* – 'To every cow its calf, to every book, its copy.'

This is THE FIRST RECORDED RULING ON COPYRIGHT. However, Columba refused to accept the ruling or to give the book back. Three thousand were slain in the ensuing battle, which was won by Columba's men. Soon afterwards, ashamed and stricken with conscience, Columba left Ireland and sailed to Iona in Scotland, where he founded his famous monastery.

Lissadell

The light of evening, Lissadell,
Great windows open to the south . . .
W.B. YEATS

Take a quiet coast road from Drumcliff, turn left between weed-covered stone gateposts, pass into woods that offer silver glimpses of the sea and open out beside a sandy bay, wind past rocky pools and deep green lawns, and there, hidden over the hill is LISSADELL, 'that old Georgian mansion' of Yeats's fond memory.

The house, built in 1830, is not pretty, but the location is spectacular.

Yeats again: 'outside it is grey, square and bare, yet set amid delightful grounds'. The view south looks out over Sligo bay while to the east, above the trees, beautiful Ben Bulben changes mood and texture with every cloud that passes.

There are two unusual design features to Lissadell. There are NO OUTBUILDINGS to distract from the simple Grecian lines – the stable block is connected to the house by a sunken tunnel. And there is NO ATTIC – the servants slept in the basement.

Lissadell was the home of the GORE-BOOTH family. During the Great Famine, Sir Robert Gore-Booth 4TH Bt., mortgaged the house in order to feed his employees.

In the 1870s THE FIRST ROE DEER IN IRELAND were introduced at Lissadell, but the herd died out in the 1920s and now there are none left anywhere in the country. There are frequent reports of sightings in the surrounding woods, but no one has been able to confirm that these elusive creatures are still living there.

EVA and CONSTANCE, grand-daughters of Sir Robert, were immortalised by Yeats as 'Two girls in silk kimonos, both/Beautiful, one a gazelle'. Eva must have been the gazelle – the poet was able to confide in her gentle nature about his unrequited love for the fervent Nationalist, MAUDE GONNE.

Constance Gore-Booth

Lissadell

Constance was an entirely different character from her sister, strong-willed and fiery, and made plain her displeasure at being woken up one night, along with the whole house-hold, by Yeats's terrified cries that he had seen a ghost on the stairs.

Highlights inside the house are the full-length murals of the Gore-Booth family painted directly on to the walls by Constance's husband, the Polish artist Casimir Markiewicz.

Like Yeats, Constance was an important figure in the Gaelic revival but, unlike Yeats, she chose to become politically active, and played a leading role in the EASTER RISING in 1916. She barricaded herself into the Royal College of Surgeons in Dublin, along with 120 Republican soldiers, and when surrendering, kissed her revolver before handing it over to her captors. A woman of great courage, outspoken and hugely popular, she escaped execution due to her high profile. In 1918 she was elected to the Westminster

Parliament as a Sinn Fein member – THE FIRST WOMAN EVER TO BE ELECTED TO THE BRITISH HOUSE OF COMMONS. She never took her seat, but served as Minister for Labour in THE FIRST DAIL (Irish Parliament).

Lissadell is home to THE LARGEST COLONY OF BARNACLE GEESE IN IRELAND.

Markree Castle

All Things Bright and Beautiful

MARKREE CASTLE is a spectacular, castellated Georgian mansion set in glorious wooded country, some 8 miles (13 km) south of the town of Sligo. Today it is a hotel – THE ONLY CASTLE HOTEL IN IRELAND RUN BY A DIRECT DESCENDANT OF THE ORIGINAL FAMILY – but in the 19th century it was at the forefront of the exciting world of astronomical discovery.

Oliver Cromwell originally granted

the land around a small fort on the banks of the River Unsin to one of his young officers, EDWARD COOPER, in 1663 and it has stayed in the Cooper family ever since. In 1830, EDWARD JOSHUA COOPER (1798–1863), who had inherited a love of astronomy from his mother, also inherited Markree and set about creating an observatory there. He insisted on having the very best available equipment, and Markree Observatory gained a reputation as 'undoubtedly the most richly furnished private observatory known'. Cooper installed THE WORLD'S FIRST CAST-IRON TELESCOPE with a 13.5-inch (34-CM) REFRACTOR LENS that WAS THE LARGEST IN THE WORLD at the time.

On 25 April 1848, Cooper's assistant ANDREW GRAHAM discovered a minor planet or asteroid called METIS – THE ONLY ASTEROID EVER TO BE DISCOVERED FROM IRELAND. Cooper and Graham then calculated and analysed the asteroid's orbit – THE FIRST TIME THIS HAD EVER BEEN DONE. They also produced the celebrated MARKREE CATALOGUE – a study that measured and recorded the positions of some 60,000 stars. Cooper also created a weather station at Markree which still functions.

Markree is the castle referred to in the hymn 'All Things Bright and Beautiful' by the lines '*the rich man in his castle, the poor man at his gate*'. MRS ALEXANDER (*see* Co. Derry, page 248), who wrote the hymn, stayed at Markree and, impressed by the view from the terrace, described it in the same hymn as '*The purple headed mountain, the river running by . . .*'

Knocknarea

Warrior Queen

The enormous cairn on the summit of KNOCKNAREA, the high hill that gazes across Sligo town towards Ben Bulben, is said to be the burial place of MAEVE, the legendary warrior Queen of Connacht.

Maeve was a noble Queen, proud of the fact that she was equal in power and wealth to her husband AILILL – except in one respect. Ailill owned a magnificent bull of superior breeding to any that she possessed. Maeve was determined that she would have a bull of like prowess but there was only one other like it in all Ireland, THE BROWN BULL OF COOLEY, and that belonged to the King of Ulster, who refused to sell it. Queen Maeve raised an army and marched to Cooley to capture the bull and was confronted by the great hero of the Red Knights of Ulster, Cuchulain (*see* Co. Louth, page 98). In the battle that followed, Maeve's

army was defeated but she managed to abduct the bull and take it back to Connacht. However, when the Ulster bull and Ailill's bull met they fought and killed each other – Maeve's honour was satisfied, although not in the way she had intended.

It is said that to remove a stone from Maeve's cairn brings terrible bad luck – perhaps that is how this huge monument has survived vandals and bounty hunters for so many thousands of years.

Spread across an area of 1.5 square miles (3.8 sq km) in fields below Knocknarea, to the south, is CARROWMORE, THE LARGEST GROUP OF MEGALITHIC TOMBS IN THE BRITISH ISLES.

Well, I never knew this
ABOUT
COUNTY SLIGO

Classiebawn Castle

The Victorian Baronial CLASSIEBAWN CASTLE, which looms like Dracula's lair above a bare, rockbound peninsula jutting out into the wild Atlantic near Mullaghmore, used to

be the holiday home of EARL MOUNTBATTEN OF BURMA. The castle was built for the British Prime Minister LORD PALMERSTON, who sat on the cliff tops watching it rise.

Palmerston bequeathed Classiebawn to his private secretary, who was also his wife's grandson, EVELYN ASHLEY, LORD MOUNT TEMPLE, who completed the building in 1874. Lord Mount Temple was the grandfather of Lord Mountbatten's wife. In 1979 Lord Mountbatten was murdered when his boat, *Shadow V*, was blown apart by a bomb, off the coast at Mullaghmore. One of Mountbatten's grandsons, Nicholas Knatchbull, and a local boy Paul Maxwell, were also killled in the explosion. Another passenger, Doreen, Lady Brabourne, died shortly afterwards from her wounds.

LOUGH GARA, which lies in the south-east corner of Co. Sligo, is the site of THE BIGGEST GROUP OF CRANNOGS SO FAR DISCOVERED IN THE BRITISH ISLES. A crannog is a Bronze Age dwelling place, consisting of wattle huts erected on an artificial island constructed out of logs, stones, mud and clay, and defensively positioned in the middle of a lake or marshland. They could only be reached by boat, or an irregular submerged causeway.

The scientist who first studied and explained FLUORESCENCE and PHOSPHORESCENCE, GEORGE STOKES (1819–1903), was born in the Rectory at SKREEN, Co. Sligo.

The LOST SILVER BELL OF SLIGO ABBEY is thought to lie at the bottom of LOUGH GILL, but only the purest of heart can hear its pealing.

WILLIAM HIGGINS (1763–1825), who introduced the use of letters and numbers to denote chemical elements, such as H for Hydrogen and O for Oxygen (as in H_2O for water), was born at COLLOONEY.

Leinster

CITY OF DUBLIN

Dubh Linn – 'dark pool'

Dublin Custom House – designed by James Gandon and completed in 1791

City of Dublin

Fair City

DUBLIN, CAPITAL CITY OF THE REPUBLIC OF IRELAND, is one of the most beautifully situated cities in Europe, on the banks of the RIVER LIFFEY beside wide Dublin Bay. As a centre of literature, art and learning, and with a rich architectural heritage, it is often referred to as 'A WESTERN ATHENS'.

The oldest evidence of life in the Dublin area is a 4,000-years-old pre-historic burial site located where EUROPE'S LARGEST WALLED URBAN PARK now stands – PHOENIX PARK. The zoo in the park was opened in

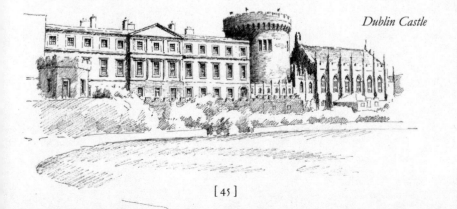

Dublin Castle

1831 and is THE FIFTH-OLDEST PUBLIC ZOO IN THE WORLD. CAIRBRE, the roaring lion that became the world-famous trademark of MGM studios, was born here in 1927.

In Celtic times Dublin was called *Baile-Atha-Cliath*, 'Town of the Hurdle Ford'. The present name is derived from the Gaelic *Dubh Linn*, meaning 'black pool'. The site of the original black pool is underneath the gardens of DUBLIN CASTLE. The castle itself, which was built in 1228, occupies THE ONLY HIGH GROUND IN THE OLD CITY.

It was over Dublin Castle that the BRITISH UNION FLAG, better known as the UNION JACK, was FLOWN FOR THE VERY FIRST TIME, on 1 January 1801 to signal the ACT OF UNION between Great Britain and Ireland.

Danish KING SIGTRYG IN 1038, it is UNIQUE IN THE BRITISH ISLES IN BEING OF DANISH ORIGIN. The subsequent Cathedral was commissioned in 1172 by STRONGBOW, whose tomb is represented inside by a later effigy. Lying next to it is a small, truncated figure reputed to be Strongbow's son, cut in half by his father for being a coward.

In 1486, LAMBERT SIMNEL, Pretender to the throne of Henry VII, was crowned King Edward VI of England in Christ Church Cathedral. Supporters of the English House of York led by GERALD FITZGERALD, Deputy Lieutenant of Ireland, claimed that 10-year-old Simnel was Edward, Earl of Warwick, nephew of Edward IV. Together they invaded England with an army of Irish and German troops

Two Cathedrals

Strongbow and Swift

CHRIST CHURCH CATHEDRAL is THE OLDEST CATHEDRAL IN IRELAND and THE OLDEST STONE BUILDING IN DUBLIN. Originally founded by the

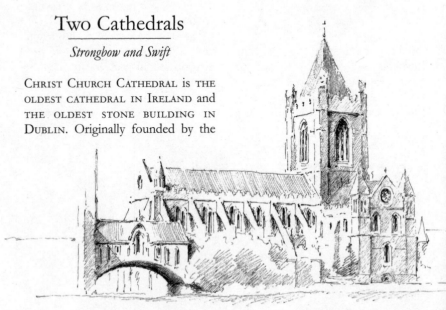

> *Strongbow was the name given to the Norman knight Richard de Clare, Earl of Pembroke, who invaded Ireland in 1170 at the request of the exiled King of Leinster, Diarmait MacMurrough (see Co. Leitrim, page 16). He married MacMurrough's daughter and became King of Leinster, but his increasing power worried Henry II, who did not want a rival power on his western borders and forced Strongbow to hand over his lands to the Crown.*

but were defeated at the BATTLE OF STOKE in 1487. Simnel served the rest of his life in Henry VII's kitchens.

Thirteenth-century ST PATRICK'S CATHEDRAL is both THE LONGEST AND THE LARGEST CHURCH IN IRELAND. William III's GENERAL SCHOMBERG, who died at the BATTLE OF THE BOYNE in 1690, is buried here with an epitaph on his black marble tomb written by JONATHAN SWIFT. Swift, who was Dean of St Patrick's for 32 years from 1713 until he died in 1745, is buried in the nave close to

ESTHER JOHNSON, his 'STELLA'. In the north transept is an ancient wooden door pierced with a jagged hole, the origin of the expression 'to chance your arm'. In 1492, during a dispute with the EARL OF KILDARE, the EARL OF ORMONDE took refuge in the Chapter House. Kildare cut a hole in the door and thrust his arm through in a gesture of reconciliation – taking the chance that Ormonde might cut it off. The courageous move worked and the two made peace.

The FIRST PERFORMANCE OF HANDEL's *Messiah* was given by the combined choirs of St Patrick's Cathedral and Christ Church at the Music Hall in Dublin's FISHAMBLE STREET in 1742.

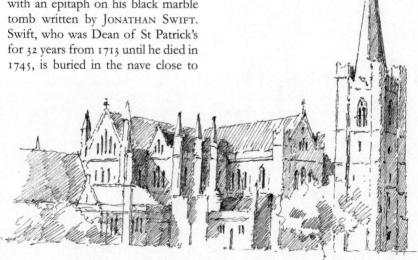

JONATHAN SWIFT was born near St Patrick's Cathedral at 7 Hoey's Court (now demolished) in 1667. Educated at Trinity College, he spent some time in England, where he met and tutored 'Stella' before returning to Ireland in 1694. Stella came herself to Ireland some time later and it is possible that they were married in 1716, although very little is known about their relationship. When Stella died in 1728 Swift was deeply saddened, and he carried a lock of her hair amongst his papers for the rest of his life. Swift obviously had a powerful effect on his young students, for another pupil of his, Esther Vanhomrigh, 22 years his junior, followed him to Ireland in 1712. Swift nicknamed her 'Vanessa', but broke off the relationship in 1723 and Vanessa never recovered, retiring heartbroken to her home at Celbridge Abbey (*see* Co. Kildare, page 67), where she died shortly afterwards.

When he had time, Swift was a shrewd political commentator, and his best-known literary work, *Gulliver's Travels*, is a bitter satire on the relationship between England and Ireland. In his last years Swift contracted Ménière's Disease, an ear illness that led Swift himself and others to think that he was going mad. His condition prompted him to establish IRELAND'S FIRST LUNATIC ASYLUM, ST PATRICK'S HOSPITAL, in 1735. As Swift himself put it:

> He gave the little wealth he had
> To build a house for fools and
>   mad;
> And show'd, by one satiric touch,
> No nation wanted it so much.

Well, I never knew this
ABOUT
CITY OF DUBLIN

The fortified area around Dublin controlled by the English after they had settled there in 1171 was known as THE PALE. This gives us the English expression 'BEYOND THE PALE', meaning 'beyond civilisation' or 'uncivilised'.

St Audoen's Church near Christ Church Cathedral is THE OLDEST CHURCH IN DUBLIN. The 12th-century tower is THE OLDEST CHURCH TOWER IN ALL IRELAND and contains IRELAND'S OLDEST CHURCH BELLS, three of them dating from 1423.

TRINITY COLLEGE, founded in 1592 by QUEEN ELIZABETH I, is IRELAND'S OLDEST UNIVERSITY. Catholics did not attend in any numbers until 1970. Its two greatest treasures are the *Book of Kells*, THE MOST BEAUTIFUL BOOK IN THE WORLD, and THE OLDEST IRISH HARP IN EXISTENCE, which possibly belonged to BRIAN BORU, THE FIRST KING OF ALL IRELAND.

Laid out in 1664, ST STEPHEN'S GREEN IS THE EARLIEST AND LARGEST OF DUBLIN'S SQUARES and was the model for NEW YORK'S CENTRAL PARK. In the north-west corner stands a huge statue of the 18th-century nationalist leader WOLFE TONE, by EDWARD DELANEY (1967). It is affectionately known as 'Tonehenge'.

MARSH'S LIBRARY beside St Patrick's Cathedral is THE OLDEST LIBRARY IN IRELAND. It was founded in 1701 by ARCHBISHOP NARCISSUS MARSH and built in the garden of the Bishop's Palace – now a police station. Most of the books are in their original oak bookcases and the library still possesses a number of caged-off alcoves where readers were locked in with rare or valuable books.

The magnificent offices of the BANK OF IRELAND, across the road from Trinity College, were completed in 1739 and were originally designed by James Gordon as THE FIRST PURPOSE-BUILT PARLIAMENT BUILDING IN EUROPE. The Bank of Ireland bought the building after the dissolution of the Irish Parliament in 1800.

LEINSTER HOUSE, where the IRISH DAIL (Parliament) now sits, was built in 1745 for the DUKE OF LEINSTER and was THE BIGGEST PRIVATE HOUSE IN DUBLIN. JAMES HOBAN based his design for the WHITE HOUSE in

Washington on Leinster House (*see* Co. Kilkenny, page 77).

The ROTUNDA was built in 1745 and is THE WORLD'S OLDEST MATERNITY HOSPITAL.

THE GUINNESS BREWERY opened in 1759 at ST JAMES'S GATE and is THE BIGGEST BREWERY IN EUROPE.

MELLOWS BRIDGE, built in 1764, is THE OLDEST BRIDGE IN THE CITY OF DUBLIN STILL IN USE. It takes Queen Street across the Liffey to the south quays. Originally named QUEEN'S BRIDGE after George III's wife, it was renamed in 1923 as QUEEN MAEVE BRIDGE and, in 1942, as Mellows Bridge in honour of LIAM MELLOWS (1892–1922), a republican soldier executed during the Irish Civil War.

The word 'QUIZ' was INVENTED IN DUBLIN. In 1780 a Dublin theatre manager, JAMES DALY, made a bet that he could introduce a meaningless word in to the English language within 24 hours. He hired a posse of schoolboys to chalk up the word 'quiz' on every available wall or surface in the city and soon Dublin was agog to know what was going on. And that is how we came by one of the most commonly used words in the world.

Dublin's GREAT SOUTH SEA WALL, built in 1748–90, stretches for nearly

5 miles (8 km) from O'Connell Bridge to Poolbeg and is THE LONGEST SEA WALL IN EUROPE.

THE HA'PENNY BRIDGE was built in 1816 and is so called because, until 1916, pedestrians had to pay a toll of ONE HA'PENNY to cross. It is THE OLDEST IRON BRIDGE IN IRELAND.

THE ABBEY THEATRE opened in 1904, with W.B. YEATS and LADY GREGORY as directors. Its aim was to promote new Irish playwrights and it always managed to be provocative and controversial. In 1907 there were

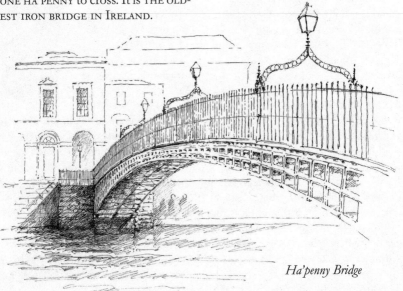

Ha'penny Bridge

All those with a fear of injections have a Dublin doctor, FRANCIS RYND (1801–61), to thank. In 1844, at the Meath Hospital in Heytesbury Street, Dr Rynd made a number of puncture holes in his patient's face using an improvised syringe made out of tubing. He then allowed morphine solution to flow through the tubing and into place underneath the skin. This was the first time such a procedure had been used. It proved painless and successful and led directly to the modern-day hypodermic syringe.

riots at the first night of JOHN MILLINGTON SYNGE's *The Playboy of the Western World*, when audiences objected to the play's portrayal of Irish peasantry as lawless and immoral. There were more riots in 1926 at the premiere of SEAN O'CASEY's *The Plough and the Stars*, with its questioning of the romantic view of Irish nationalism and rural life.

ST VALENTINE, the patron saint of lovers, is buried in the WHITEFRIARS STREET CARMELITE CHURCH. His

the Grand Canal in Dublin. In 1926 Jones won a gold medal with the car in the Ireland 24-hour trials. In 1928 he collaborated with DICK HUMPHREYS and BEN PARSONS to produce three more cars. They were called Thomond after the area of Co. Limerick and Co. Clare where the makers hailed from. None of the four Thomonds are thought to have survived, although a Thomond did appear on an Irish stamp in 1989.

ORSON WELLES made his acting debut at Dublin's GATE THEATRE at the age of 16 in 1931. JAMES MASON also made his first appearance here. Because of their often controversial content the Abbey and Gate theatres during the 1920s and '30s were known as SODOM AND BEGORRAH.

The FLAVOURED CRISP was invented in Dublin by JOE MURPHY, who first produced the 'TAYTO' CHEESE AND ONION CRISP at his works in O'Rahilly's Parade, off Moore Street, in 1954.

remains were presented as a gift by Pope Gregory XVI to the founder of the church, DR JOHN SPRATT, in appreciation of Spratt's good works and charismatic preaching while in Rome. St Valentine was a priest who blessed Christian marriages at a time when marriage had been banned by Claudius II, who believed that married men were reluctant to leave their families and enlist in the army. Valentine was arrested and beaten to death on 14 February AD 269. While in prison he helped to restore the sight of his jailer's daughter. When she opened the note he had sent her on his last night it was signed 'FROM YOUR VALENTINE'.

THE FIRST CAR EVER MADE IN THE IRISH FREE STATE was a THOMOND, built in 1925 by JAMES A. JONES at his garage in Haddington Road, by

DUBLIN'S NEWEST LANDMARK is the THE SPIRE OF DUBLIN, which soars above O'Connell Street in front of the General Post Office. Unveiled on 21 January 2003, it is made of stainless steel and, at 394 ft (120 m) high, it is THE TALLEST SCULPTURE IN THE WORLD. It replaced NELSON'S PILLAR, blown up by the IRA in 1966.

NELSON'S PILLAR, erected in 1808, was 134 ft (41 m) high and enclosed a spiral staircase giving access to a viewing platform. The head from Nelson's Pillar was retrieved and can be seen at an exhibition in Dublin's Civic Museum. While he was up there Nelson looked down upon Catholic Emancipation, the Great Famine, the Land War, the Gaelic Revival, the Easter Rising, the Troubles and the visit of PRESIDENT JOHN F. KENNEDY in 1963 – THE FIRST-EVER VISIT TO IRELAND OF A SITTING AMERICAN PRESIDENT.

The Spire of Dublin

BORN IN CITY OF DUBLIN

JONATHAN SWIFT (1667–1745) *7 Hoey's Court* Satirist and Dean of St Patrick's.

RICHARD STEELE (1672–1729) *Bull Alley just north of St Patrick's Cathedral* Dramatist and essayist who founded *The Tatler* (1709) and *The Spectator* (1711) magazines.

EDMUND BURKE (1729–97) *12 Arran Quay (demolished)* Political philosopher. 'All that is necessary for the forces of evil to win in the world is for enough good men to do nothing.'

RICHARD BRINSLEY SHERIDAN (1751–1816) *12 Upper Dorset Street* Actor and dramatist (*School for Scandal, The Rivals*).

DUKE OF WELLINGTON (1769–1852) *24 Upper Merrion Street* British Prime Minister and victor of the Battle of Waterloo.

THOMAS MOORE (1779–1852) *12 Aungier Street* The Irish Poet and Ireland's National Songwriter (*Irish Melodies*).

JOSEPH SHERIDAN LEFANU (1814–73) *Royal Hibernian Military School (now St Mary's Hospital)* Novelist (*In a Glass Darkly, Uncle Silas*).

SIR WILLIAM WILDE (1815–76) Ophthalmologist and archeologist, father of Oscar Wilde, called Oscar after a king of Sweden whose eyesight Sir William had restored.

MRS CECIL FRANCES ALEXANDER – *née* HUMPHREYS (1818–95) *25 Eccles Street* Hymn writer.

SIR CHARLES VILLIERS STANFORD (1852–1924) Composer.

OSCAR WILDE (1854–1900) *21 Westland Row* Poet, novelist, playwright (*The Ballad of Reading Gaol, The Picture of Dorian Gray, The Importance of Being Earnest*).

GEORGE BERNARD SHAW (1856–1950) *3 Synge Street* Playwright (*Pygmalion, Saint John, Man and Superman*), awarded the NOBEL PRIZE FOR LITERATURE in 1925.

OLIVER ST JOHN GOGARTY (1878–1957) *5 Parnell Square* Surgeon, poet, writer.

PATRICK PEARSE (1879–1916) *27 Pearse Street* Writer and nationalist, executed in 1916 for his part in the Easter Uprising.

SEAN O'CASEY (1880–1964) *85 Upper Dorset Street* Playwright (*The Shadow of a Gunman, Juno and the Paycock, The Plough and the Stars*).

ELIZABETH BOWEN (1899–1973) *15 Herbert Place, off Lower Baggot Street* Novelist (*The Death of the Heart, The Heat of the Day*).

BRENDAN BEHAN (1923–64) *Russell Street, off Mountjoy Square* Writer and dramatist (*Borstal Boy, The Quare Fellow, The Hostage*).

BRENDA FRICKER TV and film actress (*My Left Foot, Home Alone 2*), in 1945.

GABRIEL BYRNE Film actor (*Point of No Return*), in 1950.

COLM MEANEY TV and film actor (*Star Trek*), in 1953.

RODDY DOYLE Booker Prize-winning novelist (*The Commitments, A Star Called Henry*), in 1958.

BONO (Paul Hewson) Lead singer of rock band U2, co-founder of LIVE AID, in 1960.

SINEAD O'CONNOR Singer, in 1966.

COLIN FARRELL TV and film actor (*Ballykissangel*), in 1976.

COUNTY CARLOW

COUNTY TOWN: CARLOW

ceather-lough – 'four lakes'

The ruins of Duckett's Grove – a Gothic fairy tale built in 1830 by William Duckett

Carlow Town

Drop Dead

CARLOW, the tiny county town of County Carlow, sits pleasantly on the east bank of the River Barrow, some 50 miles (80 km) south of Dublin. Its proudest possession is a grand classical COURT HOUSE built in 1830 by WILLIAM MORRISON, ONE OF THE MOST MAGNIFICENT COURT HOUSES IN IRELAND. It is based on the TEMPLE OF ILISSUS, a temple beside the Ilissus river at Piraeus, sacred to the Muses, and seems surprisingly sumptuous for such a small place – one suggestion is that there was a mix-up with the town of CORK and that Carlow got the Court House meant for Cork while Cork got Carlow's.

Carlow's ancient Norman castle WAS THE FIRST IN THE COUNTRY TO HAVE A FOUR-TOWERED KEEP. It also used to be one of the finest castles in Ireland, until *'a ninny pated physician of the name of Middleton'* got hold of the place in 1814 and tried to

Carlow Court House

convert it into a lunatic asylum by blowing it up. His intention had been to merely diminish the thickness of the walls, but he badly miscalculated how much explosive to use: the destruction was terrible to perceive. One eyewitness account talks of the 'portentous and amazing nodding of the towers' and of 'gigantic pieces of the ruin rolling down the castle mount to the very doors of the humble cabins on the opposite side of the road'. Two towers and a bit of wall are all that remain.

Carlow's most famous son was the REV. SAMUEL HAUGHTON (1821–97), inventor in 1866 of the 'HAUGHTON DROP'. This was a humane way of hanging someone, so that the drop would be long and far enough to break the victim's neck and not leave them dangling, still alive, to be slowly strangled. In medieval days, hanging was not meant to kill, being merely a prelude to drawing and quartering. Now that drawing and quartering was no longer considered acceptable, Haughton felt that the hanging part

of the execution should be brought up to date too. To this end, he calculated that a person weighing 140 lb (63.5 kg) would need to fall 15 ft (4.6 m) to achieve a clean break. The Haughton Drop was eventually adopted at public hangings throughout Europe.

Carlow Town is the location of IRELAND'S FIRST SUGAR BEET FACTORY.

Leighlinbridge

Blue Sky Thinking

LEIGHLINBRIDGE is an old Irish village of narrow, winding streets, huddled about a Black Castle and a handsome bridge built in 1320, ONE OF THE OLDEST BRIDGES IN IRELAND STILL IN USE. For such a small place it has had a quite disproportionate influence on the world.

At 10 o'clock on the evening of 28 November 1999 a meteorite fell on Leighlinbridge – THE LAST RECORDED FALL OF A METEORITE, IN THE

Leighlinbridge

SECOND MILLENNIUM AD, ANYWHERE IN THE WORLD.

It is somehow appropriate that the sky should fall on Leighlinbridge, for it was a son of Leighlinbridge who taught us much of what we know about the sky – in particular WHY THE SKY IS BLUE. JOHN TYNDALL was born in the GARRISON HOUSE, LEIGHLINBRIDGE, in 1820, the son of a policeman. Despite a rudimentary education he developed a keen interest in physics – indeed he was THE FIRST SCIENTIST SPECIFICALLY REFERRED TO AS A 'PHYSICIST'. His main interest was the atmosphere, and he discovered that there were dust particles in the air that scattered different wavelengths of sunlight in different degrees – with the shorter blue wavelength more strongly scattered than the red. The thicker the atmosphere, the more blue light is removed, hence a rising or setting sun looks deeper red because it is seen through a deeper layer of atmosphere.

A sure sign of Tyndall's influence in the world of science is the number of scientific processes that carry his name. There is the TYNDALL EFFECT, TYNDALL BLUE and the TYNDALL CONE, all connected with the actions described above, and a TYNDALLO-METER, which measures the diffusion of light.

Tyndall was THE FIRST MAN TO

John Tyndall

PROVE THE GREENHOUSE EFFECT ON
CLIMATE CHANGE and THE FIRST TO
ACCURATELY MEASURE ATMOSPHERIC
POLLUTION.

In another field he devised
TYNDALLISATION, a form of food
sterilisation similar to Pasteurisation
but more effective and much
favoured in Europe.

He also invented the MODERN FOG-
HORN and the FIREMAN'S RESPIRATOR,
but perhaps his most innovative
invention was the LIGHT PIPE, with
which he showed that light can be
trapped in water and moved along a
pipe – a discovery that led directly to
the FIBRE OPTIC CABLES now widely
used in modern technology.

Finally, Tyndall's interest in the
movement of glaciers required him
to become a fine mountaineer, and
he was THE FIRST MAN TO CLIMB THE
WEISSHORN (14,780 ft/4,505 m) in
Switzerland.

Plagued by ill health in his old age,
Tyndall died in 1893 when his wife
mistakenly gave him an overdose of a
sleeping draught thinking it was for
indigestion.

Borris House

A Lady and a Gentleman

BORRIS HOUSE at BORRIS is the ancestral home of the great Carlow family
of KAVANAGH. In 1778 LADY
ELEANOR BUTLER, one of the famous
'LADIES OF LLANGOLLEN', was imprisoned at Borris by her family, after she
had tried to elope with her friend
SARAH PONSONBY. Borris House was
then owned by Eleanor's brother-in-
law, THOMAS KAVANAGH. Eleanor
eventually managed to escape and join
Sarah at Woodstock (*see* Co. Kilkenny,
page 77).

The most remarkable member of
the Kavanagh family to live at
Borris was ARTHUR MACMURROUGH
KAVANAGH in the 19th century, who
was born without arms or legs and
had to be carried everywhere. He
overcame his disabilities with great
courage and to such a degree that
he was able to write, ride, shoot
and paint, and became an MP and
Privy Councillor. He travelled widely
throughout Asia and gained a
reputation as a fearless tiger hunter.

Borris House

The village of Borris, as seen today, is largely his creation and he was a much-loved local character, supremely unselfconscious. He exclaimed to one of his friends on a trip to Abbeyleix, 'It's an extraordinary thing – I haven't been here for five years but the station-master recognised me!'

FAMOUS SONS OF COUNTY CARLOW

WILLIAM DARGAN (1799–1867), known as 'THE FATHER OF IRISH RAILWAYS'. Dargan was the engineer responsible for building THE FIRST RAILWAY IN IRELAND from Dublin to Dun Laoghaire in 1833 (*see* Co. Dublin, page 61).

CARDINAL PATRICK MORAN (1830–1911), Archbishop of Sydney and AUSTRALIA'S FIRST CARDINAL, born in Leighlinbridge.

CAPTAIN MYLES KEOGH, one of Ireland's 'WILD GEESE' (*see* Co. Limerick, page 182). He was born in ORCHARD HOUSE near LEIGHLIN-BRIDGE on 25 March 1840. As aide to General Custer, he died heroically in CUSTER'S LAST STAND at the BATTLE OF THE LITTLE BIGHORN, Montana, in 1876. Keogh's was the only body not mutilated by the Indians after the battle and the Sioux Chief RED HORSE spoke afterwards of an officer 'who rode a horse with four white

Captain Keogh

feet' as the bravest he had ever seen. COMANCHE, Keogh's horse, had four white feet and was THE ONLY SURVIVOR OF THE BATTLE. He was rescued and taken to Fort Lincoln and nursed back to health. Orders were issued that no one should ever ride him again – the only time in American history when such an order has been given by the Cavalry. When Comanche died he was stuffed and put on show at the University of Kansas in Lawrence, where he can still be seen.

Well, I never knew this
ABOUT
County Carlow

Carlow is THE SECOND-SMALLEST COUNTY IN THE REPUBLIC OF IRELAND.

In the middle of a field some 2 miles (3 km) outside Carlow Town is BROWNE'S HILL DOLMEN, a 5,000-year-old portal tomb that has the BIGGEST CAPSTONE IN EUROPE, weighing in at over 100 tons.

If the slender spire of the ADELAIDE MEMORIAL CHURCH that soars above the tiny village of MYSHALL near Bagenalstown seems familiar, that is because the design is based on the 404-ft (123-m) spire of Salisbury cathedral – the tallest spire in Ireland or Britain. The church was built, by her father, in memory of CONSTANCE DUGUID, who died in a riding accident in the 1880s, just having become engaged.

JOHN WATSON of BALLYDARTON, LEIGHLINBRIDGE, killed THE LAST WOLF IN IRELAND at BALTINGLASS, just across the border in Co. Wicklow, in 1786. As more and more landlords began to put sheep on their lands, the wolf, which had been common in Ireland and even kept as a pet in Celtic times, became a pest. The Irish wolfhound, allegedly descended from FINN McCOOL's mighty hound BRAN (*see* Co. Antrim, page 221), was bred for the purpose of hunting it down, with such success that by the end of the 18th century the wolf was quite extinct in Ireland.

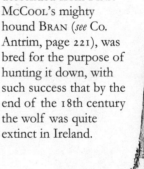

John Watson's grandson ROBERT, also of Ballydarton (a fine 19th-century Gothic house just outside the village), was a celebrated Master of Foxhounds who loved fox-hunting so much that he was convinced he would be reincarnated as a fox. He was buried, at his own request, in a fox earth, to cries of 'Gone away!'

IRELAND'S FIRST POLO CLUB was founded in 1872 by HORACE ROCHFORT of CLOGRENANE in Co. Carlow.

BAGENALSTOWN, built by one of the Bagenals of nearby DUNLECKNEY MANOR, was intended to be a 'New

VERSAILLES'. However, only the tiny, but exquisite, classical Court House was ever completed.

DUCKETT'S GROVE near Carlow town, a spectacular Gothic fantasy built in 1830, now in ruins, has THE BIGGEST CASTELLATED GATEWAY IN IRELAND.

Gateway at Duckett's Grove

County Dublin

County Town: Dublin

Dubh Linn – 'dark pool'

Howth Castle

Howth

Open House

There is always an extra place laid at the dinner table in HOWTH CASTLE. This custom dates from 1575, when pirate queen GRACE O'MALLEY sailed into Howth harbour on her way back from seeing Queen Elizabeth in England (*see* Co. Mayo, page 20). She paid a visit to the castle but was refused admittance because the family was at dinner. Grace was outraged by this snub, and when she happened upon the lord of the castle's heir, playing with his friends, it was but the work of a moment for her to abduct

the boy and take him off to her home on the coast of Mayo, Rockfleet Castle. Her ransom demand was that the doors of Howth Castle should forevermore be left open at meal times and that no one in search of food and shelter be turned away. The Lord of Howth agreed to her wishes and the pledge is honoured to this day.

It was on to the east pier at Howth that a good number of the guns used by the IRISH VOLUNTEERS (*see* Co. Antrim, page 221) during the 1916 EASTER RISING were smuggled ashore in 1914. They were transported here on board his yacht *Asgard* by ERSKINE CHILDERS, in a scenario straight out of his spy novel written a few years earlier, *The Riddle of the Sands*. Childers's wife Rita and three friends sailed on the yacht with him to help allay the suspicions of the patrolling British Navy. In 1922 Childers was arrested by the Irish Free State for carrying a weapon and executed by firing squad. His son ERSKINE HAMILTON CHILDERS became IRELAND'S FOURTH PRESIDENT in 1973.

Portmarnock

From East to West

On 24 June 1930 the Australian aviator CHARLES KINGSFORD SMITH took off from the sands of PORTMARNOCK in an attempt TO FLY THE ATLANTIC FROM EAST TO WEST. On board as navigator was CAPTAIN PADDY SAUL, son of a Dublin coal merchant, who had answered an advert in the *Irish Times* earlier that month. The plane was a Fokker monoplane called the *Southern Cross*, in which Kingsford Smith had already become THE FIRST MAN TO FLY ACROSS THE PACIFIC in 1928.

In that same year, 1928, on 12–13 April, a BREMEN aircraft co-piloted by the Dublin-born fighter pilot CAPTAIN JAMES FITZMAURICE had flown from BALDONNEL airfield south of Dublin to NEWFOUNDLAND, ON THE FIRST TRANSATLANTIC

FLIGHT FROM EAST TO WEST. However, the Bremen had fallen through the ice on landing and been unable to carry on, and Kingsford Smith wanted to make it all the way to New York. In this he was successful, reaching Harbor Grace in Newfoundland in one piece some 32 hours after leaving Portmarnock, and carrying on to New York the next day.

Two years later in 1932, JIM MOLLISON, the husband of aviator AMY JOHNSON, took off from Portmarnock Sands in a DE HAVILLAND PUSS MOTH and reached Newfoundland 31 hours later, having achieved THE FIRST SOLO TRANSATLANTIC CROSSING FROM EAST TO WEST.

Rathfarnham

Love and Hell Fire

At the beginning of the 19th century RATHFARNHAM was the scene of one of Irish history's most tragic love affairs – that of ROBERT EMMET and his great love SARAH CURRAN. Sarah was the daughter of a lawyer, JOHN CURRAN, who lived, with his family, at THE PRIORY in Rathfarnham. She was extraordinarily pretty and vivacious, with thick auburn ringlets and captivating blue eyes that enchanted all who met her.

Robert Emmet was a wild and headstrong nationalist, born in Co. Kerry in 1778. While at Trinity College he joined Wolfe Tone's UNITED IRISHMEN and supported the

1798 REBELLION, which caused his expulsion from college and flight to France, where he tried to enlist the support of Napoleon. He returned to Ireland in 1802 and planned an attack on DUBLIN CASTLE to inspire his fellow Irish to rise up against the ACT OF UNION. As the headquarters of English rule ever since the Normans had built a fortress there in 1228, Dublin Castle was a hugely symbolic target for revolutionaries and nationalists.

Whenever he could, Emmet would slip into the Priory to see Sarah, despite her father's disapproval. Although John Curran had defended many of the United Irishmen on trial after 1798, he was worried that Sarah's relationship with Emmet would put her and her family in danger. However, Sarah was smitten with the dashing and passionate young rebel and they became secretly engaged.

Then Emmet's plot went horribly wrong when his powder store accidentally blew up. His followers took to the streets and in the ensuing brawl the Lord Chief Justice, LORD KILWARDEN, was dragged from his carriage and killed. Emmet was captured a few days later and sent to Kilmainham Gaol.

From his cell, he entrusted a letter for Sarah to the prison warden, GEORGE DUNN, but was betrayed when Dunn went to the authorities. Soldiers were sent to search the Priory. Sarah's sister Amelia just managed to burn the incriminating correspondence between Emmet and Sarah while the soldiers were occupied downstairs, but Sarah was later thrown out of the house by her father for endangering all their lives. She took refuge with friends in Cork (*see* Co. Cork, page 158). Emmet was put on trial and sentenced to death. His final speech has subsequently served as an inspiration for generations of Irish revolutionaries: 'Let no man write my epitaph . . . When my country takes her place among the nations of the earth, then, and not until then, let my epitaph be written.'

On 20 September 1803, Robert Emmet was hanged and then beheaded in Dublin. To this day no one is certain where his body is buried, although several Dublin churches claim his remains. It seems likely that once it was safe, he was secretly interred in the family church of St Peter's in Aungier Street (now demolished). Sarah never recovered from her grief. She married a soldier named Robert Sturgeon and moved to Sicily, but her heart was broken and she died in 1808. Her sad story inspired a poem by the Irish poet THOMAS MOORE:

She is far from the land where her
  young hero sleeps,
And lovers are round her, sighing:
But coldly she turns from their
  gaze, and weeps,
For her heart in his grave is lying.

An unmissable and hugely daunting landmark near Rathfarnham is the

Hell Fire Club

black ruin that crowns the horizon, atop nearby MOUNT PELIER. This is a hunting lodge built in 1725 by Speaker WILLIAM CONOLLY (*see* Co. Kildare, page 67), owner of RATH-FARNHAM CASTLE, whose grounds spread over much of the Wicklow Mountains. After his death, the lodge was acquired by the notorious HELL FIRE CLUB, founded at the EAGLE TAVERN on Cork Hill in Dublin by RICHARD PARSONS, 1ST EARL OF ROSSE. The club, whose members were all rich, aristocratic young bucks, would meet to drink, gamble, and generally behave badly, presided over by a large black cat. Stories abounded of debauchery, womanising and satanic rituals at the lodge, and since it was built on the site of an ancient burial ground, using stones from the old tombs, and was very possibly cursed, these tales have the ring of truth about them. Certainly the hilltop silhouette is chilling.

The playwright JOHN MILLINGTON SYNGE (1871–1909) was born at 2 Newtown Villas in Rathfarnham.

Well, I never knew this
ABOUT
COUNTY DUBLIN

IRELAND'S FIRST RAILWAY AND THE WORLD'S FIRST SUBURBAN COMMUTER RAILWAY LINE opened between DUBLIN and DUN LAOGHAIRE in 1834.

IRELAND'S ONLY NUDIST BEACH is at FORTY FOOT LEAP, beneath the Sandycove Martello tower, in DUN LAOGHAIRE.

ROBERT FREDERICK XENON GELDOF, rock star and co-founder of LIVE AID, was born in DUN LAOGHAIRE in 1951.

Singing star RONAN KEATING (Boyzone) was born in SWORDS in 1977.

WILLIAM BUTLER YEATS (1865–1939) was born in a cottage (now demol-

Malahide Castle

ished) in Sandymount Avenue, near SANDYMOUNT CASTLE, SANDYMOUNT.

MALAHIDE CASTLE was occupied by the TALBOT family for 791 years from 1185 until 1976, making it THE OLD-EST INHABITED CASTLE IN IRELAND TO BE LIVED IN CONTINUOUSLY BY THE SAME FAMILY. On the morning of the BATTLE OF THE BOYNE in 1690, 14 members of the family had breakfast together in the dining room at Malahide. None of them ever returned.

The GRAND HOTEL at MALAHIDE was once owned by DR JOHN COLOHAN, who imported THE FIRST PETROL-DRIVEN CAR INTO IRELAND, a BENZ, in 1898. The Australian aviator CHARLES KINGSFORD SMITH stayed at the hotel in 1930 before flying across the Atlantic from PORT-MARNOCK SANDS (*see* Portmarnock, page 62).

The key battle in Irish history was fought at CLONTARF in 1014. THE FIRST TRUE KING OF ALL IRELAND, BRIAN BORU, here defeated the pagan Danes who had colonised Dublin, losing his own life in the conflict. A good way inland now, Clontarf was beside the sea in those days, before the great land reclamation schemes, and little remains to commemorate or conjure up an idea of the battle scene except a Brian Boru Avenue and Brian Boru's Well.

BRAM STOKER (1847–1912), author of *Dracula*, was born in 15 Marino Crescent, CLONTARF.

IRELAND'S FIRST RECORDED MANNED BALLOON FLIGHT landed at Clontarf on 19 January 1785, after a short flight from the gardens of LEINSTER HOUSE in Dublin. On board was 30-year-old RICHARD CROSBIE from Co. Wicklow.

The first manned balloon flight across the Irish Sea was completed in 1817 by Windham Sadler (1796–1824), who took off from Portobello Barracks in Dublin and landed in Holyhead.

Maureen O'Hara, film actress (*Rio Grande*, *The Quiet Man*, *Big Jake*), was born in Ranelagh in 1920.

The first catamaran, the *Experiment*, was designed and built in Dublin by Sir William Petty (1623–87) and launched on 22 December 1662. The *Experiment* won the world's first recorded open yacht race, held in Dublin Bay in January 1663. Sir William Petty was the author of the Down Survey (1655–6), the first mapping of all Ireland.

James Joyce (1882–1941) was born at No. 41 Brighton Square in Rathgar. His greatest novel, *Ulysses*, is the story of just one day in Dublin – 16 June 1904, the date of Joyce's first walk out with his muse Nora Barnacle, the woman who was to become his wife (*see* Co. Galway, page 5). *Ulysses* begins at the Martello tower in Sandycove, where Joyce stayed for some time with Oliver St John Gogarty (*see* Mayo, page 20), and which is now a museum in Joyce's memory.

The world's first commercial atmospheric railway was opened in 1844 between Dun Laoghaire and Dalkey. It was designed and built by Isambard Kingdom Brunel and operated for 10 years until 1854.

Dalkey is a breezy seaside village with stunning cliff views along the coastline and across Dublin Bay, and a quaint, unspoilt main street with little shops and a couple of historic castles. George Bernard Shaw lived in Dalkey as a boy from 1866 to 1874 at Torca Cottage on Dalkey Hill. Today the author Maeve Binchy, former Ferrari Formula One racing driver Eddie Irvine, and singer Van Morrison all live on Sorrento Road, while film director Neil Jordan lives on Sorrento Terrace and U2 band member David Evans (The Edge) lives in Sorrento Cottage. BBC presenters Gloria Hunniford and John Simpson and *Late Late Show* host Pat Kenny live around Bulloch Harbour, while singer Lisa Stansfield lives in Mount Henry on Torca Road.

Alfred Harmsworth, Lord Northcliffe (1865–1921), the newspaper tycoon who founded the London papers *Daily Mail* and *Daily Mirror*, was born in Chapelizod.

COUNTY KILDARE

COUNTY TOWN: NAAS

Chille-darruigh – 'the church under the oak'

Kildare Cathedral

Kildare

Eternal flame

KILDARE CATHEDRAL stands on the site of the original *Chille-darruigh* or 'church under the oak' where ST BRIGID set up her religious cell in AD 490. St Brigid is Ireland's most famous saint after St Patrick and was THE FIRST WOMAN IN IRELAND TO TAKE UP THE WORK OF THE CHURCH. In her church, she enjoined that a fire should be kept burning continuously 'for the benefit of the poor and for strangers'. GERALD CAMBRENSIS writes: 'nuns and religious women are so careful and diligent in supplying and recruiting the fire with fuel that

from the time of St Brigid it hath remained always unextinguished'. It was finally extinguished at the time of the Reformation, but St Brigid's memory still burns bright and her feast day, 1 February, still brings women to Kildare from all over the world to celebrate *Feile Bride*.

Over the door of the cathedral is a constantly replenished cross woven from rushes, known as ST BRIGID'S CROSS. It was first plaited by the saint as she was converting a dying pagan to Christianity and protects people from bad luck and illness. St Brigid's Cross was chosen as their symbol by RTE, the Irish national broadcasting organisation.

By the middle of the 19th century

Castletown House

the cathedral had fallen into a ruinous state and the DUKE OF LEINSTER took himself off around Ireland, dressed as a beggar, to raise funds for the rebuilding.

Leixlip

Salmon and Guinness

The riverside village of LEIXLIP is the site of the ORIGINAL GUINNESS BREWERY, founded by brothers ARTHUR AND RICHARD GUINNESS in 1755. Four years later, in 1759, Arthur, in great trepidation, signed a 9,000-year lease on a site at ST JAMES'S GATE in Dublin, with a view to expanding the business. It did expand and is now THE BIGGEST BREWERY IN EUROPE. The Leixlip brewery produced a traditional ale but, at St James's Gate, Arthur decided to try and brew a new kind of beer from London that had a rich, black colour from using roasted hops. It was called PORTER because it was popular with the porters at London markets such as Borough and Billingsgate.

Leixlip Castle

There is a plaque on the main street in Leixlip, commemorating the brewery, and it is thought that a couple of restored stone cottages just off the road are all that remain of the original brewery complex. Since 1958, Leixlip Castle has been lived in by Desmond Guinness, who formed the Irish Georgian Society there in that same year.

Arthur Guinness, born at nearby Celbridge, is buried in a vault beside the ruins of the round tower at Oughterard.

Leixlip is also the site of the world's first hydraulic fish lift. The famous salmon leap, or *Laz Hlaup*, after which the village is named, was compromised by the building of a hydroelectric generating plant on the river. The salmon needed another way to get to their spawning grounds upriver and so two engineers, Jim Dooge and Anthony Murphy, came up with a salmon lift that works like a lock. Fish enter the lock through a narrow, downstream inlet that funnels the water and produces turbulence, reminiscent of a waterfall, to attract the salmon. Gates are closed behind them, the lock is flooded and the upstream gate is opened to allow the fish to swim on.

Today, Leixlip might be renamed as *Leixchip* or even *Siliconlip* – it is the European headquarters of the computer chip manufacturers Intel, who make Pentium processors there. Hewlett Packard also own a large works at Leixlip, making cartridges for their inkjet printers.

Castletown
A Bit Cramped . . .

The pretty village of Celbridge, on the Liffey, is home to Castletown, Ireland's first Palladian mansion and the largest house in Ireland. Castletown was begun in 1722 for William Conolly, Speaker of the Irish Parliament and, at the time, the richest man in Ireland. It was eventually completed by his great nephew, Tom Conolly.

It was at Castletown that Tom Conolly entertained the Devil to supper one night. Out hunting, he befriended a charming stranger and invited him home for dinner. When the guest removed his boots Conolly saw, to his horror, that the chap was possessed of cloven hoofs. A quick thinker, Conolly settled the Devil down in the dining room and retired, ostensibly to get some wine, but in fact to summon the local priest. When the good man of the cloth arrived he tried to shoo the Devil away by throwing his breviary at him, but the book missed and cracked a mirror. Nonetheless, the Devil was scared off and vanished through the hearthstone and up the chimney. Today, you can still see the cracked mirror and the shattered hearthstone in the dining room.

The last private owner of Castletown was the 6th Lord Carew, who was married to the only daughter of the 15th Earl of Lauderdale. When asked what it was like to live in the largest house in

Ireland, Lord Carew answered: '*My wife thinks it a bit cramped – it is the smallest house she has ever lived in!*'

Castletown, saved by Desmond Guinness from demolition in 1967 and now owned by the Irish state, is open to the publlic.

The design of Castletown greatly influenced that of LEINSTER HOUSE in Dublin which, in turn, inspired the architect of the WHITE HOUSE in Washington, JAMES HOBAN (*see* Co. Kilkenny, page 77).

Kilkea Castle

Monkeying around . . .

KILKEA CASTLE near Athy, built in 1180, is a claimant for THE OLDEST CONTINUOUSLY INHABITED CASTLE IN IRELAND and was closely associated with the powerful FITZGERALD family, Earls of Kildare and Dukes of Leinster.

Kilkea Castle

Kilkea Castle and Lord Kildare
Are more than any woman can
  bear.

This wistful couplet was written in the 1880s by the beautiful but bored MARCHIONESS OF KILDARE, about life at Kilkea Castle with her kind, rather dull husband. She was lucky. One particular family member, the 16th-century 'WIZARD EARL', was anything but dull and apparently still haunts the castle. Fond of dabbling in magic, he was trying one day to convince his somewhat sceptical wife that he could turn himself into a bird. But, and here is the rub, only if she, his wife, showed no fear – should she do so, he warned, he would disappear for ever. As promised the Earl did turn himself into a bird and his wife, playing her part to perfection, showed supreme indifference, indeed, carried on as though nothing unusual were happening. Unfortunately, at that moment the castle cat strolled in, spotted the bird and, as cats do, made a spring for it. The Earl's wife screamed in alarm and the 11th Earl of Kildare vanished away.

That would have seemed to be that – lessons were learned, etc, etc, life went on. Except that, every seven years since then, the Earl rises from his enchanted sleep beneath the nearby Rath of Mullaghmast, gallops on a white, silver-shod charger into the same room from which he disappeared, and then rides away to the

Curragh, no doubt for a bit of a flutter.

High up on the Haunted Tower at Kilkea, it is possible to see the rough carving of a monkey on the end of a chain, clinging to the wall. This monkey features prominently on the FitzGerald coat of arms, and for a very good reason. In the 13th century, the infant John FitzGerald (who was to become the 1st Earl of Kildare) was asleep in Woodstock Castle, a nearby family seat at Athy, when fire broke out. Everyone evacuated the building in an orderly manner and lined up on the lawn to enjoy the blaze. Some time later a manservant enquired about the welfare of the young master and it was realised that no one had thought to snatch the child from his room, which by now had been reduced to ashes. Imagine the relief when a monkey, a member of the castle's menagerie, appeared at a lancet window of the only surviving tower, with the baby John in his arms. The future Earl was safe!

The monkey had rescued their
*　fancied prey,*
And placed him in yonder tower.
For centuries now hath the
*　monkey been*
In his dark unconscious rest;
But emblazoned still is his image
*　seen*
In the proud Fitzgerald's crest.

JONATHAN SWIFT gained sweet revenge on a contemporary Earl of Kildare, with whom he was having a disagreement, by mischievously lampooning the monkey story in *Gulliver's Travels*. He includes an episode where Gulliver is carried off and force-fed by an ape in Brobdingnag.

The castle is now a hotel.

Straffan

Full Steam Ahead

Inside a small, reconstructed church, reached by a winding driveway off a quiet country lane, near the undemonstrative village of STRAFFAN, you can gaze upon one of the true wonders of the modern world, THE VERY FIRST 'AUTOMOBILE' IN EXISTENCE. This is THE FIRST SELF-PROPELLED FOUR-WHEELED OBJECT EVER CREATED, a small working model of a steam engine made in 1797 by the Cornish pioneer RICHARD TREVITHICK, as a real-life blueprint for the engineers who had to put together his revolutionary machines. This tiny, shiny thing of beauty changed our world for ever, and to look upon it is momentous.

It is the Crown Jewel of the magical STRAFFAN STEAM MUSEUM, which tells the story of inventors and engineers from James Watt to William Dargan and contains a

fascinating collection of steam memorabilia and machinery, most of it used in Ireland and all fully restored and pristine. Highlights are a scale model of *Colossus*, the locomotive that ran on IRELAND'S FIRST RAILWAY from Dublin to Dun Laoghaire (*see* Co. Dublin), and a vast, steam-powered laundry machine used by the nuns from a nearby nunnery.

The museum's newest and quirkiest treasures are two cobbled stones from the courtyard in Belfast where JOHN BOYD DUNLOP developed his pneumatic tyre. The cobbles bear groove marks made by the world's first pneumatic tyres as they were tested by being ridden round and round in the yard.

The KILDARE GOLF AND COUNTRY CLUB in Straffan is the home of the 2006 RYDER CUP.

Ballitore

Endurance

Neat little BALLITORE village was founded in 1685 by ABEL STRETTEL and JOHN BARCROFT and was THE FIRST PLANNED QUAKER TOWN IN EUROPE. In 1726 another Quaker, ABRAHAM SHACKLETON, set up a school here which was attended by EDMUND BURKE from 1741 to 1744.

Abraham Shackleton's most celebrated descendant was the explorer ERNEST SHACKLETON (1874– 1922), born at KILKEA HOUSE, second in a family of 10 children. He was a member of ROBERT FALCON SCOTT'S first expedition to the South Pole in 1901 and led his own attempt in 1907, which got within 100 miles (160 km) of the Pole, nearer than anyone else at that time.

After AMUNDSEN became the first man to reach the Pole in 1911, Shackleton determined to be the first to cross the whole continent and sailed for Antarctica in 1914, just as World War One broke out. His ship was named *Endurance* after the family motto '*Fortitudine vincimus*' – 'By endurance we conquer'.

Endurance reached the Antarctic but became trapped in the ice for 10 months, before breaking up. The crew then spent six days on the open seas in three small boats before they made it to the uninhabited ELEPHANT ISLAND. Shackleton and five others took one of the boats and left to find help on SOUTH GEORGIA, 800 miles (1,300 km) away. They reached safety after 16 hellish days, in May 1916. Three months later the men on Elephant Island were finally rescued, nearly two years after the start of their expedition. Their adventures and epic tales of survival captured the imagination of the world. Shackleton may not have succeeded in his endeavours but, as SIR EDMUND HILLARY, first man to climb Mt Everest, said, '*when disaster strikes and all hope has gone, get down on your knees and pray for Shackleton*'. Ernest Shackleton died on South Georgia in 1922 and is buried there.

Another member of the Shackleton family who found fame of a sort was Ernest's brother FRANK, who was implicated in the mysterious case of the THEFT OF THE IRISH CROWN JEWELS. The Irish Crown Jewels were the insignia of the ORDER OF ST PATRICK, the Irish equivalent of England's Order of the Garter. Instituted by GEORGE III in 1783, they consisted of a star and a badge, encrusted with rubies, diamonds and emeralds, and were held in DUBLIN CASTLE.

In 1907, on the eve of a visit to Dublin by EDWARD VII, the Jewels went missing. There were no signs of forced entry, indicating an inside job. SIR ARTHUR VICARS, the Ulster King of Arms responsible for the safety of the Jewels, was blamed for their disappearance and forced to resign, but many think the real culprit was his assistant, the flamboyant Frank Shackleton, who was named as the villain by Vicars in his last will and testament. Shackleton, full of charm and wit but always in financial difficulties, was one of a circle of homosexuals who lived in Dublin Castle and was suspected of indulging in orgies of an 'unnatural nature' within the castle walls. It is possible that he was being blackmailed and needed money. It is also possible that the King ordered the investigation to be hushed up for fear of revealing that his own brother-in-law, the 9TH DUKE OF ARGYLL, was one of those indulging in the orgies. The Jewels have never been found.

About 1 mile (1.6 km) to the west of Ballitore is the RATH OF MULLAGHMAST, under which the Wizard Earl of Kildare is reputed to be sleeping (*see* Kilkea Castle, page 70).

Well, I never knew this
ABOUT
COUNTY KILDARE

Kildare is IRELAND'S FLATTEST COUNTY, contains THE GREATER PART OF THE WORLD'S LARGEST PEAT BOG, the BOG OF ALLEN, and has MORE MILES OF CANAL THAN ANY OTHER COUNTY IN IRELAND.

ST PATRICK'S COLLEGE at MAYNOOTH was founded by the English, with help from EDMUND BURKE, in 1795 so that Catholic priests would not have to go to post-Revolution France to study, where they might pick up dangerous ideas. It is reputed to be THE BIGGEST SEMINARY IN THE WORLD. The yew trees in the college gardens are some of the OLDEST TREES IN IRELAND, over 1,000 years old.

Maynooth was also at the forefront of electrical research, thanks to its pioneering Professor of Science, REV. NICHOLAS CALLAN (1799–1864). In 1836, in his laboratory at Maynooth, he invented the ELECTRIC INDUCTION COIL and THE WORLD'S FIRST TRANSFORMER. He also created what were, in their time, the WORLD'S BIGGEST BATTERY and the WORLD'S MOST POWERFUL MAGNET. His designs are used in modern electric motors and car engine ignitions, and many of his inventions and instruments can still be seen in the Science Museum at Maynooth.

CELBRIDGE ABBEY was the home of ESTHER VANHOMRIGH, Swift's 'Vanessa' (*see* City of Dublin, page 48). There is a rustic bench down by the river where she would retire to

ponder on her tragic love for Swift, whose eventual rejection hastened her early death.

At BODENSTOWN, not far from Celbridge, is the grave of THEOBALD WOLFE TONE (1763–1798). There are commemorations held here every year by FIANNA FAIL and SINN FEIN in honour of 'THE FATHER OF IRISH REPUBLICANISM'. Wolfe Tone was a founding member of the UNITED IRISHMEN, a brotherhood of all religions, inspired by the new ideas of

Celbridge Abbey

the French Revolution and dedicated to political reform. He went to revolutionary France to enlist help for a rising against English rule in Ireland but was later captured at Lough Swilly, in Donegal, while attempting to land with a French force during the 1798 rebellion. Taken to Dublin Castle, he slit his own throat before he could be executed.

The largest artificial lake in Ireland can be found on the Lyons demesne at Hazelhatch, owned by Tony Ryan, founder of Ryanair.

Standing in a field near Hewlett Packard, on the Celbridge Road out of Leixlip, is an ebullient, almost surreal, conical structure called The Wonderful Barn. And it is wonderful, 70 ft (21 m) tall with a staircase of 94 steps winding drunkenly upwards around the outside and looking, for all the world, like a fairground helter-skelter. It was put up on the Castletown estate in 1743 to give employment to the local tenants and provide an eastern vista from the house. Not just a folly, the barn was used to store grain.

Remodelled in 1747, Moore Abbey at Monasterevin, one-time ancestral home of the Earls of Drogheda, is one of only two surviving examples of a large-scale mid-18th-century Gothic house in Ireland (the other is the Gothic façade of Castle Ward in Co. Down). It had the reputation of being a very cold house. When the Earl of Clonmel came to stay in the 19th century, he brought with him a hugely heavy trunk which took a whole team of footmen to haul up the stairs. At the top it burst open and was found to be packed full of coal. In the 1920s the house was rented out to Count John McCormack, the operatic tenor (*see* Co. Westmeath, see page 120), who was prone to wander the grounds down by the River Barrow singing 'Song of my Heart'. The house is now a hospital.

The Curragh comes from an old Irish word for race course, which is appropriate since it is home to Ireland's premier race courses, The Curragh, where the Irish Derby is

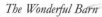

The Wonderful Barn

run, and PUNCHESTOWN, where NATIONAL HUNT meetings take place. At TULLY, just south of Kildare, which lies in the heart of The Curragh, is the NATIONAL STUD, a state-owned bloodstock farm founded by the eccentric COLONEL WILLIAM WALKER in 1900. Walker achieved great success by running his stud with the aid of astrology – he had skylights put into all the stables so that the horses could be directly influenced by sunbeams and moonlight.

In 1910, next to the National Stud, Colonel Walker, by now LORD WAVERTREE, opened his JAPANESE GARDENS, widely regarded as THE FINEST JAPANESE GARDENS IN EUROPE. They were laid out between 1906 and 1910 by the Japanese garden designer TASSA EIDA and his son MINORU. The gardens take the form of an allegorical journey of the soul from Oblivion, represented by a cave, to Eternity – a Zen garden of contemplation – by way of cherry trees, bamboos, magnolias, maples, rock gardens, water features and miniature bridges.

The 'RACE THAT SAVED MOTOR SPORT', the GORDON BENNETT MOTOR RACE of 1903, was run mainly through Co. Kildare, centred on ATHY. This was THE FIRST EVENT IN THE WORLD TO BE HELD ON CLOSED ROADS. The Gordon Bennett motor races, instigated by JAMES GORDON BENNETT, proprietor of the *New York Herald*, drew competitors from all over Europe and America and the first one took place in France in 1900. In 1902 the race was won by an Englishman, SELWYN EDGE, in a Napier car and, in accordance with the competition rules, England was to host the 1903 race. However, motor racing was forbidden in England and so the organisers turned to Ireland for a suitable racecourse, which they found at Athy, although some improvements had to be made to the local roads, such as flattening out banks and corners and smoothing the road surface in places. The 1903 race was won by CAMILLE JENATZY in a Mercedes. The Gordon Bennett Races paved the way for Grand Prix racing, which began in France in 1906.

DONNELLY'S HOLLOW, a natural amphitheatre at the eastern end of THE CURRAGH, was the venue for THE MOST FAMOUS BOXING MATCH IN IRISH HISTORY, when, in 1815, the giant Irish fighter DAN DONNELLY beat the English champion GEORGE COOPER. A small obelisk commemorates the occasion and Donnelly's footprints as he left the 'ring' are preserved.

COUNTY KILKENNY

COUNTY TOWN: KILKENNY

Cill Chainnigh – 'St Cainneach's church'

St Candice's Cathedral, Kilkenny

Kilkenny City

Butlers and Witches

The city of KILKENNY, lying on a small hill above the River Nore, is generally regarded as IRELAND'S LOVELIEST INLAND CITY. Many of the buildings are made from the local black polished limestone known as KILKENNY MARBLE, which gives the city its nickname of the 'MARBLE CITY'.

In 1366 the STATUTES OF KILKENNY were enacted, aimed at preventing the English settlers from becoming too Irish. On pain of death or imprisonment they were forbidden to speak the Irish language, marry an Irish person, wear Irish clothes or use an Irish name, and the two communities were kept entirely separate, living in different parts of the city – there are still areas of Kilkenny called ENGLISHTOWN and IRISHTOWN.

ST CANDICE'S CATHEDRAL, built in

the 13th century, stands on the site of ST CAINNEACH'S CHURCH (*Cill Chainnigh*), from which Kilkenny takes its name. It is the SECOND-LARGEST MEDIEVAL CATHEDRAL IN IRELAND, after St Patrick's in Dublin.

JONATHAN SWIFT, BISHOP BERKELEY and playwrights WILLIAM CONGREVE and GEORGE FARQUHAR were all educated at KILKENNY COLLEGE, which was founded in 1666.

The splendidly situated KILKENNY CASTLE was the seat of the powerful BUTLER family from the 14th century until 1935. In the 18th century it was the home of LADY ELEANOR BUTLER, one of the celebrated LADIES OF LLANGOLLEN (*see* Woodstock, page 80). When EDWARD VII visited the castle in 1904, he asked who all the people lining up to meet him were. '*They are the Butlers,*' came the reply. '*Well, why aren't they serving the bloody drinks then?*' retorted the monarch. The castle was given to the city in 1967.

DAME ALICE KYTELER was born at KYTELER'S HOUSE in Kilkenny in 1280, daughter of a banker. She was fabulously beautiful and when her father died in 1298 she inherited his business and became prosperous as well. She extended her house and turned it into an inn where wealthy young men would come and vie for her attention. She made four very good marriages to rich men, all of whom died after feasting well at the inn, and left her their fortunes. Their suspicious deaths, allied to tales of orgies and satanic rituals, sparked an inquisition ordered by an English bishop obsessed with witchcraft, and Dame Alice was found guilty and sentenced to be burned at the stake. She managed to escape and flee to London, leaving her maid to be incinerated in her stead. Today you can dine at the medieval KYTELER'S INN, on the site of Dame Alice's home.

Kilkenny Castle

Callan

*Fizzy Drinks, Canned Ham
and Steam*

The little town of CALLAN, a few miles south of Kilkenny, is a quiet, unassuming place, and yet from here have sprung a surprising number of iconic American institutions, including THE MOST POPULAR SOFT DRINK IN THE WORLD; THE WHITE HOUSE; THE PADDLE STEAMER; and ONE OF THE WORLD'S PIONEERING MEAT PACKERS.

In the 17th century WILLIAM CANDLER, an army officer, brought his family to live in Callan, on land granted to him by Oliver Cromwell. A number of his descendants emigrated to America and settled in Atlanta. In 1891, the pharmacist ASA GRIGGS CANDLER (1851–1929) purchased the formula for COCA-COLA, which had been developed by another pharmacist from Atlanta, JOHN S. PEMBERTON, as a tonic for minor ailments. Candler proved to be

a brilliant marketing man and, under his guidance, Coca-Cola went on to become one of the world's most recognisable brands. Asa's son Howard, who himself became chairman of Coca-Cola, built a sumptuous house in Atlanta and called it 'CALLANWOLDE' as a tribute to his family's Irish roots.

JAMES HOBAN (1762–1831), who was born in DESART, just outside Callan, studied architecture in Dublin and emigrated to America in 1789. He built the SOUTH CAROLINA STATE HOUSE and then won the competition to design the new presidential mansion in Washington, which he based on LEINSTER HOUSE in Dublin. GEORGE WASHINGTON requested that the building be reduced to two storeys for economic reasons. In 1812 the WHITE HOUSE was burned down by the British, and Hoban supervised the restoration work,

Callanwolde

Leinster House, Dublin

Hoban's original White House design

The White House, today

completed in 1817. Since then the White House has been enlarged with the addition of the North and South Porticos and the East and West Wings. James Hoban has appeared on both Irish and American stamps.

In 1824 Hoban designed ROSSEN-ARRA HOUSE, a large country home in Kilmaganny, south of Callan. The artist SIR JOHN LAVERY (*see* Belfast, page 211) spent his last few years at Rossenarra, which had come into the possession of his wife's family. He died there in 1941. During the 1970s Rossenarra belonged to the American novelist RICHARD CONDON, author of *The Manchurian Candidate* and *Prizzi's Honor*.

The parents of ROBERT FULTON (1765–1815), THE MAN WHO INVENT-ED THE PADDLE STEAMER, came from Callan, emigrating to Philadelphia just before he was born. Fulton also invented a hand-cranked SUBMARINE called the *Nautilus*. In his novel *20,000 Leagues under the Sea*, JULES VERNE based CAPTAIN NEMO'S SUBMARINE the *Nautilus* on Fulton's prototype.

PATRICK CUDAHY was born in Callan on St Patrick's Day in 1849 and was only three months old when his family moved to Milwaukee, Wisconsin. Aged 13, Patrick started to work for the meat-packing company PLANKINTON AND ARMOUR. He soon worked his way up to become a part-ner and eventually owner, changing the name of the firm to PATRICK CUDAHY. His company gained a rep-utation for innovation, particularly in the area of meat preservation, and WAS ONE OF THE FIRST IN THE WORLD TO PRODUCE CANNED HAMS, SLICED DRIED BEEF AND ITALIAN-STYLE SAUSAGE. It was also THE FIRST MEAT-PACKING COMPANY IN THE WORLD TO INSTALL A 'SHARP' FREEZER. (This is a type of air freezer that freezes very fast at very low temperatures – as in the phrase 'a sharp frost'.)

Woodstock

Love and Scandal

WOODSTOCK, a fine 18th-century house near INSTIOGE, featured prominently in the scandalous tale of the LADIES OF LLANGOLLEN. In the

1770s, SARAH PONSONBY (1755–1831), a shy and sensitive girl, lived here with her cousins, SIR WILLIAM AND LADY FOWNES. A few miles away, at KILKENNY CASTLE, lived the much older LADY ELEANOR BUTLER (1739–1829), considered something of a bookworm, and living under the threat of being dispatched to a convent, as it was thought she would never marry. They met, became firm friends and, in 1778, decided to run away together.

Their families were scandalised by what they considered an unnatural relationship. The girls were hunted down, forced to return home, and Lady Eleanor was sent under house arrest to relatives at BORRIS (*see* Co. Carlow, page 54). She managed to escape and made her way to Woodstock, where she climbed in through a window and hid in Sarah's room for 24 hours before being discovered. Seeing there was nothing to be done, their families relented and let the girls leave Ireland. They found their way to Wales, where they settled in a beautiful half-timbered house at Llangollen called PLAS NEWYDD.

Here they lived out the rest of their lives together as 'THE LADIES OF LLANGOLLEN'.

Woodstock passed on to the TIGHE family when Sir William Fownes's daughter married WILLIAM TIGHE. His daughter-in-law was the poetess MARY TIGHE, author of a volume of love poems called *Psyche*. She died at Woodstock in 1810, aged just 37, and there is a beautiful sculpture of her by FLAXMAN inside a small mausoleum in the village churchyard.

Woodstock was burnt to the ground in the 1920s, but the gardens remain and are open to the public.

Woodstock

Well, I never knew this
ABOUT
COUNTY KILKENNY

Jerpoint Abbey

JERPOINT ABBEY near Thomastown was once THE RICHEST ABBEY IN IRELAND. It has a 15th-century decorated cloister that is UNIQUE AMONGST IRISH CISTERCIAN ABBEYS, and also boasts THE TALLEST TOWER OF ANY CISTERCIAN CHURCH IN IRELAND.

DUNMORE CAVE near Kilkenny City has THE FINEST CALCITE FORMATIONS FOUND ANYWHERE IN IRELAND.

JAMES O'NEILL left Kilkenny for America in 1854 when he was only five years old. His son, born in New York in 1888, grew up to be the playwright EUGENE O'NEILL (*The Iceman Cometh, Long Day's Journey into Night*).

DUISKE ABBEY at Graiguenamanagh, founded in 1207, is THE LARGEST CISTERCIAN ABBEY IN IRELAND. It now performs as the parish church.

JENKINSTOWN, a 19th-century Gothic house near Ballyragget, was renamed 'Ballyshambles' by an early 20th-century owner, the 4th Lord Bellew, after the makeshift central corridor linking the two wings of the house collapsed, leaving him cut off from his servants, who lived in the other wing. The original centre block had burned down some time in the 1880s and never been rebuilt.

Beneath the massive tower of GOWRAN CHURCH, a few miles south-east of Kilkenny, is an altar tomb that bears the figure of a man in vestments. This is THE OLDEST INSCRIBED MONUMENT IN IRELAND. A translation of the Latin inscription reads: '*Ralph, known as Julianus, while he lived was kind and generous to those in need. March 1253.*'

The man after whom the Californian town of BERKELEY, with its famous University, is named, philosopher BISHOP GEORGE BERKELEY (1685– 1753), was born at

Bishop Berkeley

DYSART CASTLE near THOMASTOWN, now a romantic ruin. He founded 'IMMATERIALISM', a school of thought particularly influential in the New World, which believes that reality is 'that which can be perceived in the mind'. What can be perceived must exist and what cannot be perceived cannot exist – '*esse est percipi*' – 'to be is to be perceived'. From 1734 he served for 20 years as a hugely popular BISHOP OF CLOYNE.

COUNTY LAOIS
(formerly QUEEN'S COUNTY)

COUNTY TOWN: PORTLAOISE

Lugaid Laigne – name of a legendary warrior

The Rock of Dunamase – Ireland's 'Acropolis'

Portarlington

Excuse mon French

PORTARLINGTON takes its name from SIR HENRY BENNET, who became the 1ST EARL OF ARLINGTON and provided us with the first '*a*' in the word CABAL. The original Cabal was Charles II's notorious Committee for Foreign Affairs that took its name from the initial letters of five of its members – CLIFFORD, ARLINGTON, BUCKINGHAM, ASHLEY, AND LAUDERDALE. Many of their decisions were deeply unpopular or made in secret, hence the word cabal has come to mean 'a group of people who intrigue or meet furtively to bring about their own agenda'.

In the 17th century a large number of refugee HUGUENOTS settled in Portarlington and the town has a definite French feel to it, with tall, handsome houses that turn their backs to the street in typical French style, with extensive gardens and orchards. There are two churches, the 'ENGLISH', now disused, and the 'FRENCH', where there are many tombstones with inscriptions in French.

DAME NINETTE DE VALOIS (1898–2001), FOUNDER OF THE ROYAL BALLET, was born EDRIS STANNUS in Co. Wicklow, and spent much of her childhood at her grandfather's house, THE ELMS, near Portarlington.

The Elms

IRELAND'S FIRST TURF-FIRED POWER STATION opened in 1950, just to the north of Portarlington.

Killeshin

Beauty and Beards

KILLESHIN is one of Ireland's special, hidden places. It is tranquil and soothing. Nothing much seems to happen here, and the drowsy Irish air hangs heavy with scents and moisture. Killeshin used to be the chief town of Co. Laois, growing up around a monastery founded in the 5th century by ST COMGHAN. Now, almost nothing remains except the entrance to the monastery, ONE OF THE FINEST OF THE IRISH ROMANESQUE DOORWAYS LEFT IN THE COUNTRY, dating from the 11th century. On the capitals are carvings of exquisite detail, human faces, some shaven, some with beards or moustaches. Everywhere there are chevrons and intertwining shapes.

There is a rare inscription in Gaelic, ONE OF ONLY THREE KNOWN IN IRELAND, but unfortunately it is too worn to be able to read clearly.

There used to be a round tower here too, 103 feet (31 m) high, but it was knocked down in 1705 by a farmer, worried that it might fall on his sheep.

At nearby TIMAHOE, there *is* still a round tower, 11th-century and THE MOST RICHLY DECORATED ROUND TOWER IN IRELAND. High off the ground there is a Romanesque doorway that shows carvings of bearded heads similar to those at Killeshin, probably carved by the same craftsmen.

William Dargan

Father of Irish Railways

THE MAN WHO CHANGED THE FACE OF IRELAND, Co. Laois's most famous son, WILLIAM DARGAN, was born near Killeshin on 28 February 1799. He worked for some time as an apprentice to the pioneering Scottish engineer THOMAS TELFORD and helped to construct the London-to-Holyhead road across the mountains of North Wales. This was the main route from London to Dublin, and Dargan was determined that the Irish portion of the road should be the equal of the British. He returned to Ireland, set up his own contracting company and built the HOWTH-TO-DUBLIN

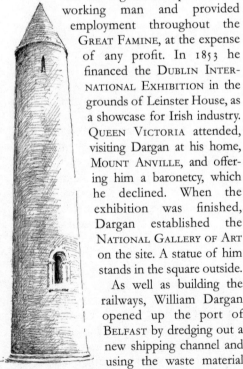

Timahoe

road, thus completing the London-to-Dublin link. At that time HOWTH was the terminus for boats from HOLYHEAD.

In 1831, Dargan won the contract to build IRELAND'S FIRST RAILWAY from the new port of DUN LAOGHAIRE to DUBLIN, again finishing off the highway to London.

The success of this project, which he completed in one year, despite having to overcome huge engineering difficulties, led to many other railway contracts, and Dargan ended up building most of Ireland's railways, some 800 miles (1,290 km) in all.

He was a great champion of the working man and provided employment throughout the GREAT FAMINE, at the expense of any profit. In 1853 he financed the DUBLIN INTERNATIONAL EXHIBITION in the grounds of Leinster House, as a showcase for Irish industry. QUEEN VICTORIA attended, visiting Dargan at his home, MOUNT ANVILLE, and offering him a baronetcy, which he declined. When the exhibition was finished, Dargan established the NATIONAL GALLERY OF ART on the site. A statue of him stands in the square outside.

As well as building the railways, William Dargan opened up the port of BELFAST by dredging out a new shipping channel and using the waste material to create the artificial

Emo Court

Queen's Island that HARLAND AND WOLFF now occupies. He also developed the seaside resort of BRAY, along the lines of Brighton, and built many miles of canal, including the ULSTER CANAL.

In 1866 he was badly injured falling from his horse and, unable to maintain control of his many enterprises, he died in 1867, bankrupt and broken. He is buried in GLASNEVIN CEMETERY.

A spoonful of honey will catch more flies than a gallon of vinegar.

Never show your teeth unless you can bite.

quotes from WILLIAM DARGAN

The eye-catching new cable-stayed bridge that carries the LUAS tram line at TANEY CROSS, near DUNDRUM town centre, has been named the WILLIAM DARGAN BRIDGE in honour of the Father of the Irish Railways.

Emo Court

Open House

EMO COURT, a palatial neo-classical house 4 miles (6.4 km) south of Portarlington, was built and designed for the Earl of Arlington by JAMES GANDON in 1790. Gandon was best known as the architect of Dublin's Custom House, and Emo Court is THE ONLY PRIVATE COUNTRY HOUSE HE EVER DESIGNED.

There is a 1-mile-long (1.6 km) avenue of WELLINGTONIAS leading up to the front of the house, planted in 1850. These trees are considered to be THE FINEST OF THEIR KIND IN EUROPE. When EDWARD VII visited, the entire length of the avenue was laid with carpet.

Another part of Gandon's commission was to build a church at nearby COOLBANAGHER, which he did – ST JOHN THE EVANGELIST – THE ONLY CHURCH HE EVER BUILT.

Emo Court is owned by the Office of Public Works and is open to the public.

Rock of Dunamase

Acropolis of Ireland

The great ROCK OF DUNAMASE rises 150 ft (45 m) above the flat plain near Portlaoise, and is THE MOST IMPORTANT HISTORICAL SITE IN CO. LAOIS. There has been a fortress here since the Iron Age, although the ruins seen here today are from the 12th-century castle of DIARMAIT MACMURROUGH, King of Leinster, who passed the site on to his son-in-law, STRONGBOW. 'DUNNUM' was considered notable enough for the Greco-Egyptian map maker PTOLEMY to include it on his celebrated world map in AD 140.

There is reputed to be treasure buried beneath the Rock, guarded by a huge hound called BANDOG, with slavering jaws and red, flaming eyes. Some think the treasure might be the lost Irish Crown Jewels (*see* Co. Kildare, page 67)!

The Rock of Dunamase presides over the GREAT HEATH or *Magh Rechet*, a huge plain, not dissimilar to The Curragh, yet little known. The vegetation is so unlike the surrounding landscape that the Heath can be seen clearly from space. In Celtic times it was the site of the *Aenach Carmain*, a festival hosted by the King of Leinster to celebrate *Lughnasa*, or the beginning of harvest time.

Somewhat neglected, considering its significance, this ancient place is rather off the tourist trail, which only adds to the sense of history and timelessness. It is well worth a visit.

Well, I never knew this
ABOUT
COUNTY LAOIS

THE FIRST QUAKER SCHOOL IN IRELAND was opened at MOUNT-MELLICK in 1677.

THE REPUBLIC OF IRELAND'S FORE-MOST MALE CONVICT PRISON is at PORTLAOISE.

HEYWOOD GARDENS, south of Abbeyleix, is one of the few gardens in Ireland designed and landscaped by SIR EDWIN LUTYENS and GERTRUDE JEKYLL.

THE PASS OF THE PLUMES, near Portlaoise, is so named because of the huge number of English plumed helmets that were left strewn across the marshy valley floor, after the Earl of Essex's men were defeated here by OWEN MACRORY O'MOORE in 1599.

DR BARTHOLOMEW MOSSE (1712–59), founder of THE WORLD'S FIRST PURPOSE-BUILT MATERNITY HOSPITAL, the ROTUNDA in Dublin, was born in Port Laoise, where his father was the Rector.

As you come into the little market town of BALLINAKILL, on the road from Abbeyleix, there are two trees known as the TOLL TREES. This is where visitors to the town had to pay a toll before they could enter.

The pretty village of DONAGHMORE, west of Abbeyleix, was used as the location for the 1994 film *All Things Bright and Beautiful*, starring GABRIEL BYRNE, KEVIN McNALLY and TOM WILKINSON.

POET LAUREATE CECIL DAY-LEWIS (1904–72) was born in BALLIN-TUBBERT, near Stradbally. Under the name NICHOLAS BLAKE he also wrote popular detective novels. He is the father of Oscar-winning actor Daniel Day-Lewis (*My Left Foot*, *Last of the Mohicans*, *Gangs of New York*).

An OAK TREE growing in the demesne at ABBEYLEIX is registered as 700 YEARS OF AGE – THE OLDEST OAK TREE IN IRELAND. The village of Abbeyleix is home to 'Morrissey's', which, both inside and out, is one of the finest examples of a traditional Irish pub.

COUNTY LONGFORD

St Mel's Cathedral, Longford, completed in 1893

Goldsmith Country

A Writer's Childhood

OLIVER GOLDSMITH (1728–74), one of the greatest natural writers in the English language, was born in a tumbledown farmhouse at PALLAS, a small hamlet to the east of BALLYMAHON. His father, the REV. CHARLES GOLDSMITH, farmed the surrounding fields while assisting his wife's uncle at the church in KILKENNY WEST in Co. Westmeath. The farmhouse is no longer there but the site is well marked and can be reached across fields.

Goldsmith was baptised in the nearby village church at FORGNEY, where there is a memorial window to him.

The family moved to LISSOY, just across the border in Co. Westmeath, when Oliver was two years old. His first school was here but he later went to school in EDGEWORTHSTOWN.

ARDAGH is a very attractive estate

village north of Ballymahon. Although the village as we see it today was largely laid out in the mid-18th century by the FETHERSTON family, it has a long history. ST PATRICK founded a church here in the 5th century, installing his nephew ST MEL as bishop. ST BRIGID spent some time at the monastery as a young nun before going to Kildare (*see* Co. Kildare, page 67). St Mel is said to be buried somewhere beneath the ruins of the stone cathedral that replaced his wooden one.

In 1744 the young Oliver Goldsmith turned up in Ardagh on his way home from school and booked into ARDAGH HOUSE, under the misapprehension that it was an inn. The Fetherstons, whose home it was, played along, providing him with supper and a room. Oliver was particularly taken with the Fetherston daughters, thinking they were servant girls, and made clumsy attempts to seduce them. When all was revealed in the morning Goldsmith was mortified, but the embarrassing incident provided him with the plot for his most successful play *She Stoops to Conquer*. Ardagh House is now a school.

Other works of Oliver Goldsmith are *The Vicar of Wakefield* and *The Deserted Village*.

Don't let us make imaginary evils, when you know we have so many real ones to encounter.

Our greatest glory consists, not in never failing, but in rising every time we fall.

You can preach a better sermon with your life than with your lips.

Ask me no questions and I'll tell you no fibs.

quotes from OLIVER GOLDSMITH

Edgeworthstown

Revolution, Road Building and 'Riting

The EDGEWORTH family settled in what was to become EDGEWORTHS-TOWN in 1583. The first member of the family to come to prominence was HENRY ESSEX EDGEWORTH, born in the RECTORY in 1745. When Henry was four years old his father ROBERT went over to the Catholic Church and moved his family to Toulouse in France. Henry took Holy Orders and went as a priest to Paris, where he became confessor to LOUIS XVI's sister MADAME ELIZABETH. By now he was known as ABBÉ DE FIRMONT, after FIRMOUNT, the family

The Rectory

Edgeworthstown House

home, which still exists, some 3 miles (5 km) north of Edgeworthstown. He attended Louis XVI on the scaffold, and was by his side as the guillotine fell – his robes were drenched in the French King's blood. In the ensuing frenzy de Firmont was able to escape through the mob to Poland, where he died in 1807.

Henry's cousin was RICHARD LOVELL EDGEWORTH (1744–1817), an unsung hero of invention and innovation. He inherited EDGE-WORTHSTOWN HOUSE in 1782 and set about remodelling it inside, knocking down walls to create light and space. He put in a self-styled central heating system, making Edgeworthstown House THE FIRST CENTRALLY HEATED HOUSE IN IRELAND, and filled the house with gadgets, such as sideboards on wheels and leather straps on the doors to prevent them from banging. Out in the yard, an ingenious pump fed water to cisterns

in the house and automatically dispensed halfpennies to beggars for each half-hour they spent at turning the handle.

During his lifetime Richard Lovell Edgeworth developed, amongst other things, an early bicycle, an aerial telegraph system that could send a signal from Dublin to Galway in eight minutes, advanced carriage suspension springs, a horse-drawn railway for carrying peat across the estate, and a vehicle with caterpillar tracks that could traverse the local bogland. His finest achievement was the new road he laid across the estate, incorporating two ground-breaking design features that revolutionised road building for ever. The first was a camber, whereby the centre of the roadway was arched a little higher than the sides to allow rainwater to drain away. The second was a top layer of small broken stones or chips that were compressed into a hard, smooth surface as vehicles passed over them. These innovations were adopted by road builders everywhere and foreshadowed John Macadam's techniques by three years.

Richard married four times and had 22 children. His eldest daughter was the writer MARIA EDGEWORTH (1767–1849), best known for novels such as *Castle Rackrent* and *Ormond*. During the Great Famine she wrote *Orlandino* to raise funds for the relief of poverty and suffering, and even though she was approaching her eighties, she distributed food and clothes and wrote to her friends with appeals for help. Such was her fame that when a food parcel arrived from America addressed simply to 'Miss Maria, Ireland', it was delivered straight to her door. Apart from occasional visits to London, Maria spent almost all her life in Edgeworthstown. She died at the age of 82 and is buried alongside her father in the family vaults in St John's churchyard. Inside the church is a lovely writing table, inlaid with marble, a gift to Maria from SIR WALTER SCOTT, who was a great admirer of her work.

Also buried in St John's churchyard is Oscar Wilde's sister ISOLDE, who died while staying at the Rectory in Edgeworthstown.

Edgeworthstown House is now run as a nursing home.

Newtowncashel

Beauty from the Bog

NEWTOWNCASHEL, or 'CASHEL', is a pretty hilltop village close to LOUGH REE, IRELAND'S FIFTH-LARGEST LAKE and THE SECOND-LARGEST ON THE RIVER SHANNON. In 1980 the village, deep in the heart of Ireland, achieved the unique accolade of winning both the NATIONWIDE CARE AWARD and the NATIONAL TIDY TOWNS COMPETITION.

The approach to the village along the (relatively) main road is enhanced by *Home Coming*, a graceful sculpture of waterbirds that provides a tantalising glimpse of Cashel's distinctive secret. As you pass through the village there are more sculptures and, at the centre, a rock fountain. All are the work of the artist MICHAEL CASEY and his son KEVIN.

Michael Casey has been creating beauty out of bogwood for 30 years, in his small workshop just down the road at BARLEY HARBOUR, on the shores of Lough Ree. His studio is a seductive place, strewn with pieces of wood, oak, pine, yew, all of different sizes, shapes and textures, waiting for Michael to carve them into life.

Mother and Child

Bogwood comes from the remnants of ancient forests that have been buried beneath the peat bogs of Ireland for thousands of years, impregnated and preserved by the solvents and moisture in the peat. As the peat bogs are dug for fuel and fertiliser so more pieces of wood come to light. Michael scours the local bogland areas for likely examples, takes them home to dry and then waits for the shapes to emerge naturally from the wood. Sometimes this can take a while – one piece rested in his studio for 11 years before he spotted CUCHULAIN on his horse. Michael makes frequent visits to THE BURREN (*see* Co. Clare, page 149), seeking inspiration from the fantastical forms to be found within this vast limestone landscape.

As well as gracing exhibitions, private collections, churches, towns and villages across Ireland and Britain, Michael's unique sculptures have been sent around the world. Two of his works formed the centrepiece of Ireland's entry into the OSAKA GARDEN AND GREENERY EXPOSITION of 1990 in Japan.

Michael Casey's workshop at Barley Harbour, where he works with his son Kevin, can be visited by appointment.

Two miles (3 km) away at CORLEA is THE ONLY KNOWN EXAMPLE OF AN EARLY IRON AGE ROAD IN IRELAND. In 1984, peat cutters uncovered a great oak timber roadway that had lain hidden under the bog for centuries. The road, dating from 148 BC, was constructed by laying oak planks across pairs of parallel runners made from birch and ash. It ran for over half a mile across the bog, connecting a small drumlin, a source of bog iron, to the mainland. This road, capable of carrying wheeled traffic, is THE LARGEST OF ITS KIND YET DISCOVERED IN EUROPE. There is evidence of other similar tracks in the area, indicating the presence of a whole sophisticated road system.

Granard

Harping on . . .

At 534 feet (162.8 m) high, THE MOTTE OF GRANARD IS THE HIGHEST NORMAN MOTTE IN IRELAND. A small, very old, market town, Granard is also famous for its HARP FESTIVAL, which is held every year in August. The seat of the EARLS OF GRANARD is CASTLE FORBES, a spectacular 19th-century Gothic-style castle at NEWTOWNFORBES, a little north of Longford.

BORN IN GRANARD

KITTY KIERNAN (1892–1945), fiancée of MICHAEL COLLINS (*see* Co. Cork, page 158). She met Collins when he came to stay at her brother's hotel, the GREVILLE ARMS, during the 1917 Co. Longford by-election. In 1996 NEIL JORDAN made a film called *Michael Collins*, starring LIAM NEESON in the title role. Kitty Kiernan was played by JULIA ROBERTS.

Former Irish National Hunt champion jockey FRANK BERRY, now racing manager for J.P. McMANUS (*see* Co. Limerick, page 182).

Legendary show jumper EDDIE MACKEN.

From Longford to America

Father of New York and the OK Corral

In 1690 CHARLES CLINTON was born on the Earl of Granard's estate at Newtownforbes, north of Longford. In 1722 he married ELIZABETH DENISTON from a neighbouring family. Even though they were Presbyterians, these were difficult times in Ireland, then under the Penal Laws. In 1729 Clinton chartered a ship, the *George and Anne*, and sailed for the New World along with his wife and children and 150 other Presbyterians from the Longford area.

Four months later they landed at CAPE COD, MASSACHUSETTS, and founded a small colony on the Hudson river, north of New York, which they called LITTLE BRITAIN. In 1739 the Clintons had a son, GEORGE, who became a friend of GEORGE WASHINGTON and a general in the Revolutionary army during the War of Independence. He was made NEW YORK'S FIRST GOVERNOR and is known as the FATHER OF NEW YORK,

having served for 21 years, longer than anyone before or since. His statue represents New York in the Capitol Building in Washington.

George Clinton was also VICE PRESIDENT to THOMAS JEFFERSON and JAMES MADISON. His nephew, DeWITT CLINTON, was several times Mayor of New York City as well as Governor of New York State and State Senator.

On the *George and Anne* with the Clintons were the McCLOUGHRYS from NEWTOWNFORBES. Two of their direct descendants, TOM and FRANK McLAURY, were part of the Clanton gang gunned down at TOMBSTONE, ARIZONA, by WYATT EARP, during the GUNFIGHT AT THE OK CORRAL in 1881.

Carrigglas Manor

Mr Darcy

CARRIGGLAS MANOR, near Longford, originally belonged to the Bishops of Ardagh. In the 17th century it was left to Trinity College, Dublin, who

Carrigglas Manor

in the 18th century leased it to the Newcomen family. In 1794, SIR WILLIAM NEWCOMEN approached JAMES GANDON, architect of Dublin's Custom House, to build a house and stables at Carrigglas. The house was never built but the stables were and they are superb – THE ONLY EXAMPLE OF DOMESTIC OUTBUILDINGS BY GANDON (*see* Emo Court, Co. Laois, page 87). Gandon also erected a grand entrance gate for the park, acknowledged as THE FINEST SET OF GATES IN CO. LONGFORD.

Quite a controversial figure, Sir William Newcomen owned a bank in Castle Street, Dublin (now Government offices), and was MP for Co. Longford. He was suspected of being bribed to support the ACT OF UNION in 1801, against the wishes of his constituents. Certainly a sub-

stantial debt that he owed to the Government was written off and his wife was raised to the Irish peerage, becoming Baroness Newcomen of Mosstown and, later, Viscountess Newcomen. In 1825 her son THOMAS, VISCOUNT NEWCOMEN, committed suicide after the family bank failed – perhaps because of a backlash from his father's political manoeuvrings.

After the Newcomens, Carrigglas Manor was leased to CHIEF JUSTICE THOMAS LEFROY, who eventually bought the freehold and rebuilt the house, in Tudor Gothic style, in 1837. JANE AUSTEN would often visit while she was staying at Edgeworthstown. She found Lefroy immensely attractive and modelled the character of MR DARCY in *Pride and Prejudice* on him.

Well, I never knew this
ABOUT
County Longford

St. Mel's Cathedral in Longford is an impressive Renaissance-style building, with a noble portico and belfry and what is generally regarded to be THE FINEST INTERIOR OF ANY CLASSICAL CHURCH IN IRELAND. The building of the cathedral, begun in 1840, was interrupted by the Famine and it was not completed until 1893.

County Longford was very badly affected by the Great Famine and many of its people had to emigrate. A large number went to ARGENTINA, where a descendant of one of these families, EDEL MIRO O'FARRELL, became PRESIDENT OF ARGENTINA in 1914.

The poet PADRAIC COLUM (1881–1972), one of the founders of the ABBEY THEATRE in Dublin, was born in Longford.

At 916 ft (279 m), CAIRN HILL is THE HIGHEST POINT IN CO. LONGFORD. There is a local saying used when referring to someone with exceptionally good sight – '*He could see a speck on the top of Cairn Hill.*'

INIS CLOTHRANN, one of the larger islands in LOUGH REE, is where QUEEN MAEVE (*see* Co. Sligo, page 36) met her death. She was slain here while bathing, struck by a stone from the sling of FORBAID, a Prince of Ulster.

COUNTY LOUTH

COUNTY TOWN: DUNDALK

lubhadh – 'plain'

13th-century barbican of St Lawrence's Gate, Drogheda

Dundalk

Bubble Cars and Pop

DUNDALK, county town of Louth, used to be at the northern extent of the English Pale and is the last big town in Ireland before the border with the North.

In 1316, the year after he had been crowned KING OF IRELAND, EDMUND BRUCE, brother of ROBERT THE BRUCE, KING OF SCOTLAND, made Dundalk his capital. He died defending it, just up the road at FAUGHART, in 1318.

ST PATRICK'S CATHEDRAL, in the centre of the town, was built between 1835 and 1847 and is modelled on KING'S COLLEGE CHAPEL, CAMBRIDGE, in England.

By the main street, in St Nicholas Church of Ireland cemetery, there is a fine obelisk, 30 feet (9 m) high, which stands as a monument to the poet ROBERT BURNS and his sister AGNES (1762–1834). It was erected in 1859, on the centenary of the poet's birth, as a tribute to his genius, from the people of Dundalk. Agnes Burns is buried in the cemetery here. In 1818 she had come to live at STEPHENSTOWN, just outside Dundalk, where her husband was the estate manager for the FORTESCUES. Also employed on the estate at that time was the family of THOMAS CALLAN (*see* American Heroes, page 102).

For three years, from 1959 until 1961, Dundalk was THE HOME OF THE BUBBLE CAR. The DUNDALK ENGINEERING COMPANY produced the HEINKEL KABINE bubble car from the modified cockpits of old Heinkel bombers. This was one of the first cars to use MONOCOQUE CONSTRUCTION TECHNIQUES, and those made in Dundalk were known as HEINKEL IRELANDS.

HARP LAGER is brewed, by Guinness, in Dundalk.

Today, Dundalk's most famous export is family pop band THE CORRS, all of whom were born here.

Out in Dundalk Bay stands DUNDALK LIGHTHOUSE, looking for all the world like something from the War of the Worlds. Built in 1849, it perches on top of slender iron legs that are fixed firmly on to the soft seabed, using a screw pile system devised by the blind engineer ALEXANDER MITCHELL (1780–1868). Before Mitchell's screw piles it had been impossible to anchor lighthouses, or any other structures, on sandy terrain, but the technique is now in use around the world and Dundalk can boast one of the finest early examples to be found anywhere.

Drogheda

Heads and Tales

DROGHEDA is a Norse settlement on the Boyne estuary, fortified by the Normans, and it is still an important seaport. In 1494, Parliament met here to enact the infamous POYNINGS'S LAW, introduced by LORD DEPUTY EDWARD POYNINGS, which decreed that no law passed by the Irish parliament would be legal until approved and passed by the English Privy Council. Poynings's Law remained in force, in one form or another, until the ACT OF UNION in 1801.

The centre of Drogheda is dominated by ST PETER'S ROMAN CATHOLIC CHURCH, whose greatest treasure is the embalmed head of BLESSED OLIVER PLUNKETT, ARCHBISHOP OF ARMAGH and PRIMATE OF ALL IRELAND. Plunkett was born at LOUGHCREW in Co. Meath in 1629 and sent to Rome for his education. He was ordained in 1654 and remained in Rome, since it was unsafe to return to Ireland, where Catholics were being ruthlessly persecuted. In 1669 he was appointed ARCHBISHOP OF ARMAGH and he took up his post in 1670. The next few years were spent trying to restore the battered Catholic Church, but when persecutions broke out again in 1673, Plunkett had to go into hiding. He refused to be exiled and endeavoured to minister and protect his flock as best he could.

In 1678 in England, a young troublemaker called TITUS OATES managed to persuade CHARLES II that there was a 'POPISH PLOT' to kill the King and replace him with the Catholic JAMES II. In the frenzy of anti-Catholic hysteria that followed, Plunkett was arrested and, after a kangaroo trial, hanged, drawn and quartered at TYBURN in London, in 1681. He was THE LAST CATHOLIC EVER TO BE EXECUTED FOR HIS FAITH IN ENGLAND. As his remains were being incinerated, friends snatched his head from the flames and it eventually ended up in the church at Drogheda, where it is lovingly preserved in a glass case, the scorch marks still visible. Also in the church is the door from Plunkett's prison cell at NEWGATE PRISON in London. In 1920 Blessed Oliver Plunkett became THE FIRST IRISH MARTYR TO BE BEATIFIED. In 1975 he was made a saint, THE FIRST

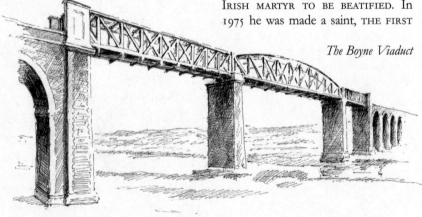

The Boyne Viaduct

NEW IRISH SAINT FOR OVER 700 YEARS since ST MALACHY, founder of Ireland's first Cistercian abbey at Mellifont, was canonised in 1199.

In 1791, the actress ELIZA O'NEILL was born in Drogheda, daughter of an actor–manager. A stunning beauty, Eliza's performance as JULIET on her theatrical debut in London was a sensation, and she went on to become ONE OF IRELAND'S GREATEST ACTRESSES. In 1819 she married WILLIAM WRIXON, Irish MP for Mallow, later SIR WILLIAM WRIXON-BECHER, 1st BT.

THE BOYNE VIADUCT, which carries the Dublin-to-Belfast railway 90 ft (27.4 m) above the river at Drogheda, is one of the wonders of the industrial world. It was opened in 1855 and designed by the Scottish engineer SIR JOHN MACNEILL, using a lattice-work of cast-iron girders that was relatively light but strong enough to bear the weight of a fully laden train. It was THE FIRST SUCH BRIDGE EVER BUILT and, at 508 ft (155 m) in length, THE LONGEST CAST-IRON STRUCTURE IN THE WORLD at that time. The view of Drogheda from the bridge is stupendous.

in Louth, CUCHULAIN was known as SETANTA. At the age of seven, he picked a fight with CULANN THE SMITH'S savage watchdog and killed it with a hurling stick. As penance he took over the animal's role as a guard, earning the name CUCHULAIN or 'CULANN'S HOUND'.

He was 17 when QUEEN MAEVE OF CONNACHT sent her army to capture the BROWN BULL OF COOLEY (*see* Co. Sligo, page 36), prized possession of his lord, the King of Ulster. Cuchulain was forced to defend the kingdom on his own because the RED KNIGHTS OF ULSTER were incapacitated by labour pains – a curse put upon them by the goddess MACHA for their maltreatment of a pregnant woman. Cuchulain was unaffected because he came from Leinster and he kept Maeve's army at bay single-handedly. Maeve eventually got her revenge by luring Cuchulain to his death using sorcerers.

Cuchulain is the 'patron saint' of all Irish fighters and a statue of him stands in Dublin's General Post Office to commemorate the leaders of the 1916 Easter Rising.

Cuchulain

Patron Saint of Irish Warriors

THE DUN OF DEALGA, a rocky mound just outside DUNDALK, was the birth-place of Ireland's most famous mythological hero, CUCHULAIN.

During his early years growing up

Cuchulain by Michael Casey

American Heroes

Conspicuous gallantry

THOMAS J. CALLAN was born at RATHIDDY in 1853. His parents worked for the FORTESCUES, big Co. Louth landowners, before emigrating to America some time in the 1860s. Thomas joined the US army in 1876 and went on to win AMERICA'S HIGHEST AWARD FOR VALOUR, THE CONGRESSIONAL MEDAL OF HONOR, for 'conspicuous gallantry . . . as a member of the water party in the Little Big Horn River fight'.

JENNIFER HODGERS, born in CLOGHERHEAD in 1843, emigrated to America when she was a young girl and went on to become THE SMALLEST MAN IN THE COMPANY – Company G of the 95th Illinois Infantry. At the outbreak of the American Civil War, Jennifer disguised herself as a man and joined up to fight for the Northern cause. She fought bravely at Vicksburg, the Red River campaign and the Battle of Nashville, and ended her service in 1865, aged 22, her secret undiscovered. She lived the rest of her life as a man, but her undoing was a car accident in 1911, when she was 68. She was taken to the Veterans Hospital for treatment and gave the staff there a considerable shock. It was nonetheless agreed that, in light of her courageous military service, she should be allowed to keep her soldier's pension.

Monasterboice

Ireland's Greatest Treasure

Turn off the noisy Dublin road, down a dusty country lane, through waving fields of green, and there, like a gem cast upon the grass, is MONASTERBOICE, perhaps the sweetest place in all Ireland. Founded in the 5th century by ST BUITE, an unassuming disciple of St Patrick, this place hides beneath his mantle, and the busy world passes it by. Enfolded in a small square churchyard on the side of a hill, embowered in trees, is a trove of ancient riches unsurpassed in Europe. Unmolested by the hand of officialdom, unspoiled and unselfconscious, Monasterboice does not lay out its beauties in neat, ordered ranks but hides them, haphazard, in clutter. You must wander along winding paths and clamber over broken monuments to find them. Red-breasted robins, a whole colony of them, accompany you, hopping from tomb to tomb, singing their hearts out. And suddenly it stands before you, four-square, surprisingly big, unprotected from the elements or the vandals, yet good as new, the 10th-century HIGH CROSS OF MUIREDACH. This is IRELAND'S GREATEST TREASURE, a picture gallery in stone, a display of such sublime power it takes your breath away.

Muiredach's Cross, 18 ft (5.5 m) tall, is so named because of the inscription on the base which reads, '*A prayer for Muiredach by whom this cross was made*'. The west face tells the story of Christ, while the east face depicts scenes from the Old Testament, Adam and Eve, David

and Goliath, Moses smiting the rock, the Last Judgement.

Nearby is the TALL CROSS, THE TALLEST IN IRELAND, 21 ft (6.4 m) high, just as beautifully carved, but more worn. Overlooked and hiding against a wall is an exquisite smaller cross which, in any other place than this, would seem magnificent.

Guarding them all is a slender, sinuous, Round Tower, its cap missing but still over 100 ft (30 m) tall, THE SECOND-HIGHEST ROUND TOWER IN IRELAND after the one on SCATTERY ISLAND, CO. CLARE. Monasterboice is Ireland at its loveliest.

Well, I never knew this
ABOUT
COUNTY LOUTH

COUNTY LOUTH is IRELAND'S SMALLEST COUNTY.

The tiny village of LOUTH, now just a handful of dwellings, was once important enough to give its name to the county. St Patrick established a church here and appointed ST MOCHTA as THE FIRST BISHOP OF LOUTH.

ARDEE CASTLE, midway between Drogheda and Dundalk, is THE LARGEST FORTIFIED MEDIEVAL TOWER HOUSE IN IRELAND.

The picturesque little fishing village of CARLINGFORD is THE OYSTER CAPITAL OF IRELAND, and holds a

popular oyster festival in August. The border with Northern Ireland runs along the middle of CARLINGFORD LOUGH. ST PATRICK landed at Carlingford in AD 432, at the start of his mission to convert Ireland from paganism to Christianity.

FAUGHART was the birthplace, in AD 453, of ST BRIGID (*see* Co. Kildare, page 67).A shrine was dedicated here in her honour in 1933.

EDWARD BRUCE, self-styled KING OF IRELAND (*see* Dundalk, page 98), was killed at FAUGHART HILL in 1318. He is thought to be buried in the churchyard on the hill.

MELLIFONT ABBEY, pleasantly situated on the banks of the little River Mattock, was founded in 1142 by ST MALACHY, and was THE FIRST CISTERCIAN MONASTERY TO BE BUILT IN IRELAND. Here are THE EARLIEST EXAMPLES OF GOTHIC ARCHITECTURE IN IRELAND. The most interesting remains are those of a UNIQUE 13TH-CENTURY 'LAVABO', where monks would wash their hands in a fountain before dining. Ireland's 'HELEN OF TROY', DEVORGILLA, whose elopement led to the Norman invasion of Ireland in 1169, is buried beneath the chancel pavement. She retired here at the end of her life and died in 1193 at the age of 85. WILLIAM OF ORANGE used the abbey for his headquarters during the BATTLE OF THE BOYNE in 1690 (*see* Co. Meath, page 105).

COUNTY MEATH

COUNTY TOWN: NAVAN

an Mhi – 'the middle'

The passageway at Newgrange

Boyne Valley

Valley of the Kings

A journey along the mellow, undulating BOYNE VALLEY is a journey back to the dawn of the Irish nation. The name comes from an Irish princess, BOINNE, who was drowned in the river. BRU NA BOINNE or 'THE PALACE OF THE BOYNE' is the wellspring of Irish civilisation, where IRELAND'S FIRST SETTLERS sailed up the river and began to farm the fertile soil, creating dwelling places and communities, and leaving behind a wealth of monuments and mysteries.

Newgrange

NEWGRANGE, best-known and most visited of all the Boyne Valley burial chambers, is THE FINEST AND BEST-PRESERVED PASSAGE GRAVE IN EUROPE. It was built around 3200 BC, making it 500 YEARS OLDER THAN THE PYRAMIDS and 1,000 YEARS OLDER THAN STONEHENGE. It is an engineering masterpiece, constructed by a Stone Age people who possessed no wheels or metal tools. At dawn on the winter solstice (21 December), the first rays of the rising sun flood into the tomb, through an ingenious roof box above the entrance, and illuminate the central burial chamber – making Newgrange THE OLDEST SOLAR OBSERVATORY IN THE WORLD. Anyone who wishes to witness this remarkable experience inside the chamber can enter a lottery for one of the few places made available each year – and pray it isn't cloudy.

One mile west of Newgrange is KNOWTH, which has two passage graves and THE GREATEST COLLECTION OF MEGALITHIC ART IN EUROPE – stones carved into a gallery of patterns, swirls, chevrons, lozenges, squares, concentric circles, zigzags, triangles and more.

Hill of Slane

The HILL OF SLANE is where St Patrick kindled THE FIRST FLAME OF CHRISTIANITY IN IRELAND. The year was AD 433 on the eve of the Druid festival of BELTAINE. A bonfire was lit on the ROYAL HILL OF TARA, as was the tradition, and KING LOIGHAIRE decreed that no other bonfires should be allowed. But then, to the north, a new fire sprang to life in defiance of the edict. It was the FIRST PASCHAL FIRE IN IRELAND, lit by St Patrick where it could be seen by everyone as a direct and symbolic challenge to the authority of the pagan King and his Druids. Loighaire sent his troops to arrest St Patrick and bring him to Tara under sentence of death. Face to face with the King, St Patrick picked a SHAMROCK from the grass and used it to explain the HOLY TRINITY. By using an ancient Irish symbol, St Patrick defused the King's anger and won his respect. From that moment, he was permitted to preach his gospel across all of Ireland.

Slane Castle

There is a group of ruins on the summit of the Hill of Slane, including a 15th-century church tower. The steps are broken and uneven and the climb is dark, but the stupendous view from the top, over the Boyne valley from Trim to the sea and across to the Hill of Tara, makes the effort all worthwhile.

At the foot of the hill, sitting in parkland beside the attractive village of Slane, is SLANE CASTLE, home to the EARL and COUNTESS OF MOUNT CHARLES and famous since 1981 for its rock concerts. Artists who have appeared here include U2, OASIS, QUEEN, BRUCE SPRINGSTEEN, REM, BOB DYLAN, GUNS N' ROSES, MADONNA, BRYAN ADAMS, VAN MORRISON, NEIL YOUNG, DAVID BOWIE and THE ROLLING STONES. The castle has reopened after a fire in 1991.

Hill of Tara

The Seat of High Kings until the 11th century, the HILL OF TARA is the historic, political and spiritual centre of Celtic Ireland. It was also at the HUB OF IRELAND'S ANCIENT TRANSPORT NETWORK, with five major chariot tracks radiating out to the north, south and west linking Tara with other important settlements.

There is not much left on the Hill apart from the view. On a clear day, HALF THE COUNTIES OF IRELAND can be seen from here. A rough-looking stone thrusts up from the ground inside one of the hilltop circles. This is THE LIA FAIL or STONE OF DESTINY, beside which Kings would be crowned – on the inauguration of a true King the stone would give out a roar of approval.

The oldest structure on the hill is a passage tomb known as the MOUND OF THE HOSTAGES, recalling the tradition that High Kings would

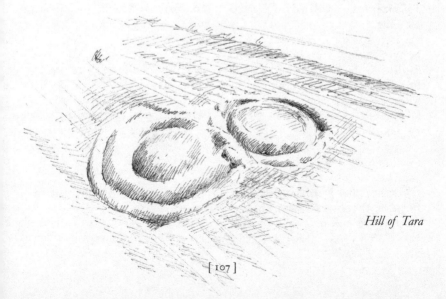

Hill of Tara

Trim Castle

keep as hostages the eldest sons of their vassal kings, to ensure good behaviour.

In 1899 a group calling themselves the British Israelites dug up the hillside, convinced that the ARK OF THE COVENANT was buried inside. They didn't find it but they did manage to upset a host of Irish history lovers including W.B. YEATS.

Trim

TRIM CASTLE, completed in 1224 and covering an area of over 3 acres (1.2 ha), is THE LARGEST NORMAN CASTLE IN THE REPUBLIC OF IRELAND. The castle was the home of the ROYAL MINT until the 15th century and RICHARD II confined his cousin HENRY OF LANCASTER (later Henry IV) here in 1399.

Trim Castle provided a spectacular location for the 1995 film *Braveheart*, starring MEL GIBSON.

On the opposite bank of the River Boyne is TALBOT'S CASTLE, a beautiful fortified manor house built in 1415 by SIR JOHN TALBOT. In 1717 it

was bought by ESTHER JOHNSON (Swift's 'Stella'), and she sold it, for a handsome profit to Swift, the very next year. He then sold it on, for an even greater profit, and it was converted into a school. ARTHUR WELLESLEY, the future DUKE OF WELLINGTON, went to school here. He spent much of his childhood at nearby DANGAN CASTLE (now a ruin), his father's country house, and also lived in Trim for a while.

IRELAND'S OLDEST COMPLETE AND UNALTERED BRIDGE, dating from 1393, crosses the River Boyne at Trim.

A half-mile east of Trim is the ruined abbey of ST PETER AND ST PAUL, built in 1206. In the hedge by the road there is a gate known as the ECHO GATE. If you stand at the gate facing the abbey and call out across the fields, a perfect echo returns from the distant ruins.

The Battle of the Boyne

THE BATTLE OF THE BOYNE, although perhaps not the most important, is nonetheless THE MOST FAMOUS BATTLE IN IRISH HISTORY. It was fought on 1 July 1690 between the forces of the Catholic JAMES II, whose men were encamped on DONORE HILL, south of the river, and the Protestant WILLIAM OF ORANGE, whose army crossed from the north bank at SLANE, OLDBRIDGE and GROVE ISLAND. The result of the battle was to be the suppression of Catholicism in Ireland for the next 300 years. The most high-profile casualty was William's GENERAL SCHOMBERG, cut down by the Irish cavalry as he rallied his troops at Oldbridge.

As it became clear that the battle was lost, and with his army retreating to DULEEK, James fled to Dublin. He commented to his hostess LADY TYRCONNEL, 'Your countrymen can run very fast it must be owned.' To which her tart reply was, *'In this, as in every other respect, Your Majesty surpasses them, for you have won the race.'*

There is an Interpretive Centre about the battle at Oldbridge.

Loughcrew

Ireland's Secret

Deep in the drowsy heart of Ireland, scattered across the bare hilltops, gazing down on 17 counties, and with just the wind for company, is lonely LOUGHCREW. At rest for 6,000 years, this is Ireland's most secret tourist spot, THE LARGEST COMMUNITY OF PASSAGE GRAVES IN THE WORLD, made up of what are very possibly THE OLDEST MAN-MADE DWELLINGS ON THE PLANET.

There are two main groups of cairns laid out on neighbouring hills, some roofed with wonderful engravings, some exposed and weathered. They were plundered by amateurs and bounty-hunters in the early years of the 20th century, but the locusts moved on and left the atmosphere intact. Maybe they did Loughcrew a favour, for the dead eye of officialdom has so far remained focused on richer fare at Newgrange, and has not yet swivelled its soulless gaze in this direction. There are no buses to bring you here, no guides to tell you what to see, no café, no entrance fee. Here you can wander alone amongst our earliest ancestors, see what they once saw, feel what they once felt, maybe dream what they once dreamt. There is solitude, communion, a sense of wonder.

The most prominent feature is the romantically named CAIRN T on CARNBANE EAST. Sit on the HAG'S CHAIR, a massive slab of stone set into the mound, and make a wish. Or you can obtain the key, and a torch, from the café at LOUGHCREW HOUSE and explore the passageway and central chamber by yourself. Shut the gate behind you, sit there in the dark, and listen to the murmurings . . .

LOUGHCREW GARDENS, down in the valley, are an altogether gentler affair, ONE OF THE FEW 17TH-CENTURY LANDSCAPED GARDENS IN IRELAND. They are being painstakingly restored to their original

Loughcrew House,
before the fire of 1964

glory by CHARLES AND EMILY NAPER, whose family have been here since 1655. A yew walk, grottoes, rockeries, a physic border, water features, sculptures, a medieval motte, fairy glades for children, lawns and woodland, are all laid out around the ancient tower house where BLESSED OLIVER PLUNKETT was born in 1629 (*see* Co. Louth, page 98).

Making a romantic vista across the fields is a gigantic Athenian Ionicportico, almost all that is left of the cursed LOUGHCREW HOUSE.

Three times will Loughcrew be consumed by fire. Crows will fly in and out of the windows. Grass will grow on its doorstep.

And, sure enough, the large neo-classical mansion, first built in 1823 by C.R. COCKERELL, burned to the ground three times, the last time in 1964, just as the present owner, Charles Naper, was about to move in. Today the family live in the converted stable block next door.

Well, I never knew this
ABOUT
COUNTY MEATH

TURLOUGH O'CAROLAN (1670–1738), LAST OF THE IRISH BARDS (*see* Co. Roscommon), was born at NOBBER, north of NAVAN.

TARA MINE to the north-west of Navan is THE LARGEST ZINC MINE IN THE WORLD.

MEATH was originally the fifth province of Ireland and included Westmeath, which was made a separate county during the PLANTATION OF MARY TUDOR.

> *The Plantations involved the confiscation of lands by the English Crown, mainly from Irish Catholics, with the aim of resettling those lands with Scottish and English Protestants loyal to the Crown. The two major Plantations were the* MUNSTER PLANTATION *in 1586 (under Elizabeth I) of land in the counties of Cork, Kerry, Limerick and Waterford, and the* ULSTER PLANTATION *in 1609 (under James I) of land in the counties of Armagh, Cavan, Donegal, Derry, Fermanagh and Tyrone.*

ST ULTAN'S school in Navan bears a plaque commemorating the birthplace of FRANCIS BEAUFORT (1774–1857), inventor of the BEAUFORT WIND SCALE. His 13-point scale, which went from zero as based on the amount of sail a man o' war could safely hoist. Beaufort also set in train one of the pivotal events of world history when he arranged for a young naturalist called CHARLES DARWIN to join HMS *Beagle*, on her epic voyage to the South Seas – the trip that spawned Darwin's THEORY OF EVOLUTION. Beaufort knew of Darwin through his relationship to RICHARD LOVELL EDGEWORTH (*see* Co. Longford, page 90), who was both his BROTHER-IN-LAW – Beaufort's sister FRANCES was Edgeworth's fourth wife – and his FATHER-IN-LAW – Beaufort was married to Edgeworth's daughter HONORA. Richard Lovell Edgeworth was a member of the LUNAR SOCIETY, a group of thinkers and innovators who would meet in Birmingham on the Monday nearest the full moon to discuss how to change the world. A fellow member was ERASMUS DARWIN, Charles Darwin's grandfather.

DULEEK is a small village set between Navan and the coast. Its name comes from *Daimh Liag*, meaning 'stone house', and it is here that St Patrick is said to have built THE FIRST STONE CHURCH IN IRELAND. A priory was built on the site in 1192, and it is the remains of this building that can be seen at Duleek today.

PIERCE BROSNAN (*James Bond, Remington Steele, The Thomas Crown Affair*) was born in Co. Meath in 1953. He came into the world at ST MARY'S

HOSPITAL, DROGHEDA – the hospital is actually just in Co. Meath, not Co. Louth. His parents lived in Navan, where Brosnan grew up.

EUROPE'S ONLY OFFICIAL HORSE-RACE MEETING HELD ON A BEACH takes place along the golden sands at LAYTOWN, south of Drogheda.

Just outside Navan are the ruins of
ATHLUMNEY CASTLE, burnt down by
its Catholic owners twice – once in
1649 to stop it falling into the hands
of OLIVER CROMWELL and once in
1690 to deny WILLIAM OF ORANGE.

Athlumney Castle

'WE'LL KEEP THE RED FLAG FLYING
HERE . . .' Indeed they do in
CROSSAKEEL, west of Kells, with a
fine memorial to JIM CONNELL
(1852–1929), author of the famous
song adopted as their anthem by the
INTERNATIONAL LABOUR MOVEMENT.
Connell was born at KILSKYRE, Co.
Meath, and made a rousing speech
here at Crossakeel in 1918.

JOHN WATSON (1856–1908), of
BECTIVE, Co. Meath, formulated the
official rules for the game of polo. He
was the great grandson of the JOHN
WATSON who killed the last wolf in
Ireland (*see* Co. Carlow, page 54).

The neat village of KELLS, lined with
smart Georgian houses, is the birthplace of *'the most beautiful book in the
world'*, the BOOK OF KELLS, now in
Trinity College Library in Dublin.
Kells Abbey was founded in AD 550
by ST COLUMBA, and the celebrated
book was written by monks from
Iona who fled here in AD 806 to
escape the Danes. There are some fine
remains, including the 9th-century
St Columba's House, a Round Tower
and a High Cross that was used as a
gallows during the uprising of 1798.

Just outside Kells is HEADFORT
HOUSE, built in the mid-18th century
for the 1st Earl of Bective, and which
contains THE ONLY COMPLETE EXAM-
PLE OF A ROBERT ADAM INTERIOR IN
IRELAND. The house is now a school.

Not far from Kells is the HILL OF
TAILTE. RATH DUBH on the summit

was the site of the *Aonach Tailteann*, the great Games organised by the High Kings in honour of QUEEN TAILTE. The Games, a sort of Irish Olympics, predate the Greek Olympics and were held here from 600 BC or earlier until the Norman invasion of 1169. Since 1924 they have been sporadically revived in one form or another.

The BOYNE CORACLE or 'CURRAGH' was used from Neolithic times right up until the 1930s and was THE OLDEST TYPE OF VESSEL TO SURVIVE IN THE BRITISH ISLES. It was made from hazel rods and tanned cowhide, and St Patrick is believed to have rowed from Scotland to Ireland in a Boyne Curragh.

COUNTY OFFALY

Birr Castle, set amongst Ireland's largest private gardens

Tullamore

Give every man his Dew . . .

TULLAMORE is the county town of Offaly and THE BIGGEST TOWN ON THE GRAND CANAL outside Dublin. In 1785 CHARLES BURY inherited the Tullamore estates, and during the celebrations to mark his ascendancy a hot air balloon was released, got caught on a chimney and blew up. In the resulting conflagration most of Tullamore was burnt down. Over the next 50 years it was rebuilt by the Burys into a prosperous market town.

Two miles outside Tullamore is CHARLEVILLE FOREST, built for the Burys by FRANCIS JOHNSTON between 1798 and 1812, and THE LARGEST GOTHIC-STYLE CASTLE IN IRELAND. It also boasts THE FINEST GOTHIC INTERIORS OF ANY HOUSE IN IRELAND. The staircase in the castle is said to be haunted by Charles Bury's eight-year-old daughter, who was killed while sliding down the banisters.

Tullamore's most famous export is TULLAMORE DEW whiskey, first distilled in the town in 1829 by MICHAEL MOLLOY, who also built the Tullamore Distillery. The 'DEW' is derived from the initials of a later manager of the Distillery, DANIEL E. WILLIAMS. In 1947 IRISH MIST liqueur was produced here. Tullamore Distillery is no longer

operational and both drinks are now made elsewhere, but the Distillery building and original gates have been preserved.

Birr

Parsonstown

The attractive town of BIRR, for a while PARSONSTOWN, with its bustling Georgian streets and rambling castle, is Ireland's beating heart. EMMETT SQUARE, in the middle of the town, is reputed to be THE GEOGRAPHICAL CENTRE OF IRELAND.

BIRR CASTLE was begun in the 1620s by SIR LAWRENCE PARSONS, whose family later became EARLS OF ROSSE. The 1st Earl of Rosse started the HELL FIRE CLUB in 1735 (*see* Co. Dublin, page 61). Gothicised in the 19th century, the castle is still their family home and not open to the public. Inside is what the topographer THOMAS DINELY described in 1681 as 'the fairest staircase in Ireland'. It is also ONE OF THE EARLIEST WOODEN STAIRCASES IN IRELAND.

Birr Castle was the model for Kinalty Castle in HENRY GREEN'S novel *Loving*, which made it a very appropriate location for the 1996 BBC film of the novel.

The castle gardens, THE LARGEST PRIVATE GARDENS IN IRELAND, are open to the public. They are full of natural beauty and man-made wonders, and a walk around them is a fascinating experience.

Squatting plumb centre of the gardens, and completely unmissable, is the 'LEVIATHAN OF PARSONSTOWN', a vast telescope built in 1845 by WILLIAM PARSONS, the 3RD EARL OF ROSSE. For 70 years this was the LARGEST TELESCOPE IN THE WORLD.

Leviathan of Parsontown

Housed in a tube 54 ft (16.5 m) long – IRELAND'S LONGEST BARREL – is a 72-inch (183-cm) mirror, and the whole contraption is connected to a series of pulleys and weights supported by sturdy walls 56 ft high and 72 ft long (17 x 22 m). The telescope is referred to in Jules Verne's science fiction novel *From the Earth to the Moon*. It has been fully restored and can regularly be seen in operation.

Below the castle walls the River Camcor tumbles over a small waterfall, and in 1879 the 4th Earl installed a water wheel here, which drove a turbine that provided both the castle and the town with electricity – making Birr THE FIRST TOWN IN THE WORLD TO BE LIT BY ELECTRICITY.

Ireland's oldest iron suspension bridge

Crossing the river just upstream from the waterfall is the delicate ironwork of a small suspension bridge built around 1820, THE OLDEST BRIDGE OF ITS KIND IN IRELAND.

Elsewhere in the grounds can be found THE TALLEST GREY POPLAR in the world and an avenue of box hedges, 300 years old and 40 ft (12 m) high, THE TALLEST BOX HEDGES IN THE WORLD.

Housed in the stables is the Birr historic science centre, which tells the story of the incredible inventions and achievements of the Parsons family.

WILLIAM PARSONS, 3RD EARL OF ROSSE (1800–67), constructed the world's largest telescope with which he discovered the WHIRLPOOL NEBULA in 1845. He also experimented with steam-powered carriages in the grounds of Birr Castle. In 1869 his cousin MARY WARD was thrown from one of these carriages, at Birr, and killed. She was IRELAND'S FIRST MOTORING FATALITY.

MARY FIELD (1813–85) was the 3rd Earl's wife, an heiress who funded her husband's projects. She was a talented person in her own right, particularly in the field of photography. Her pictures of the Rosse telescope were exhibited at THE WORLD'S FIRST PHOTOGRAPHIC EXHIBITION in London and she was THE FIRST RECIPIENT OF A MEDAL FROM THE PHOTOGRAPHIC SOCIETY OF IRELAND. Her darkroom, ONE OF THE EARLIEST DARKROOMS IN THE WORLD, has been re-created in the stables, which themselves were designed by Mary Field. An enthusiastic blacksmith, she also created and built the magnificent iron gates at the entrance to the park.

LAURENCE PARSONS, 4TH EARL OF ROSSE (1840–1908), harnessed Birr's first electricity supply and devised an accurate way of measuring the moon's temperature, using his father's equipment.

CHARLES PARSONS (1854–1931) was the youngest son of the 3rd Earl. He grew up and was educated largely at Birr and made his own far-reaching contribution to the modern world by inventing THE STEAM TURBINE and building THE WORLD'S FIRST TURBINE-POWERED SHIP, THE *Turbinia*.

Clonmacnoise

The Loveliest Doorway in Ireland

CLONMACNOISE was founded by ST CIARAN in 545, at a remote spot on a rise set above a wide bend of the RIVER SHANNON, old Ireland's most

important highway. Although a popular tourist spot, there is something about the panoramic views of the slow, sinuous Shannon, winding through flat green meadows, HOME TO IRELAND'S RAREST SPECIES OF BIRD, THE CORNCRAKE, that raises you above the throng and imbues a sense of peace and calm.

The site of the monastery includes three high crosses, two round towers, the remains of eight churches and several hundred grave tablets,

Temple Finghin

THE LARGEST COLLECTION IN EUROPE. The smaller round tower, an integral part of TEMPLE FINGHIN, is UNUSUAL IN HAVING AN ACCESS DOOR AT GROUND LEVEL. In the walls of the cathedral is a 15th-century WHISPERING DOOR – such are the acoustics that if you stand just in the doorway and whisper, you can be heard anywhere inside the building.

Whispering Door

The tiny one-room church was built in 1167 by Ireland's 'Helen of Troy', Devorgilla (*see* Co. Leitrim, page 16), and the gorgeous little Romanesque west doorway exquisitely frames a graceful chancel arch and the trees beyond, a picture of ravishing loveliness. Few people seem to make the effort to come here, one of the most restful and enchanting spots in Ireland.

Oak posts from THE OLDEST KNOWN BRIDGE IN IRELAND have recently been uncovered down by the river below Clonmacnoise. Dating from AD 804 they are visible underwater as a double row of vertical wooden posts that carried a long-distance highway across the river. The bridge was nearly 400 ft (120 m) long and the roadway raised about 20 ft (6 m) above the riverbed.

When you tire of the crowds, take a short walk along the raised pathway to the secluded ruins of the little NUN'S CHURCH, and there contemplate with wonder THE MOST BEAUTIFUL DOORWAY IN IRELAND.

Nun's Church

Well, I never knew this
ABOUT
COUNTY OFFALY

A few miles west of Tullamore are the sad and secluded ruins of the great monastery of RAHAN, founded in the 6th century by ST CARTHACH.

A walk through cow pastures leads to three scattered small churches. If you can gain access to the largest, which has been horribly cemented to look like an electricity sub-station, you will be amazed to find inside an exceptionally beautiful small Romanesque chancel arch and A GLORIOUSLY FLAMBOYANT ROUND ROMANESQUE EAST WINDOW, UNIQUE IN ITS DESIGN. Despite being shamelessly neglected, the wondrous beauty of these simple antique treasures makes one pause awhile.

At the end of the 17th century CHARLES CARROLL of BALLYMACADAM CASTLE near CADAMSTOWN, Co. Offaly, emigrated to Maryland in America. The O'CARROLLS were an ancient Irish Catholic family who had been gradually dispossessed of their lands and properties by the Normans and various Protestant plantations. Charles, known as 'THE SETTLER', was determined to revive the family fortunes in the New World. He succeeded. His grandson CHARLES CARROLL, 'THE SIGNER', became THE RICHEST MAN IN AMERICA. He was THE ONLY CATHOLIC TO SIGN THE AMERICAN DECLARATION OF INDEPENDENCE and THE LAST OF THOSE WHO SIGNED TO DIE, in 1832, at the age of 95.

The massive, ruined, creeper-covered keep of CLONONY CASTLE sits within its well-preserved bawn beside the road near CLOGHAN. The grass is mown but the gate is firmly locked against vandals and litter, so one can only gaze through bars at the limestone tablet lying under a tree beside the tower. Here lie ELIZABETH AND MARY, cousins of Henry VIII's second Queen, the tragic ANNE BOLEYN. After she was beheaded her family were exiled to Ireland, and the two cousins lived out their days in this remote, forgotten place.

> *A bawn is the walled enclosure next to or surrounding a Plantation-era castle or tower house (15th–17th century).*

County Westmeath

County Town: Mullingar

Iarmhidh – 'west of the middle'

The 'Jealous Wall' at Belvedere House

Belvedere

The Jealous Wall

Standing tall in front of BELVEDERE HOUSE, near Mullingar, is the 'JEALOUS WALL' – THE LARGEST FOLLY IN IRELAND.

Belvedere House, THE FIRST BOW-ENDED HOUSE IN IRELAND, was built on the shores of LOUGH ENNELL in 1740 as a 'villa' or fishing lodge for ROBERT ROCHFORT, one of Ireland's richest men. Rochfort, whose seat was GAULSTON PARK a few miles away at ROCHFORTBRIDGE, was very proud of his pretty young wife, and when he discovered in 1743 that she had been having an affair with his younger brother Arthur, his rage knew no bounds. He chased Arthur out of Ireland and imprisoned his wife at Gaulston, where she was forbidden to see anyone apart from elderly servants. He meantime lived the life of a carefree bachelor at Belvedere, throwing lavish parties and rising through the ranks of

Belvedere House

society to become the Earl of Belvedere and a Major-General in the Army.

Rochfort's unfortunate wife managed to escape from Gaulston once, but was turned in by her cruel father VISCOUNT MOLESWORTH when she appealed to him for help. She eventually remained incarcerated for 31 years, unable even to see her children. Arthur, the brother, tried to sneak back into Ireland, but was caught and sued by Rochfort for adultery, ending his days in the debtors' prison in Dublin.

In the meantime, Rochfort quarrelled with another of his brothers, GEORGE, who lived across the fields from Belvedere at ROCHFORT HOUSE. Rochfort, by now the EARL OF BELVEDERE, was so incensed by the sight of his brother's house, which was much more magnificent than his own, that he erected an enormous sham ruin, the JEALOUS WALL, to blot out the view.

'THE WICKED EARL', as Rochfort became known, died in 1744 and Belvedere was inherited by his son, who sold Gaulston and released his mother. She, by now, had gone slightly wild, talking to the portraits and wandering through the house with a strange, unearthly look that alarmed the staff. Her voice was never raised above a whisper and she emerged from Gaulston pale, starting at noises, and blinking in the light. CHARLOTTE BRONTË, in her novel *Jane Eyre*, is said to have based Mr Rochester's unbalanced wife, locked away in the tower room at Thornfield Hall, on Rochfort's unfortunate spouse.

Gaulston was burned down in 1920, while ROCHFORT HOUSE, which changed its name to TUDENHAM PARK, is now a shell. Belvedere and the Jealous Wall are still standing and can be visited.

In the 1920s Belvedere was the home of LIEUTENANT-COLONEL CHARLES HOWARD-BURY (1881–1960), who LED THE FIRST-EVER EXPEDI-

TION TO MOUNT EVEREST in 1921. Although this expedition did not reach the summit, it mapped the way for all the subsequent attempts.

In the early 18th century a regular visitor to Gaulston House was JONATHAN SWIFT. While wandering along the banks of Lough Ennell, he noted how small the people on the opposite shore seemed, and this gave him the idea for the tiny Lilliputians in *Gulliver's Travels*. LILLIPUT HOUSE, named in his honour, is open for accommodation.

Hill of Uisneach

Centre of Ireland

There are several places in Ireland that claim to be at the centre of it all. EMMETT SQUARE in BIRR (*see* Co. Offaly, page 114) is one, and there are two other, rather tentative, rival locations. In Co. Westmeath there is a tall obelisk that marks the spot on a hill near GLASSAN and in Co. Roscommon there is HODSON'S PILLAR, a stunted stone stump, on an island in Lough Ree. In fact, THE GEOGRAPHICAL CENTRE OF IRELAND is to be found in eastern Co. Roscommon, at a point 2 miles (3 km) south of ATHLONE.

However, for the ancient peoples of Ireland there was only one possible site, the HILL OF UISNEACH, near Ballymore, which rises above the surrounding bog-land to a height of 600 feet

(183 m). Here was the sacred heart of Ireland, Seat of High Kings, ancient place of assembly, site of the festival of BELTAINE, marking the start of summer, and the place of the Druid Fire Cult of SAMHAIN, which celebrates the final harvest, summer's end, and is THE ORIGIN OF HALLOWEEN.

Uisneach lies on one of the five chariot roads radiating out from the Hill of Tara, and St Patrick is believed to have given the veil to St Brigid here – the Catholic Church often used important pagan sites for Christian rituals.

Today, the Hill of Uisneach is a rather nondescript, soulless place, fenced off by farmers and decidedly unwelcoming. If you do manage to find the right hill and the decrepit bramble-covered gate, and make the climb to the summit, you will soon realise why this was such a significant place. YOU CAN SEE TWO-THIRDS OF IRELAND FROM HERE, 22 COUNTIES IN ALL, and the view is simply breathtaking.

There are plenty of broken monuments strewn about on the hilltop, reflecting the activities that took place here. The most commanding is the CATSTONE, a huge limestone

boulder that resembles a cat about to pounce on a mouse. It marks the pagan heart of Ireland.

This should be a celebrated spot, but maybe its very anonymity is what makes its unexpected discovery so moving.

Daramona

Hotspots

County Westmeath was home to one of Ireland's remarkable group of 19th-century amateur astronomers. There was Edward Cooper and his extraordinary refractor at MARKREE CASTLE (*see* Co. Sligo, page 36), William Parsons, with his huge telescope at BIRR (*see* Co. Offaly, page 114), and here in Westmeath there was WILLIAM WILSON (1851–1908) with his dome, set up in the garden of his home at DARAMONA in STREET in 1871.

Using a 12-inch (30-cm) telescope made by HOWARD GRUBB of Dublin, Wilson took a series of high-quality photographs of nebulae and

the stars, considered the best yet produced, but he truly came to prominence as THE FIRST MAN TO MEASURE THE TEMPERATURE OF THE SUN.

Assisted by P.L. GRAY, and utilising a differential radio-micrometer, he estimated the temperature at 6,590 degrees centigrade – modern science calculates it to be 6,075 degrees centigrade, so Wilson was extraordinarily accurate, considering the simplicity of his equipment. In 1898 Wilson took THE FIRST-EVER PHOTOGRAPH OF A SUNSPOT. He also made experiments with X-RAYS and it is possible that in 1898 he took THE WORLD'S FIRST X-RAY PHOTOGRAPH.

Many of William Wilson's photographs survive, and his telescope went to the University of London's observatory at Mill Hill in North London. It is now in Liverpool Museum. Wilson is buried in the family plot at Street, Co. Westmeath. His house and observatory fell into disrepair.

William Wilson's nephew, who was born at Daramona, was KENNETH EDGEWORTH (1880–1972), a cousin

Daramona

of the Edgeworth family from Co. Longford. He studied astronomy at Daramona, and in 1949 was the first person to suggest that there might be material and debris from newly formed planets orbiting on the outer edges of the solar system. In 1992 Edgeworth was proved right, when a faint object was seen beyond Neptune from an observatory in Hawaii, but the phenomenon was named the KUIPER BELT after the astronomer GERARD KUIPER, who had espoused the same theory two years *after* Edgeworth.

There is no doubt that the 19th-century amateur astronomers of Ireland contributed mightily to our understanding of space and the galaxies, so much so that Ireland should today be a world centre of astronomy. Their undoing was the Irish weather – at Daramona, in the late 19th and early 20th century, the skies were cloudy for an average of over 250 days each year. That fact alone makes the achievements of those Irish pioneers all the more remarkable.

Fore Abbey

Seven Wonders of Fore

Monastery built on a bog
Mill without a mill-stream
Tree that will not burn
Water that will not boil
Water that flows uphill
Anchorite in a Stone
Stone lintel raised by St Fechin's prayers

The ruins of FORE ABBEY, slumbering in a secluded valley near Castlepollard, form THE LARGEST GROUP OF BENEDICTINE REMAINS IN IRELAND. This is a dreamy place, cut off from the rest of the world by a rim of low hills, and time can be happily lost wandering through the complex of venerable old buildings, ferreting out the seven wonders.

The MONASTERY, originally founded by ST FECHIN in the 7th century, is indeed BUILT ON A BOG, although what we see here today dates from the 13th century onwards. Nearby are

the stone blocks of a former MILL with NO MILL-RACE in sight. This is limestone country and the stream probably disappears underground in dry weather. No one dares to try and BURN THE TREE or BOIL THE WATER since 'illness will befall any who try'. And there really is a stream that appears to FLOW UPHILL. It leaves LOUGH LENE at the head of the valley and appears higher up on the other side of the road as a spring – the two are probably not connected, but the illusion is startling.

The ANCHORITE IN A STONE is a more solid concept. On the hillside across from the monastery is a chapel, built around a tiny stone cell that was occupied in the 17th century by THE LAST HERMIT IN IRELAND, PATRICK BEGLAN. Just below is St Fechin's original church, added to in the 12th century. Above the west door is a massive STONE LINTEL, marked with a cross inside a circle. It looks so heavy that it could only have been lifted into place by the *power of prayer*.

LOUGH LENE IS UNIQUE in that IT DRAINS BOTH EAST AND WEST. Because central Ireland is so flat there is no natural watershed, and Lough Lene balances on the cusp – one stream feeds into the RIVER DEEL and flows east into the RIVER BOYNE and the IRISH SEA, another stream runs underground to supply the spring at FORE, which then flows west into the RIVER INNY, and so to the RIVER SHANNON and the ATLANTIC.

The Children of Lir

Swansong

County Westmeath's very own wicked stepmother story centres on the wild and lonely LOUGH DERRAVARAGH.

KING LIR had four lovely children with his wife EVA. When Eva died tragically young, only his love for the children kept King Lir from despair.

Some years later he married again, to the cold but beautiful AOIFE. At first all was well, but Aoife soon became jealous of the bond between her husband and his children. When Lir was away hunting, she took the children down to Lough Derravaragh to bathe. While they were happily splashing, she laid a spell on them, turning them into swans, condemned to haunt the waters of Ireland for 900 years – the first 300 years on Lough Derravaragh. As swans, the children had sweet singing voices and people came from far and wide to hear them. Their grieving father decreed that no swan in Ireland should ever be harmed – still the law in Ireland today.

After their time on Lough Derravaragh, the swans spent their next 300 years on the storm-tossed SEA OF MOYLE off the Antrim coast and then another 300 years around INISHGLORA, Co. Mayo. With the beginning of Christianity, when St Patrick came to Ireland, the spell was broken and the children regained human form – not as the beautiful children they once were, but wizened and hideous crones. They died soon afterwards – but not before they were baptised.

To this day the swans on Lough Derravaragh sing more sweetly than anywhere else in Ireland.

Tullynally Castle, before the addition of the conservatory

Tullynally Castle

Larger than Life

TULLYNALLY CASTLE IS THE BIGGEST CASTLE IN IRELAND, a quarter of a mile (0.4 km) in circumference, spread over 2 acres (0.8 ha), with more than 120 rooms. The grounds contain IRELAND'S LARGEST KITCHEN GARDEN. In Irish, Tullynally means 'HILL OF THE SWAN', very appropriate since it sits beside Lough Derravaragh, where the Swans of Lir spent their first years.

The original tower house of the 17th century has been enlarged over time and was finally embellished into a Gothic castle in 1806. It has been the home of the PAKENHAM family, later EARLS OF LONGFORD, since 1655.

In the early 19th century Tullynally was equipped with an experimental central heating system by RICHARD EDGEWORTH of neighbouring Edgeworthstown, thus becoming THE FIRST CASTLE IN EUROPE TO HAVE CENTRAL HEATING.

A previous owner of Tullynally was EDWARD, THE 6TH EARL OF LONGFORD, for a long time on the

Board of Directors of the GATE THEATRE in Dublin. Because of its policy of charging very low prices for tickets the Gate was always in financial difficulties, and for many years Lord Longford provided funding to keep the theatre alive.

Edward was a memorable figure who weighed 24 stone (152 kg), and was so stout that he had to sit in the back seat of a car in order to drive it. MICHAEL MACLIAMMOIR, the noted Irish actor who co-founded the Gate Theatre in 1928 with HILTON EDWARDS, described him 'striding into the theatre with his sudden infectious cackle of laughter,

his magnificent expanse of grey flannel trouser, dazzling pullover and billowing breast . . .'

The 6th Earl filled Tullynally with his artistic friends such as the future Poet Laureate JOHN BETJEMAN and author EVELYN WAUGH. In the library at Tullynally is the globe that Waugh spun to decide where he should go on his travels in the 1930s – it stopped on Abyssinia (now Ethiopia).

The present owners are the authors THOMAS and VALERIE PAKENHAM, who open the castle to visitors by appointment. The grounds are open throughout the summer.

Well, I never knew this
ABOUT
COUNTY WESTMEATH

LOCKE'S DISTILLERY at KILBEGGAN was established in 1757 and is IRELAND'S LAST REMAINING EXAMPLE OF A SMALL POT DISTILLERY. There is now a museum here that tells the story of Irish whiskey making.

LISSOY, a hamlet north of Athlone, is the 'SWEET AUBURN' of OLIVER GOLDSMITH'S *The Deserted Village*. Goldsmith's family moved here from PALLAS when he was two years old and he first went to school here. A short distance to the north-east is a pub called THE THREE PIGEONS, named after the inn from *She Stoops to Conquer* (*see* Co. Longford, page 90).

ATHLONE IS THE LARGEST TOWN ON THE RIVER SHANNON and was the birthplace of THE GREATEST TENOR OF HIS DAY, COUNT JOHN McCORMACK (1884–1945). McCormack became renowned in the fields of opera and popular music for his soaring voice, amazing breath control and clear diction. In 1914 he was the first artist to record 'It's a Long Way to Tipperary'. His greatest accolade came in 1928 when he was made a Papal Count, in recognition of his efforts for Catholic charities.

KILBEGGAN RACE TRACK is IRELAND'S ONLY ALL NATIONAL HUNT RACECOURSE, where races are run under National Hunt rules.

Author J.P. DONLEAVY (*The Ginger Man*, *The Beastly Beatitudes of Balthazar B*, *The Onion Eaters*) lives at LEVINGTON PARK, a historic 18th-century house near Mullingar, where he writes and raises cattle. He was born in New York in 1926, the son of Irish immigrants.

The FIRST VICTORIA CROSS OF WORLD WAR ONE was awarded to LIEUTENANT MAURICE DEASE, born in Co. Westmeath in 1889, for extreme courage at the BATTLE OF MONS, in August 1914. Dease's father lived at LEVINGTON PARK (*see above*).

BALLINAGORE became THE FIRST VILLAGE IN IRELAND TO BE LIT WITH GAS when it was supplied with peat gas by the Perry family. The controlled fermenting of peat produced enough gas to light the Perrys' home, the village mills and the streetlights.

SOUTH HILL, a plain 19th-century manor house near the village of DELVIN, was the home of SIR THOMAS CHAPMAN (1846–1920). In the 1870s Chapman hired a governess for his daughters called SARAH LAWRENCE. They fell in love and had an affair, which resulted in two illegitimate

South Hill

Killua Castle

children. The younger of these, Thomas Edward Lawrence, grew up to be celebrated as Lawrence of Arabia. The main family seat of the Chapmans was Killua Castle near Clonmellon. In the grounds of Killua is an obelisk commemorating the planting of the first potato in Ireland by Sir Walter Raleigh. This is disputed (*see* Co. Waterford, page 199). In his letters, Lawrence of Arabia expressed a desire to one day purchase Killua Castle, but died in a motor-bicycle accident in Dorset in 1935 before he could fulfil his wish.

COUNTY WEXFORD

Wexford (Viking name) – 'west harbour'

Johnstown Castle – once owned by the Grogan family, the biggest untitled landowners in Ireland

Wexford

The North-West Passage

WEXFORD WAS THE FIRST TOWN IN IRELAND TO FALL TO THE ANGLO-NORMANS, in 1169. Today it is an attractive old walled town with narrow alleyways, crooked streets, a long quayside and a lively maritime atmosphere.

Near the old West Gate are the ruins of the priory where HENRY II SPENT LENT in 1172, doing penance for the murder of THOMAS BECKET.

OSCAR WILDE'S MOTHER, the writer and poet JANE ELGEE, known as 'SPERANZA', was born in the OLD RECTORY, SOUTH MAIN STREET

West Gate, Wexford

in 1826. (It may have been 1821 – Speranza was vague about her true age.)

Sir Robert McClure, the man who discovered the North-West Passage, was born in North Main Street, in a house next to Whites Hotel on 28 January 1807. He entered the Royal Navy in 1824 and served for a time on Admiral Nelson's flagship HMS *Victory*. In 1848 he sailed to the Arctic as First Lieutenant on the *Enterprise*, one of two ships led by Sir James Clark Ross, to search for the lost Franklin Expedition.

They failed to find Franklin but McClure returned to the Arctic as commander of HMS *Investigator* in 1850. This time he approached the Arctic from the west, entering through the Bering Strait and sailing east. On reaching Banks Island, McClure pressed on and discovered the narrow Prince of Wales Strait, between Banks Island and Victoria Island.

The *Investigator* was soon caught in the ice, but McClure was keen to learn where the strait led, so he decided to explore further by sledge. After several days he found himself looking at what would later be called Viscount Melville Sound, proof that Banks Island was actually an island. On 21 April 1851, he wrote in his journal, 'Can it be possible that this water communicates with Barrow's Strait, and shall

prove to be the long-sought North-west Passage?'

When he could get free of the ice, McClure sailed round the north-west coast of Banks Island and into the strait that now bears his name. *Investigator* became icebound again and McClure and his crew, suffering from starvation and scurvy, had to wait to be rescued by Sir Edward Belcher in 1853. They returned to London as heroes having finally proved the existence of the fabled North-West Passage. McClure was knighted in 1854.

Sir Robert McClure died in 1873 and is buried in London.

John Barry

Father of the American Navy

John Barry, 'Father of the American Navy', was born in 1745, the son of a Catholic farmer. His birthplace was a simple thatched cottage at Ballysampson, on Our Lady's Island, just outside the town of Wexford. In 1759 he went to sea with his uncle, the master of a local vessel, on a voyage to Philadelphia, where he decided to stay in order to escape Catholic persecution in Ireland.

Over the next few years he commanded several merchant ships trading with the West Indies, and gained a reputation as a brilliant sailor and popular captain. After the outbreak of the Revolutionary War with Britain, Barry gained command of the brig *Lexington*, and on 7 April 1776 he captured a British tender off the Cape of Virginia, achieving THE FIRST CAPTURE OF A BRITISH WARSHIP BY AN AMERICAN WARSHIP and becoming THE FIRST COMMISSIONED OFFICER TO CAPTURE A SHIP UNDER THE AUTHORITY OF THE AMERICAN CONGRESS.

Before the War ended Barry took part in many engagements against the British, was responsible for training a new generation of naval officers for America's nascent Federal Navy, and compiled the Naval Signals Book. As well as conducting the first engagement of the American Navy, Barry was also involved in THE LAST SEA BATTLE OF THE AMERICAN REVOLUTION. His ship the *Alliance* successfully fought off a British frigate, the *Sybil*, while escorting a Spanish bullion ship from Havana, carrying 72,000 Spanish silver dollars for Congress.

He was eventually appointed Commander-in-Chief of the American Naval Forces, by George Washington, effective from 4 June 1794. Commodore John Barry

died at his residence, STRAWBERRY HILL, outside Philadelphia, in September 1803, aged 58. A statue of him stands on Crescent Quay in Wexford, donated by the American people.

Enniscorthy

A Good Walloping

ENNISCORTHY stands on the banks of the River Slaney, a pleasant town of quiet streets and old houses, survivors of a turbulent history.

ENNISCORTHY CASTLE was restored in the 19th century by the EARL OF PORTSMOUTH, a descendant of SIR HENRY WALLOP, granted lands in Co. Wexford when he was Vice-Treasurer of Ireland in the 16th century.

Enniscorthy's most notable building is ST AIDAN'S CATHEDRAL, completed in 1848 and designed by AUGUSTUS PUGIN, architect of the HOUSES OF PARLIAMENT in London.

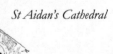

St Aidan's Cathedral

Sir Henry Wallop's *ancestor,* Sir John Wallop, *gave the family name to the English language in 1513 when, on the orders of Henry VIII, he raided the coast of Normandy in reprisal for the French burning of Brighton in Sussex. Such was the ferocity of Wallop's retribution, destroying ships and harbours and laying waste towns and villages, that a beating, or a good hiding, has been known ever since as a* 'WALLOPING'.

On 29 May, during the 1798 rebellion, Enniscorthy was captured by the Wexford Insurgents, under Father John Murphy. The town's defences were effectively destroyed by a cleverly engineered stampede of cattle which cleared the way for the rebels to advance unhindered.

Father Murphy had originally persuaded his flock to give up their weapons, but when people were driven from their homes and persecuted by the Yeomanry and his church at Boolavogue was ransacked, he took up arms at the head of a force of United Irishmen and pikemen from Wexford, who became known as the Wexford Insurgents. They met with considerable early success but were finally surrounded and defeated at Vinegar Hill, just outside Enniscorthy. Father Murphy was captured and executed at Tullow on 2 July 1798.

Father Murphy's home at Boolavogue has been restored as a museum illustrating life on an Irish farm from the time of 1798.

Annie Jameson, granddaughter of the founder of Jameson's whiskey, and mother of radio pioneer Guglielmo Marconi, (*see* Co. Galway, page 5) grew up near Enniscorthy.

Augustus Pugin also built a Gothic chapel for his friends the Powers, *of* Powers whiskey *fame, at* Edermine House, *their recently built Italianate villa, down the River Slaney.*
Today, Powers whiskey is the best-selling Irish whiskey in Ireland, *and is known as* 'the Father of all Irish whiskeys'.

Boolavogue

Kennedy

The Road to Camelot

JOHN FITZGERALD KENNEDY, THE MOST FAMOUS AMERICAN PRESIDENT OF MODERN TIMES and THE FIRST CATHOLIC PRESIDENT OF THE UNITED STATES, was descended from a Wexford family.

On a wet day in 1848 PATRICK KENNEDY, a cooper, set sail from the Wexford port of NEW ROSS to escape the Great Famine and make a new life for his family in America. Within two generations, the Kennedy family had progressed from steerage on an immigrant ship, via the slums of Boston, to being one of the richest and most influential dynasties in the world.

A little over 100 years after that wet day in Co. Wexford, JOHN F. KENNEDY was elected as the 35TH PRESIDENT OF THE UNITED STATES. In an early example of spin, his wife JACKIE later referred to their time at the White House as CAMELOT, after the mythical court of King Arthur, and certainly few Presidents before or since have evoked such passion and optimism as JFK.

In June 1963 President Kennedy, fresh from his '*Ich bin ein Berliner*' (which actually means 'I am a dough-nut') speech in Berlin, made THE FIRST-EVER VISIT TO IRELAND BY A SITTING AMERICAN PRESIDENT. For the most powerful man in the world, the highlight of the trip was enjoying a cup of tea with his kinsfolk at his ancestor's simple homestead in Dunganstown.

The Kennedy Homestead at Dunganstown near New Ross is still run by Patrick Kennedy's descendants and is open to the public.

The Kennedy Homestead, Dunganstown

Well, I never knew this
ABOUT
COUNTY WEXFORD

In the 12th century, the King of Leinster, DIARMAIT MACMURROUGH, made the village of FERNS his capital and founded an abbey there. It was to Ferns that he brought the abducted DEVORGILLA, setting in train the events that led to the Anglo-Norman invasion of 1169 (*see* Co. Leitrim, page 16). Fragments of a 12th-century High Cross near the abbey ruins are thought to mark his grave. It is believed that the head of FATHER MURPHY (*see* Enniscorthy, page 132) is buried somewhere here too.

It was on BAGINBUN HEAD at BANNOW BAY, south of Wexford, that THE NORMANS FIRST SET FOOT ON IRISH SOIL. ROBERT FITZSTEPHEN and MAURICE FITZGERALD stepped ashore here with 300 soldiers in May 1169.

ROBERT FITZSTEPHEN'S CASTLE, built in 1169 at FERRYCARRIG, WAS THE FIRST NORMAN CASTLE IN IRELAND.

The tall tower on the site today comes from a later 15th-century castle.

MERCOD BALLAGH is the first person known to have been executed by guillotine. This happened in 1307 near MERTON on the River Slaney in Co. Wexford.

A YEW TREE growing in a private garden in Co. Wexford is registered as over 1,000 years of age – THE OLDEST TREE IN IRELAND.

The lighthouse on HOOK HEAD dates from 1172 and is THE OLDEST LIGHT-HOUSE IN EUROPE. It is also ONE OF THE OLDEST OPERATIONAL LIGHT-HOUSES IN THE WORLD. There has been a beacon here, tended by monks, since the 5th century. The present stone tower was built by WILLIAM LE MARESCHALL, EARL OF PEMBROKE.

Tintern Abbey

William Le Mareschall also built Tintern Abbey, in 1200, romantically situated on the edge of a creek. It is hidden in a grove of trees and there is a charming old stone bridge across the fields, leading down to Barrow Bay. Tintern was Mareschall's way of giving thanks for his rescue from drowning, when his boat was caught in a storm off the Wexford coast. He populated the Abbey with monks from the famous Tintern Abbey in Monmouthshire, Wales.

The phrase 'by Hook or by Crooke' was supposedly coined by Oliver Cromwell when he was deciding whether to approach Waterford Harbour via Hook Head or the village of Crooke on the opposite side of the estuary.

Slaney Manor was built by the Percevals in 1828. A prominent member of the family was Spencer Perceval, shot at the Houses of Parliament in London in 1812, the

Slaney Manor

ONLY BRITISH PRIME MINISTER TO BE ASSASSINATED. Later, Slaney Manor was the home of ADMIRAL LORD BEATTY (1871–1936) of World War One fame (Battle of Jutland). He was to become THE YOUNGEST ADMIRAL OF THE ROYAL NAVY SINCE NELSON.

The CODA family emigrated from WEXFORD TOWN to America during the time of the Great Famine. Their son grew up to be the colourful Wild West figure 'BUFFALO BILL' CODY (1846–1917).

THE FIRST MAGPIES IN IRELAND arrived in Wexford Town in 1682, blown across the sea from Wales by an easterly storm.

The RAVEN NATURE RESERVE, part of an area of flat, marshy land near Wexford Harbour known as the NORTH SLOBS, is home to the IRISH HARE, a variety of hare with short ears and a white tail that is UNIQUE TO IRELAND. Also found here is the VIVIPAROUS LIZARD, IRELAND'S ONLY NATIVE REPTILE.

The SALTEE ISLANDS off Kilmore Quay make up THE LARGEST BIRD SANCTUARY IN IRELAND.

LADY'S ISLAND south of Wexford is THE ONLY PLACE IN BRITAIN OR IRELAND WHERE COTTONWEED GROWS.

It was a doctor in OULART, ARTHUR LEARED (1822–79), who invented THE MODERN STETHOSCOPE, first using two earpieces, connected by rubber tubes to a listening chamber, in 1851.

CARNSORE POINT south of Wexford is THE MOST SOUTH-EASTERLY POINT OF IRELAND.

ROSSLARE is THE SUNNIEST TOWN IN IRELAND, with an average of 4 hours and 20 minutes of sunshine every day.

COUNTY WICKLOW

COUNTY TOWN: WICKLOW

Wicklow (Viking *Vikingr Lo*) – 'Viking meadow'

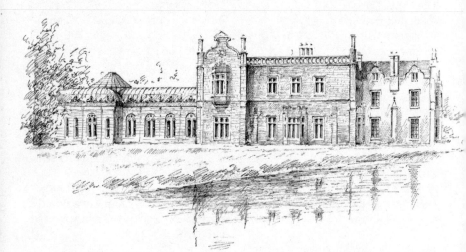

Killruddery House – set amongst the oldest surviving formal gardens in Ireland

The Vale of Avoca

*There is not in the wide world
A valley so sweet as that vale
In whose bosom the bright waters meet*
THOMAS MOORE

This soft and scented valley is a much-loved beauty spot and has attracted nature lovers and poets, such as Thomas Moore, for many years. The vale begins at THE MEETING OF THE WATERS, described above, where the Avonbeg and Avonmore rivers converge to form the Avoca.

Lying at the heart of the vale is the little village of AVOCA, more often known these days as BALLYKISS-ANGEL, after the hugely popular BBC TV series of that name, which was filmed here. It has made this tiny place, and particularly the village pub FITZGERALD's, familiar to millions across the world.

AVOCA HANDWEAVERS have been producing fine tweeds since 1723

[138]

in IRELAND'S OLDEST SURVIVING WORKING MILL.

Mining has gone on at Avoca since prehistoric times and, because of this, the area was important enough to be marked on PTOLEMY'S celebrated MAP of AD 150. Mining for copper and sulphur only ceased in 1982, making Avoca THE LONGEST-WORKING OF ALL IRELAND'S MINES.

Rumours that gold had been found 'in them thar Wicklow mountains' or, more precisely, on the slopes of CROGHAN MOUNTAIN, not far from Avoca, sparked IRELAND'S ONLY GOLD RUSH in 1795. No one got rich but, for 200 years, Croghan became IRELAND'S ONLY COMMERCIAL GOLD MINE and has been worked on and off by locals, private companies and State companies ever since.

A small open-cast gold mine opened near Omagh, in Co. Tyrone, in 2000.

At the southern end of the valley, in the village of WOODENBRIDGE, is IRELAND'S OLDEST HOTEL, the WOODENBRIDGE HOTEL, established in 1608. The bridge at Woodenbridge is now made of stone.

Fitzgerald's, Avoca

Russborough House

A Collection of Thieves

The Palladian RUSSBOROUGH HOUSE, near BLESSINGTON, is THE LONGEST HOUSE IN IRELAND, with a façade of over 700 ft (213 m), and has THE FINEST STUCCO-DECORATED ROOMS IN IRELAND. It must also be THE MOST ROBBED HOUSE IN IRELAND.

In 1952 SIR ALFRED BEIT and his wife CLEMENTINE, a cousin of the celebrated MITFORD sisters, bought the house and filled it with a magnificent series of paintings – the fabulous BEIT ART COLLECTION. This was inherited from his uncle,

Russborough House

the Alfred Beit who was a founder of the DE BEERS diamond company.

In 1974 an IRA gang broke into the house, bound and gagged 71-year-old Sir Alfred and one of his staff, dragged them into the library, and proceeded to cut a number of priceless paintings out of their frames with a screwdriver. They got away with 19 pictures in all, including a Goya, a Vermeer, two Gainsboroughs and three Rubenses.

Among the thieves was DR ROSE DUGDALE, Oxford graduate daughter of an English millionaire, who had found excitement in life by stealing from her father and falling in love with IRA gunman EDDIE GALLAGHER. She turned out to be the gang's undoing.

Their demands were that four IRA bombers in prison in London be transferred to Belfast, in return for five of the paintings. Before that could happen, the Irish police recovered the entire haul after a raid on an isolated cottage in Co. Cork. A local village policeman had grown suspicious when he heard that the cottage had been rented to a strange Frenchwoman with an English accent, who turned out to be Rose Dugdale. She was sentenced to nine years in jail.

In 1976 the Beits set up a foundation so that the house could be opened to the public and, along with the collection, preserved for the nation.

Ten years after this, in May 1986, thieves struck again, this time in the guise of Dublin arch-villain MARTIN CAHILL. He got away with £30 million worth of paintings, but seven pictures were recovered the next day and over the years most of the others were found abroad, as Cahill was unable to sell them in Ireland. There are now just two of these paintings still missing.

In 1987, Sir Alfred donated a large part of the collection to the NATIONAL GALLERY OF IRELAND.

Sir Alfred Beit died in 1994, the same year that Martin Cahill was assassinated by the IRA.

In 2001 Russborough House was ram-raided by three armed men who drove a jeep into the building and took two paintings worth £3 million, a Gainsborough and a Bellotto. These were recovered in 2002, as was a Rubens from the 1986 haul – just as thieves removed five more pictures, including two more Rubenses, in Russborough's FOURTH robbery.

Lady Beit died in August 2005.

Glendalough

St Kevin's Birds

Glendalough today – St Kevin's Church

GLENDALOUGH is not just Ireland's most sacred holy place, but also a valley of supreme loveliness. ST KEVIN, a Prince of Leinster, came here in the 6th century to live as a hermit, and it is easy to see why. It is a secret place of purple hillsides, still blue lakes and no sound but the birds and the wind in the trees.

Glendalough, alas, is no longer secret and has become ruinously popular. It should be visited on a bad day, when the clouds lower and the grey rain sweeps off the mountains and there is no companion but the mist – just as it would have been when St Kevin himself lived there. Not that the saint was able to get away entirely. He was pursued to Glendalough by a lovesick young lady called Kathleen. Thomas Moore puts it so well:

> *By that lake whose gloomy shore*
> *Skylark never warbles o'er,*
> *Where the cliff hangs high and*
>   *steep,*
> *Young Saint Kevin stole to sleep.*
> *'Here, at least,' he calmly said,*
> *'Woman ne'er shall find my bed.'*
> *Ah! The Good Saint little knew*
> *What that wily sex can do.*

On waking up in the lakeside cave that served as his bed, St Kevin found Kathleen standing naked beside him. Obviously a man of chilled steel, he seized her and flung her off the ledge and into the lake.

St Kevin was never troubled again, but visitors to the cave, which can only be reached by boat and a difficult scramble up the cliff, report that ghostly hands have been known to emerge from the water, trying to drag them back down into the icy depths . . .

St Kevin, it seems, was more patient with birds of the feathered variety. When a blackbird laid her eggs on his outstretched hand, rather than disturb her, he didn't move until the eggs had hatched some weeks later.

Despite the tourists and the buses, Glendalough is still a tranquil, mystical place, and a 10-minute walk can lose you amongst the simple monastic remains and lacustrine beauty.

County Wicklow on Film

Because of its majestic scenery, spectacular great houses and proximity to Dublin, Co. Wicklow has been chosen over the years as a location for numerous feature films and television series.

KILLRUDDERY HOUSE, 2 miles (3 km) south of BRAY, home of the Earls of Meath, is a bewitching

17th- and 19th-century creation, set within THE OLDEST SURVIVING FORMAL GARDENS IN IRELAND. They were laid out by a French gardener from Versailles. The SYLVAN THEATRE in the grounds, enclosed by a bay hedge, is THE ONLY EXAMPLE OF SUCH A THEATRE IN IRELAND.

The opening sequences of the 1989 film *My Left Foot*, starring DANIEL DAY-LEWIS as the crippled artist CHRISTY BROWN, were shot at Killruddery. Much of the film was made at ARDMORE studios in the nearby seaside town of BRAY, which was also featured in the film. Daniel Day-Lewis won BEST ACTOR OSCAR for his portrayal, while BRENDA FRICKER won the Oscar for BEST SUPPORTING ACTRESS, playing his mother.

In 1992 Killruddery was used as the country house of an evil landlord who mistreats TOM CRUISE in the RON HOWARD film *Far and Away*, starring Cruise and NICOLE KIDMAN.

In the last years of World War Two, LAURENCE OLIVIER and hundreds of extras came to POWERSCOURT HOUSE, just south of Dublin, to film *Henry V*. Powerscourt is a magnificent Palladian house with famous gardens, extensive enough for staging the spectacular battle scenes that the film required. Olivier was scarred for life when a horse galloped straight into the camera he was looking through, sending a piece of metal up through his top lip and into his gums. Subsequently, he often sported a moustache to hide the scar.

Olivier as Henry V was not the only royal personage who nearly came to grief at Powerscourt. When KING GEORGE IV visited in 1821, VISCOUNT POWERSCOURT decided to impress his royal guest by damming up the waterfall in the deer park, and then releasing the water so that it would cascade down the mountainside and provide a suitably exciting spectacle. A special bridge was built from which to view the show. The King, however, over-indulged at dinner and never got to the waterfall, which turned out to be just as well – when the water was eventually let go it deluged down in a raging torrent that swept the bridge away.

This POWERSCOURT WATERFALL, where the RIVER DARGLE tumbles 425 ft (130 m) off the Wicklow

Powerscourt House

Mountains, is THE HIGHEST WATER-
FALL IN IRELAND. It can be found 3
miles (5 km) south of Enniskerry,
in the Powerscourt Deer Park.
KING ARTHUR (NIGEL TERRY) and
LANCELOT (NICHOLAS CLAY) meet
and duel at the waterfall in the 1981
film *Excalibur,* directed by John
Boorman who lives locally.

In 2002 Powerscourt House and
gardens became the extravagant
estate of the COUNT OF MONTE
CRISTO, in the film of that name,
starring GUY PEARCE, JAMES
CAVIEZEL and RICHARD HARRIS.

LUGGALA, a magical 'gingerbread'
Gothic cottage set in the heart
of the Wicklow Mountains near
ROUNDWOOD, is the home of GARECH
BROWNE, pony-tailed member of the
GUINNESS dynasty and co-founder,
with PADDY MOLONEY, of CLADDAGH
RECORDS and THE CHIEFTAINS. In
1974 the Luggala estate became THE
OUTLANDS where SEAN CONNERY ran
riot as an EXTERMINATOR in JOHN
BOORMAN's futuristic oddity *Zardoz.*

KILCOOLE is perhaps THE MOST
RECOGNISED VILLAGE IN IRELAND, as
the setting for *Glenroe*, THE LONGEST-
RUNNING SOAP ON IRISH TELEVISION.
For 18 years the people of Ireland
were glued to their TV sets on a
Sunday evening, watching this tele-
vised evocation of life in a rural Irish
village. The series was unable to
survive the death of everyone's
favourite character, BIDDY, in a car
crash in 2000, and was taken off
the air in 2001. GLENROE FARM,
the fictional home of the central
characters, farmers DINNY AND
MILEY BYRNE, is now a tourist
attraction.

Well, I never knew this
ABOUT
COUNTY WICKLOW

COUNTY WICKLOW is known as 'THE
GARDEN OF IRELAND' and is THE
MOST HEAVILY FORESTED COUNTY IN
IRELAND.

The wonderfully beautiful GLENMAL-
URE, west of Rathdrum, is 22 miles
(35 km) in length, THE LONGEST
GLACIAL VALLEY IN THE BRITISH
ISLES. It is overlooked by WICKLOW's
HIGHEST MOUNTAIN, the imposing
LUGNAQUILLA, which rises to 3,034 ft
(925 m) above sea level.

Picturesque ROUNDWOOD looks down
on the rest of Ireland from 780 ft
(238 m) up in the Wicklow Mountains
and is THE HIGHEST VILLAGE IN
IRELAND.

At ANNAMOE, the next-door hamlet
to Roundwood, in 1720, the author
LAURENCE STERNE, then a boy of
seven, fell into the fast-running mill
race. He was taken a full turn of the
mill wheel before being plucked out
of the water by the miller, wet and

shaken but otherwise unharmed. As Sterne himself puts it, *'the story is incredible, but known for truth in all that part of Ireland, where hundreds of people flocked to see me'*.

ERSKINE CHILDERS JR, former President of Ireland, is buried nearby at DERRYLOSSERY.

TINAKILLY HOUSE, overlooking Wicklow Bay, was built in 1876 by a grateful government for ROBERT HALPIN (1836–94), captain of THE WORLD'S BIGGEST SHIP, the *Great Eastern*. As Captain of this huge vessel, Wicklow-born Halpin had been responsible for laying THE FIRST SUCCESSFUL TRANSATLANTIC CABLE from VALENTIA ISLAND TO NEWFOUNDLAND in 1866 (*see* Co. Kerry, page 171).

The handsome 17th-century stone village of SHILLELAGH, at the southern tip of the Wicklow Mountains, gives its name to the rough, knobbled cudgel of oak or blackthorn that has become such an emblem of Ireland. In medieval times the whole district was covered with magnificent oak woods, but over the years the demand for timber has seen the forest stripped. A remnant of those great woods is the TOMNA-FINNOGE OAK FOREST, standing just off the Tinahely road, which is still one of the largest oak forests in Ireland. Timber from the Shillelagh woods was used to roof some of the finest buildings in Europe, including WESTMINSTER HALL in London, the STADTHOUSE in Holland, and ST PATRICK'S CATHEDRAL in Dublin.

It was near BALTINGLASS, on the

Tinakilly House

Avondale House

western edge of the Wicklow Mountains, that JOHN WATSON killed THE LAST WOLF IN IRELAND in 1786 (*see* Co. Carlow, page 54).

A DOUGLAS FIR, 184 ft (56 m) tall, growing on the Powerscourt estate is THE TALLEST TREE IN IRELAND.

AVONDALE HOUSE, just south of RATHDRUM, was the birthplace of CHARLES STEWART PARNELL (1846–91), known as 'THE UNCROWNED KING OF IRELAND'. He was one of Ireland's greatest political leaders and the man who did more than anyone to force the issue of HOME RULE. As President of the IRISH LAND LEAGUE, he created the tactic of non-cooperation that defeated Co. Mayo

land agent CAPTAIN BOYCOTT and gave a new word to the English language (*see* Co. Mayo, page 20). He died at the young age of 45, a year after his career was ruined when he was cited in a divorce case over his affair with KITTY O'SHEA.

Charles Stewart Parnell's maternal grandfather was ADMIRAL CHARLES STEWART, commander of the USS *Constitution*, 'Old Ironsides', during the Anglo-American WAR OF 1812.

Avondale House and grounds are now owned by the state and open to the public. The Georgian house contains a MUSEUM dedicated to Parnell.

The name of a Wicklow man, JOHN KYAN (1774–1850), has gone down in the English language to describe an early kind of wood preservative, once used to treat railway sleepers, building timbers, rope and sailcloth. John Kyan's father owned the Avoca mines, which had a problem with support timbers rotting in the damp conditions. In 1812 Kyan found that by impregnating the timbers with a bichloride of mercury solution, the breakdown of the wood was greatly slowed. This process became known as 'Kyanisation' and was widely used until the discovery of creosote in the 1850s.

Munster

COUNTY CLARE

COUNTY TOWN: ENNIS

an Clar – 'level place'

*Mount Ievers Court at Sixmilebridge was built in the 1730s and is
the quintessential Irish 'tall house'*

The Burren

Unique

At the north-west corner of County
Clare is THE BURREN, 400 square
miles (1,000 sq km) of bare limestone pavement, home to A UNIQUE
COMBINATION OF PLANT LIFE found
nowhere else in the world. The
absence of frost allows mild-climate
Mediterranean species to thrive
alongside alpine and arctic plants
normally found high up in the
mountains or in tundra regions.

At CARRON, right in the heart of
the Burren, is IRELAND'S FIRST
PERFUMERY, where essential oils are
extracted from a variety of plants,

[149]

Poulnabrone Dolmen at the heart of The Burren

using traditional pot stills, then mixed with natural essences and pure Burren spring water to create delicate scents and fragrances.

Below the surface, the limestone of the Burren is riddled with underground passages, potholes and cave systems, including Pollinagollum, the longest cave in Ireland, which extends for nearly 10 miles (16 km). Near Doolin, on the western edge, in a cave called Polanionain, is the longest free-hanging stalactite in the world, hanging 23 ft (7 m) down from the roof.

Killaloe

A Smart Stone

The tiny town of Killaloe is attractively situated on the west bank of the River Shannon, at the south end of Lough Derg. In the churchyard of St Flannan's Cathedral is an exquisite small, 12th-century Oratory with a beautiful Romanesque doorway. There is an equally remarkable Romanesque

St Flannan's Cathedral and Oratory

doorway inside the cathedral, rescued from a former church. Next to this doorway is Killaloe's most special treasure, THORGRIM'S STONE, the shaft of a cross carved by a Viking over 1,000 years ago. It is THE ONLY KNOWN EXAMPLE IN THE WORLD of a bi-lingual stone with inscriptions in both Scandinavian Runes and Irish Ogham. The runic reads: 'Thorgrim carved this cross', while the Ogham writing says: 'A blessing upon Thorgrim'.

> OGHAM, THE EARLIEST FORM OF IRISH SCRIPT, *is a system of straight lines and notches corresponding to Roman letters. It can be found carved on Ogham stones throughout Ireland.*

About 1 mile from Killaloe is the green mound of KINCORA, where BRIAN BORU had his palace and possibly where he was born in 941. Boru was the first – and last – High King who effectively ruled all Ireland. He died at the moment of his greatest triumph, victory over the Vikings at the Battle of Clonfert in 1014 (*see* Co. Dublin, page 61).

Further north, on the little island of INISCALTRA, or Holy island, out in Lough Derg, is St Caimin's church, with A UNIQUE TRIANGULAR WINDOW, THE ONLY ONE OF ITS KIND IN IRELAND.

EDNA O'BRIEN, the novelist and short story writer (*Girl with Green Eyes, Time and Tide, Vanishing Ireland*), was born at TUAMGRANEY, on the edge of Lough Derg, in 1930.

John P. Holland

Dive Dive Dive

JOHN P. HOLLAND was born in LISCANNOR near the Cliffs of Moher, in 1841, the son of a coastguard. His father died in the Great Famine, and with Co. Clare being very much the land of DANIEL O'CONNELL, 'THE LIBERATOR', Holland grew up a staunch Republican. He enjoyed using his fertile mind and inventive brain to think up new ways of hurting the British, and he eventually decided that a good way to inflict real damage was to attack the British Navy by submarine, stealing up under water and hitting them at close range.

At the age of 17 he came up with the blueprint for his first submersible. It was a design that he never had to radically alter for the rest of his life. When JULES VERNE published his novel *20,000 Leagues under the Sea* in 1870, Holland was hugely motivated to try and turn his dream into a reality. Jules Verne had himself been inspired by another Irish inventor, ROBERT FULTON, who had constructed a primitive submarine called *Nautilus* (*see* Co. Kilkenny, page 77).

In 1872 Holland emigrated to Boston and joined up with the IRISH FENIAN BROTHERHOOD, an organisation dedicated to raising support for the Irish Republican cause in America. The Fenians offered Holland funding to develop his ideas and, in 1877, the *Holland No 1* was launched on the Passaic River, New Jersey, in front of an admiring crowd.

Unfortunately, as soon as it was put in the water it sank – someone had failed to insert the screw plugs. Undaunted, Holland retrieved his submarine and tried again next day, this time making several successful dives. In 1881 he unveiled the *Fenian Ram*, a three-man vessel designed as an underwater battering ram.

The Holland I submarine

Over the next few years, despite falling out with the Fenians and enduring bureaucratic interference

from the American naval authorities, Holland continued to develop and improve on his boyhood design, and in 1900 he sold *Holland VI* to the US Navy – ITS FIRST SUBMARINE. They soon bought five more, creating THE WORLD'S FIRST SUBMARINE FLEET, all of them Hollands.

Orders poured in from all over the world, and Holland even sold his machine to the old adversary who had inspired his invention in the first place – the British Navy. He built two submarines for the Japanese Navy which contributed mightily to a Japanese victory over the Russians in the RUSSIAN–JAPANESE WAR OF 1904–5.

Holland never lived to see the ultimate fulfilment of his vision. He died in 1914, just weeks before THE WORLD'S FIRST MAJOR SUBMARINE ACTION, when a German submarine sank three British cruisers in the North Sea, ushering in a new and deadly form of naval warfare.

Although he did not invent the world's first submarine, John P. Holland designed and built THE WORLD'S FIRST SELF-PROPELLED SUBMERSIBLE THAT WORKED. Only Japan gave him the recognition he deserved, when the Emperor presented him with the Rising Sun Medal.

Holland No 1 is now in the PATERSON MUSEUM in New Jersey. The *Fenian Ram* was eventually employed against the British when it was exhibited in New York in 1916 to raise money for SINN FEIN. There is a plaque to Holland's memory in

Liscannor, his birthplace, which was unveiled in 1964 on the fiftieth anniversary of his death.

Holland's submarines were fitted with THE WORLD'S FIRST SUBMARINE PERISCOPE, designed by the Irish telescope maker HOWARD GRUBB, whose father had built telescopes for all the pioneering Irish astronomers of the 19th century.

The Colleen Bawn

Murder Most Foul

On the north shore of the Shannon estuary, in the small, windswept BURRANE churchyard at KILLIMER, south-east of Kilrush, there once stood a Celtic cross at the head of a lonely grave. It bore this inscription:

Here lies the Colleen Bawn
Murdered on the Shannon
July 14th 1819 R.I.P.

The cross is gone now, dismantled by souvenir hunters. But little ELLEN HANLEY lies here still, close to where her body was washed up on the shore in the autumn of 1819, and in the same grave as Peter O'Connell, the man who found her. The flat gravestone has now been encased in concrete to protect it.

A simple and unlettered Limerick farmer's daughter, but bright, friendly and bewitchingly beautiful, she was not quite 16 when she was lured away from her uncle's house by her handsome neighbour, the rich, cruel landowner JOHN SCANLAN, of Ballykehan House. They married soon afterwards in the Old Church at KILRUSH.

Within weeks the spoilt Scanlan had tired of his bride, always more popular and beloved than he could ever be, and he was determined to be rid of her. With his servant SULLIVAN he took Ellen out into the middle of the river, intending to shoot her, but lost his nerve. Instead, he plied Sullivan with whiskey and persuaded the poor man to do the deed for him, which Sullivan did, with a musket. Then they removed her clothes, attached a rope weighted down with a rock, and threw her body over the side, where it sank from sight.

Six weeks later Ellen's bloated remains were cast up on the north shore of the Shannon. Scanlan and Sullivan had already gone into hiding, but they were both hunted down and caught. Even though Scanlan was defended in court by THE LIBERATOR, DANIEL O'CONNELL, himself, such was the horror and outrage at this hideous crime that he was sentenced to death, and on 16 March 1820 John Scanlan swung from the end of a rope at GALLOWS GREEN. His servant Sullivan suffered the same fate not long afterwards.

The tragic story of Ellen Hanley, now known to the world as 'THE COLLEEN BAWN', fired the imagination of writers and poets everywhere, and she has come to symbolise both

Irish innocence and Irish beauty. *The Colleen Bawn* was a dramatic adaptation by Dion Boucicault of Gerald Griffin's novel *The Collegians*, which was based on the story of Ellen Hanley. The play made the story famous, and hence Ellen Hanley became known by the name that Boucicault had given her – 'The Colleen Bawn'. A 'colleen' is a country girl.

Colonel Blood

Bad Blood

Colonel Thomas Blood (1618–80), born in Kilnaboy Castle, Co. Clare, more than lived up to his name.

Educated in England, he was granted land in Ireland for services to Oliver Cromwell, but at the Restoration of the Monarchy in 1660 these lands were taken away from him by Charles II. Blood devised a plot to kidnap the Lord Lieutenant of Ireland, James Butler, Duke of Ormond, from Dublin Castle, intending to hold him hostage until the Blood estates were restored. The plot was foiled and Blood's accomplices arrested, but Blood himself escaped disguised as a priest, and fled to Holland.

In 1670, after various exploits in England that left him with a price on his head, Blood tried again to abduct the Duke of Ormond, this time in England. This attempt failed too, but some think it was merely a ploy to distract attention from Blood's true objective, the plot for which he has become infamous, the theft of the Crown Jewels from the Tower of London.

Disguised once more as a parson, Blood paid a number of visits to the Tower during 1671 and befriended the Keeper of the Jewels, Talbot Edwards, even going so far as to arrange a marriage between his own fictitious nephew and Edwards's daughter. During these visits, Blood acquainted himself with the security arrangements, and on 9 May his plan swung into action.

Talbot Edwards was knocked over the head with a mallet then bound and gagged, while Blood and his companions stuffed the Crown Jewels into a sack and made off with their booty. It was unfortunate that at this precise moment the Jewel Keeper's son should choose to visit his father for the first time in years. The gang ran straight into him, the alarm was raised and they were caught red-handed.

Blood was imprisoned in the Tower, close to the scene of his crimes, but refused to answer questions to anyone but the King. When he was finally granted an audience, no one knows what he said to the King, but instead of sending Blood to the gallows Charles II gave him a full pardon, returned his Irish lands and even granted him a pension of £500 a year.

There are many who think that Blood was in fact working as an agent for the King, and that the Jewels were meant to be secretly sold abroad to boost the royal coffers. Whatever the truth, Colonel Blood lived out the rest of his days peacefully at home – as far as anyone knows.

Such was the reputation of the man from Co. Clare, that some while after he had been buried, the authorities exhumed his body, just to make sure that he was actually dead.

Well, I never knew this
ABOUT

COUNTY CLARE

MOOGHAUN HILLFORT, near Dromoland Castle, is over 2,000 years old and is THE LARGEST STONE RING FORT IN IRELAND. It was also the site of THE GREAT CLARE GOLD FIND. In 1854, workmen digging the railway line to Ennis unearthed a rough stone box full of gold ornaments. There were armlets, rings, bracelets, ingots and a crown – THE LARGEST COLLECTION OF GOLD OBJECTS EVER FOUND IN EUROPE. Much of the hoard, which dated from the Bronze Age, was dispersed amongst those who found it, although some pieces made their way to the National Museum in Dublin.

The CLIFFS OF MOHER, rising sheer out of the ocean to a height of 668 feet (204 m), are THE MOST VISITED, AND RECOGNISED, NATURAL ATTRACTION ON THE WEST COAST OF IRELAND.

In the sea off Kilkee is BISHOP'S ISLAND, or '*Oileen an Ospoig Gortaigh*', ISLAND OF THE HUNGRY BISHOP. It was named after a Bishop who fled here during a famine so that he wouldn't have to share his provisions with his flock. A storm blew up and the Bishop was trapped on the island, eventually dying of hunger.

One mile west of KILLINABOY, on ROUGHAN HILL, there used to stand the TAU CROSS, a T-shaped cross with carved human masks, one at each end. It is UNIQUE IN IRELAND and is probably a pre-Christian boundary marker. It is now in the Heritage Centre at COROFIN.

KILFENORA, on the southern edge of the Burren, is THE SMALLEST CATHOLIC DIOCESE IN IRELAND. Thanks to an ecclesiastical anomaly, it has one of the biggest names in the church for a bishop – THE POPE.

SPANISH POINT is where, in September 1588, the bodies of hundreds of drowned sailors were washed ashore from wrecked ships belonging to the scattered Spanish Armada. SIR TURLOCH O'BRIEN of Liscannor patrolled the cliffs with a body of armed men to prevent any of the survivors from landing.

The ARDNACRUSHA HYDROELECT-RICITY SCHEME on the River Shannon, north of Limerick, opened in 1929 and has been described as the 'EIGHTH WONDER OF THE WORLD'. It was built to feed THE WORLD'S FIRST NATIONAL ELECTRICITY GRID and was the prototype and inspiration for many similar schemes around the world, such as the HOOVER DAM on the Colorado river in America.

The round tower on SCATTERY ISLAND, a mile out in the River Shannon off Kilrush, is THE TALLEST COMPLETE ROUND TOWER IN IRELAND. It is 120 ft (37 m) high. The monastery on Scattery was founded by ST SENAN in the 6th century, once he had rid the island of a monster. Rather like poor St Kevin of Glendalough, St Senan came here to escape the attentions of the Fair Sex. A female saint, CANNERA, travelled from Kerry to be with him, but he turned her away – although he was kinder than St Kevin and didn't actually throw her into the sea.

SHANNON AIRPORT IS THE MOST WESTERLY INTERNATIONAL AIRPORT IN EUROPE. The WORLD'S FIRST DUTY-FREE SHOP opened here on 21 April 1947. Since the airport opened in 1945, the town of Shannon has grown up around it as IRELAND'S FIRST 'ARTIFICIAL' TOWN, designed by government, rather than developing through natural growth.

FRANCIS MacNAMARA, father-in-law of the Welsh poet DYLAN THOMAS (*Under Milk Wood*), owned the FALLS HOTEL in ENNISTYMON. His kinsman, John 'Fireball' MacNamara. was celebrated for fighting 57 duels.

Scattery Island

creating a perfect 'O'. The structure proved so strong that it lasted for over 100 years before needing major restoration.

The popular television series *Father Ted* was filmed in Co. Clare, at locations around KILFENORA, ENNISTYMON and KILLINABOY, south of the Burren. The actual PAROCHIAL HOUSE, where Father Ted and his companions lived, is at GLENQUIN, about 2 miles (3 km) north of Killinaboy.

Just outside LISDOONVARNA, home of IRELAND'S ONLY SURVIVING SPA, is the uniquely ingenious lightweight 'SPECTACLE BRIDGE', built in 1875 over the Aille river gorge by Co. Clare engineer JOHN HILL. To save on weight he removed the brickwork from the middle of the bridge,

DR PATRICK HILLERY, PRESIDENT OF IRELAND from 1976 until 1990, was born in the village of MILLTOWN MALBAY in 1923.

County Cork

The 18th-century Clock Tower at Youghal, originally a city gate and then a prison

Cork City

Butter, Bells and Beer

CORK IS THE SECOND-LARGEST CITY IN THE REPUBLIC OF IRELAND.

Ireland's reputation for churning out delicious butter dates from the late 18th century, when Cork had THE LARGEST BUTTER MARKET IN THE WORLD and Ireland was THE WORLD'S LARGEST EXPORTER OF BUTTER. The rich pastures of Munster produced a huge surplus of milk and the best way to preserve it was to turn the milk into salted butter, which could then be exported through the port of Cork to the rest of the world. KERRYGOLD, now the trademark of the IRISH DAIRY BOARD, is largely a result of that inheritance and is ONE OF IRELAND'S LARGEST EXPORTERS.

Cork has also been known as a brewing centre, since the 17th century. The oldest surviving brewery in the city is BEAMISH & CRAWFORD, which was set up in 1792 by the WILLIAMS BEAMISH and CRAWFORD, when they took over a small brewery in SOUTH MAIN STREET in the heart of the medieval city. For some 30 years, at the beginning of the 19th century, they were THE BIGGEST BREWERS IN IRELAND, until overtaken by Guinness. Now owned by Scottish and Newcastle, Beamish & Crawford still occupy their original brewery in South Main Street.

MURPHY'S ALE, founded by JAMES J. MURPHY and now owned by Heineken, has been brewed in Cork since 1856. One of the more colourful Murphy ancestors was MARIE LOUISA MURPHY, who was the mistress of

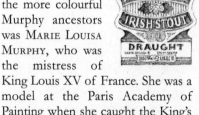

King Louis XV of France. She was a model at the Paris Academy of Painting when she caught the King's wandering eye, and was the first young lady to take up residence at the legendary PARC-AUX-CERFS (Deer Park) at VERSAILLES, where Louis housed his mistresses. Murphy fami-

ly legend has it that the money she sent back to Ireland helped to start up the Murphy business empire.

MURPHY is THE MOST COMMON SURNAME IN IRELAND and is derived from the name *Murchadh*, meaning 'sea warrior'.

The first Professor of Mathematics at University College, Cork, was GEORGE BOOLE (1815–64), inventor of BOOLEAN ALGEBRA. His book *The Mathematical Analysis of Logic*, which deals with how to convert abstract ideas into algebraic equations that can be processed by machine, helped to pave the way for modern computers and web search engines. In 1855 Boole married MARY EVEREST, niece of SIR GEORGE EVEREST, the surveyor of India after whom the world's highest mountain is named. They had five daughters, one of whom, LUCY BOOLE, became THE FIRST-EVER FEMALE PROFESSOR OF CHEMISTRY IN IRELAND OR BRITAIN.

On this I ponder, where'er I wander,
And thus grow fonder, sweet Cork,
   of thee,
With thy bells of Shandon,
That sound so grand on
The pleasant waters of the River Lee.
FRANCIS MAHONY ('FATHER PROUT')

SHANDON STEEPLE, built in 1722, is CORK'S MOST RECOGNISABLE LANDMARK, made famous by FATHER PROUT's endearing poem 'The Bells of Shandon'. Anyone may ring the bells for a small fee. The steeple clock is known as 'THE FOUR-FACED

Shandon Steeple

It will come as no surprise to anyone who has been caught behind a tractor on Irish roads that at one time Ireland had THE BIGGEST TRACTOR FACTORY IN THE WORLD. HENRY FORD opened a factory in Cork, on the site of the old Cork Park racecourse, in 1919, HIS FIRST MANUFACTURING VENTURE OUTSIDE AMERICA. In 1927, Ford moved its ENTIRE TRACTOR-MAKING BUSINESS to Cork.

LIAR' due to its habit of showing a slightly different time on each face.

The *Cork Daily Advertiser*, launched on 1 October 1836, was THE FIRST DAILY PROVINCIAL NEWSPAPER IN THE BRITISH ISLES.

Henry Ford had strong connections with Co. Cork. His ancestors had been tenant farmers in the BALLINASCARTHY area, his father William emigrating to America as a boy in 1847. There is now a HENRY FORD TAVERN in Ballinascarthy with a replica MODEL T FORD parked up across the road. Henry Ford called

Old Ford tractor factory

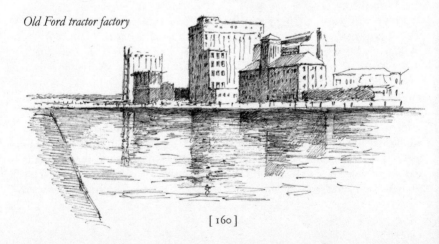

his home in Detroit FAIR LANE, after the Co. Cork birthplace of his maternal stepgrandfather PATRICK O'HERN.

Production of tractors moved to England in 1932. Ford continued to make components in Cork, but the custom-built factory closed in 1984

Cork Harbour
Tammany Hall

CORK HARBOUR claims to be THE SECOND-LARGEST NATURAL HARBOUR IN THE WORLD after Sydney, Australia, although Poole Harbour in England makes the same claim.

On the eastern shore are the ruins of WOODHILL, the house to which SARAH CURRAN fled after her lover ROBERT EMMET had been executed in 1803 (*see* Co. Dublin, page 61).

Nearby is the little ruin of DUNDANION CASTLE, from where WILLIAM PENN sailed in 1669 to found PENNSYLVANIA in America. Penn's father, ADMIRAL *William Penn* WILLIAM PENN, is said to have been born in the castle at MACROOM in 1621. Admiral Penn was later granted the castle by Oliver Cromwell in 1654.

BLACKROCK, on the edge of Cork Harbour, was the birthplace of RICHARD CROKER (1841–1922), known as 'BOSS CROKER'. His family emigrated to New York when he was

a child, and he rose through New York politics to become the boss of TAMMANY HALL, the powerful New York political machine that dominated Democratic party politics for 20 years. He survived a major corruption scandal during his time in office and returned to Ireland in 1903, a wealthy man. He lived the rest of his life on a large estate in Ireland and won the EPSOM DERBY with his horse ORBY in 1907.

> *The name Tammany came from Tamanend, the Delaware Indian chief who welcomed William Penn and signed the lost* TREATY OF SHAKAMAXON *in 1682.*

Cobh
Gateway to America

COBH is a brightly coloured, mainly Victorian, seaside town, prettily situated on Great Island, in the middle of Cork Harbour. It was once known as QUEENSTOWN in honour of Queen Victoria, who landed here in 1849, but reverted to its former name in 1920. It is dominated by ST COLMAN'S CATHEDRAL, completed in 1916 and set high on the cliffs above the town. The spire soars to nearly 300 feet (90 m) and contains a carillon of 49 bells, THE LARGEST CARILLON IN IRELAND OR BRITAIN.

During the years of the Great Famine, 1845–51, Cobh was the main port of departure for those leaving the country bound for America and Australia. Since then over two million emigrants have passed through Cobh.

HENRY FORD's father WILLIAM left for Michigan from Cobh in 1847.

On 20 December 1891, ANNIE MOORE and her young brothers sailed from Cobh on the SS *Nevada*, arriving in New York after 12 days at sea in steerage. Annie became THE FIRST-EVER EMIGRANT TO BE PROCESSED THROUGH ELLIS ISLAND when it opened on 1 January 1892. There is a statue to her outside the Cobh Heritage Centre, and also one on Ellis Island.

The OLDEST YACHT CLUB IN THE WORLD, the ROYAL CORK YACHT CLUB, founded in 1720, is based at Cobh. In 1903 THE WORLD'S FIRST MOTOR BOAT RACE, the HARMSWORTH CUP COMPETITION, was run from the Royal Cork Yacht Club headquarters to Glanmire, over a course of 8.5 miles (13.7 km).

THE FIRST STEAM SHIP TO TRAVEL BETWEEN IRELAND AND ENGLAND sailed from Cobh in 1821.

On 4 April 1838, a small Irish paddle-steamer, the *Sirius*, slipped out of Cobh on her way to becoming THE FIRST SHIP EVER TO CROSS THE ATLANTIC UNDER STEAM ALONE. She arrived in New York, almost out of fuel, 18 days later on 22 April, just hours ahead of the much bigger and faster *Great Western*.

In 1912, the 'unsinkable' *Titanic*, perhaps the most famous ship of all time, made her last stop at Cobh before sailing away to her tragic place in history. Many of her passengers had stayed for several days at Cobh, while they waited for the *Titanic* to arrive from Southampton.

On 7 May 1915, the British liner *Lusitania*,

St Colman's Cathedral

Sirius

heading for Liverpool out of New York, was torpedoed by a German submarine off THE OLD HEAD OF KINSALE near the entrance to Cork Harbour. She blew up, with the loss of 1,198 lives, including 128 Americans. This action was largely responsible for bringing the US into World War One. Many of the victims were washed up in Cork Harbour and are buried in the Old Church Cemetery just outside Cobh, while others are in the churchyard at Kinsale. Survivors were brought into Cobh to recover and many joined in a memorial service in St Colman's Cathedral, where just three years earlier there had been a service in

memory of those lost on the *Titanic*.

There are memorials to both the *Titanic* and the *Lusitania* on the waterfront in Cobh.

Blarney Castle

The Gift of the Gab

There is a stone there that whoever kisses
Oh! He never misses to grow eloquent.
'Tis he may clamber to a lady's chamber
Or become a Member of Parliament . . .
FRANCIS MAHONY ('FATHER PROUT')

Five miles (8 km) north of Cork, at the top of the ruined 15th-century keep of BLARNEY CASTLE, is IRELAND'S FIRST TOURIST ATTRACTION, the 'BLARNEY STONE'. KISSING THE BLARNEY STONE is said to bestow great eloquence or the 'gift of the gab', although actually accomplishing the kiss is not so easy. The stone is located in a fairly inaccessible spot which requires the kisser to lie down, face up, and squirm backwards underneath the parapet, while being held by the legs. Most undignified. Blarney derives its reputation from a 16th-century owner, DERMOT MACCARTHY, who managed to avoid handing the castle over to Queen Elizabeth I by placating her with soft

Blarney Castle

words and promises. She finally expostulated 'This is all just Blarney – he says he will do it but never means it!'

Midleton

Cheers

The MIDLETON DISTILLERY IS THE LARGEST WHISKEY DISTILLERY IN IRELAND. It began life as a woollen mill in 1796 but was soon lying empty. The MURPHY BROTHERS were the first to set up a distillery here, in 1820, calling themselves JAMES MURPHY & Co. They eventually merged with other local distillers to become the CORK DISTILLERS COMPANY. The family also diversified into brewing (*see* Cork City, page 158).

In 1966 Cork Distillers joined with Dublin-based distillers JOHN JAMESON and JOHN POWERS to form the IRISH DISTILLERS GROUP. All production was moved to Midleton

to take advantage of THE WORLD'S BIGGEST POT STILL, with a capacity of 31,618 GALLONS, and lower overheads. In 1975 Irish Distillers opened a new all-purpose distillery on the site. The old distillery is now a museum of whiskey.

Adrigole

Something in the Air

Looming over the village of ADRIGOLE, which is strung out along the south coast of the Beara Peninsula, is HUNGRY HILL. It gives its name to a novel by DAPHNE DU MAURIER, about the local 19th-century copper barons, the PUXLEYS (called the Brodericks in the book). When in spate, the stream running off Hungry Hill makes a magnificent spectacle, cascading 700 feet (215 m) down the mountainside.

Adrigole is where THE GLOBAL BAN ON CFCS BEGAN. The scientist SIR JAMES LOVELOCK, author of the GAIA

Midleton Distillery

theory of the earth, was sitting in the garden of his holiday cottage in Adrigole, one summer day in 1968, when he started to wonder about the thick smog that was lying across the village. Could it be caused by industrial pollution blowing across from Europe, on the east wind? Some years previously Lovelock had invented an ECD, or electron capture device, to measure air pollution. Setting one up at Adrigole, he was able to confirm that the smog was indeed industrial pollution, largely made up of CHLOROFLUOROCARBONS – CFCs. Adrigole became THE FIRST IN A WORLDWIDE NETWORK OF ATMOSPHERIC POLLUTION-MONITORING STATIONS, and further research uncovered the startling fact that CFCs were the main cause of the thinning of the ozone layer.

> *The Gaia theory postulates that the earth is a self-regulating living entity that continuously adjusts the elements to create the best physical and chemical environment to sustain life. Gaia was a Greek earth mother figure.*

Bantry Bay

Were such a bay lying upon English shore, it would be a world's wonder.
WILLIAM MAKEPEACE THACKERAY

'A BLISSFUL GLIMPSE OF PARADISE.' 'THE ADJECTIVE HAS NOT YET BEEN INVENTED WHICH COULD DO JUSTICE TO THIS EARTHLY HEAVEN.' Bantry Bay seems to speak to the poet in all who gaze upon it. A breathtaking backcloth of green mountains, warm blue seas fed by the Gulf Stream, there is certainly much to attract the visitor, and Bantry Bay has lured people here since the dawn of time.

According to the many ancient Irish annals, THE VERY FIRST PEOPLE TO INHABIT IRELAND landed at Bantry Bay. Forty years before the Great flood, Noah's niece CESAIRE, along with 150 handmaidens and three men, came ashore here and loved it so much that she stayed.

The French, in particular, seem to love Bantry Bay, for they keep coming back. They first arrived in 1689 with a large fleet full of 7,000 men, guns, ammunition and gold, to help James II in his efforts to regain the English throne. Having landed their cargo, the French turned for home but found themselves trapped by an English squadron commanded by ADMIRAL HERBERT. The French managed to fight their way out, but there were many casualties on both sides, and a number of ships were sunk.

Undaunted, 100 years later in 1796 the French gathered themselves under GENERAL HOCHE for a return visit. This time, 43 ships and 15,000 men left Brest and sailed for Bantry Bay to support the planned uprising of the UNITED IRISHMEN, led by WOLFE TONE, who was on board one of the French ships. After leaving Brest they were hit by squalls, and only 19 ships, including Tone's, reached Ireland to ride out the storm at anchor in the bay.

As Tone wrote in his diary, 'We were close enough to toss a biscuit ashore.' But they had been spotted by RICHARD WHITE, from BANTRY HOUSE, high above the bay, and the local militia was on the alert. The French weren't to know that there were only 400 men to oppose them, for a garrulous Bantry trader, who had rowed out to the ships to sell provisions, talked excitedly of thousands of British troops swarming through the town. The French, already seasick and disheartened, sailed away after scuttling one of their number, *La Surveillante*, which was too badly damaged to make it home.

Slightly marring the natural beauty of Bantry Bay, an oil terminal opened on WHIDDY ISLAND, in the middle of the bay, in 1968. In 1979 IRELAND'S WORST INDUSTRIAL ACCIDENT occurred here, when a fire on the oil tanker *Betelgeuse* killed 51 people and did immense damage to the terminal. While salvaging the *Betelgeuse* two years later, divers came across the wreck of *La Surveillante*, now an official IRISH NATIONAL MONUMENT.

Bantry Bay is IRELAND'S BIGGEST MUSSEL-PRODUCING CENTRE.

TIM HEALEY (1855–1931), FIRST GOVERNOR-GENERAL OF THE IRISH FREE STATE, 1922–7, was born in Bantry.

> *In 1946, Bantry House became the* FIRST PRIVATE HOUSE IN THE BRITISH ISLES TO BE OPENED REGULARLY TO THE PUBLIC.

Bantry House

Well, I never knew this
ABOUT
COUNTY CORK

COUNTY CORK IS THE LARGEST COUNTY IN IRELAND, at 3,000 SQ MILES (7,800 SQ KM).

FASTNET ROCK, 4 miles (6 km) south-west of Clear Island, is IRELAND'S SOUTHERNMOST POINT. It was THE LAST PIECE OF IRELAND that those sailing for America out of COBH would see, and is known as 'THE TEAR DROP OF IRELAND'.

able to spy on what was going on through a hole in the temporary wall that had been erected there, while the house was undergoing renovation work. She was discovered when she dislodged a brick, but her getaway was thwarted by Tyler the butler, on guard outside the door. It was decided that the only way to ensure Elizabeth's silence was to admit her into the Lodge, where she would be bound by a vow of secrecy, and so she took her place in history.

Doneraile Court

Some time around 1710, at DONERAILE COURT, 17-year-old ELIZABETH ST LEGER became THE ONLY WOMAN IN HISTORY TO BE INITIATED AS A FREEMASON. She had fallen asleep unnoticed in the dark of the library one evening, unaware that a secret ceremony was about to be held in the room next door. When she awoke she heard voices and was

Fastnet gives its name to a classic yachting race run every other year from the ISLE OF WIGHT to FASTNET ROCK, and back to PLYMOUTH, a total distance of 615 miles (990 km). In 1979, the biggest-ever entry of 303 boats was hit by violent storms and 17 people lost their lives.

In 1993 the platform of the tiny railway station at MILLSTREET, near

Macroom, had to be lengthened to accommodate an influx of visitors from all over Europe, when the EUROVISION SONG CONTEST was held there in the GREEN GLENS EQUESTRIAN ARENA. Millstreet was chosen because one of the directors of the host television broadcaster, RTE, was born there.

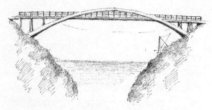

MIZEN HEAD IS THE MOST SOUTH-WESTERLY POINT OF IRELAND. The lighthouse there is reached by a graceful suspension footbridge, made of prefabricated concrete. When it was built in 1909 it was THE LARGEST CONCRETE SUSPENSION BRIDGE IN THE WORLD, and THE FIRST TO BE PREFABRICATED. BROW HEAD, on the Mizen Peninsula, is THE SOUTHERNMOST POINT IN MAIN-LAND IRELAND.

THE WORLD'S FIRST RECORDED STEEPLECHASE was run in 1752 between the church steeples of DONERAILE and BUTTEVANT. Steeples were used to mark the start and finish lines as they were the tallest and most prominent landmarks around.

The poet EDMUND SPENSER (1552–99) lived at KILCOLMAN CASTLE, near Doneraile, for eight years in the late 16th century, and wrote his most notable work, *The Faerie Queene*, while he was there. In the Irish rebellion of 1598 the castle was looted and burned and Spenser's baby son perished in the flames. Spenser never recovered from the tragedy and died the next year. The ivy-covered ruins of Kilcolman Castle stand on high banks above a small, secluded lough, where wild irises grow amongst the reeds – it is both tranquil and melancholy, the perfect place for a poet.

Near Fermoy is CASTLE HYDE, a fine Georgian house built in 1801 for the Hyde family, ancestors of DOUGLAS HYDE, FIRST PRESIDENT OF IRELAND

Castle Hyde

(*see* Co. Roscommon, page 29). It is now owned by the dancer MICHAEL FLATLEY, of *Riverdance* fame.

A MONTEREY CYPRESS tree growing at INNISHANNON, 39 ft (12 m) in circumference, has THE WIDEST GIRTH OF ANY TREE IN IRELAND.

MYRTLE GROVE in YOUGHAL, a bustling town at the mouth of the RIVER BLACKWATER, is one of the finest of the few genuine Tudor houses left in Ireland. SIR WALTER RALEIGH lived here from 1588 to 1589, and here he planted THE FIRST POTATO IN IRELAND. (Killua Castle in Co. Westmeath makes the same claim, as does Matrix Castle in Co. Limerick.) Here also, a bucket of water was thrown over him as he was smoking THE FIRST PIPE OF TOBACCO EVER SEEN IN THE BRITISH ISLES, by a startled ser-vant who thought his master was on fire. (This story is also told of SHERBORNE CASTLE, Raleigh's home in Dorset in England.) EDMUND SPENSER gave the first reading of his newly written poem *The Faerie Queene* to Raleigh, as they sat under a yew tree in the garden at Myrtle Grove.

KINSALE is known as THE GOURMET CAPITAL OF IRELAND, thanks to its huge variety of restaurants of every nationality. For a while Kinsale was the home of flamboyant TV chef KEITH FLOYD. It is one of Ireland's most attractive small towns, with winding streets and a jaunty Spanish feel to it – perhaps not surprising, as the town was occupied by the Spanish for ten weeks in 1601.

DURSEY ISLAND, off the tip of the Beara Peninsula, is connected to the mainland by IRELAND'S ONLY CABLE CAR, licensed to carry three passengers and one cow.

Myrtle Grove

In CASTLETOWNHEAD stands DRISHANE, the Georgian home of EDITH SOMERVILLE (1858–1949), best remembered for her fox-hunting novels *Some Experiences of* and *Further Experiences of an Irish R.M.* Edith also collaborated with her cousin VIOLET MARTIN (1862–1915), who wrote as 'Martin Ross', on travel and children's books. They are buried in adjacent graves in the village churchyard.

From 1936 until 1938 international motor races were run on the CARRIGROHANE race track that ran west from VICTORIA CROSS, on the outskirts of Cork, to CARRIGROHANE STATION. The track was famous for its 3-mile (4.8-km) 'CORK STRAIGHT'.

JAMES HICKEY, great-grandfather of US President JOHN F. KENNEDY, was born near CLONAKILTY BAY in 1837.

Today CLONAKILTY is renowned for its BLACK PUDDINGS.

SARAH CURRAN, fiancée of ROBERT EMMET (*see* Co. Dublin, page 61), is buried in the churchyard at NEWMARKET, near Mallow, birthplace of her father J.P. CURRAN (1750–1817).

In 1631, more than 100 inhabitants of the seaside town of BALTIMORE were carried off as slaves by Algerian pirates. This Baltimore is not the namesake of the Baltimore in Maryland, America. That takes its name from the Baltimore estates, in Co. Longford, of the CALVERT family (LORDS BALTIMORE).

The charismatic Nationalist leader MICHAEL COLLINS (1890–1922) was born in WOODFIELD FARM near CLONAKILTY. In 1919 he founded the IRA (IRISH REPUBLICAN ARMY), and for ten days in 1922 he was HEAD OF STATE of the IRISH FREE STATE, before being ambushed and murdered at Bandon in Co. Cork by Irish Republicans opposed to the ANGLO-IRISH TREATY of 1921.

Near ARDGROOM on the Beara Peninsula is THE BALLYCROVANE OGHAM STONE, standing just over 17 ft (5.2 m) high, THE TALLEST OGHAM STONE IN EUROPE.

COUNTY KERRY

COUNTY TOWN: TRALEE

Ciar Riacht – 'Ciar's kingdom'

*St Mary's Cathedral, Killarney, completed in 1855, is considered the finest example
in Ireland of Augustus Pugin's work*

The Rose of Tralee

An Irish Beauty

*She was lovely and fair as the rose of
the summer,
Yet, 'twas not her beauty alone that
won me.
Oh no! 'Twas the truth in her eyes ever
beaming
That made me love Mary, the Rose of
Tralee.*

In August each year, every Irish county and many Irish emigrant communities from around the world send one of their prettiest girls to Tralee to compete for the title of THE ROSE OF TRALEE.

The festival is based on the love song 'THE ROSE OF TRALEE', written in the 19th century by WILLIAM MULCHINOCK, a wealthy young man in love with his family's maid, MARY O'CONNOR. Because of the difference in social status, their love was frowned upon and William was encouraged to emigrate. When he returned some years later Mary was dead, stricken by tuberculosis, and the heart-broken William poured out his sorrow in song.

The modern festival revives an annual carnival of the bygone days before mass emigration and reunites Irish people from all over the world.

Ballybunion

Bon Voyage

The joyously named BALLYBUNION is a popular seaside resort with a lovely beach at the mouth of the River Shannon, and also the unlikely terminus for THE WORLD'S FIRST POWER-DRIVEN PASSENGER-CARRYING MONORAIL.

In 1880, the Frenchman CHARLES LARTIGUE (1834–1907) sat in the Algerian desert, chewing an onion and watching the camel trains go by. He noticed how they could carry very heavy loads, as long as they were evenly balanced. Applying that principle, he experimented with a length

of monorail that ran for 50 miles (80 km) across the desert, using mules to pull trains of panniers along the rail, which was raised 2 feet (60 cm) above the sand. The experiment worked.

Inspired by his success, Lartigue rigged up a demonstration model and took it to London. There were only two takers. One was Lyon in France, where a rail was built but never used, the other was Ballybunion. Here, Lartigue built a rail that ran for 9 miles (14.5 km) through Co. Kerry, from BALLYBUNION inland to LISTOWEL. It opened for business in 1888.

It was quite a sight. The engines had to be specially built to straddle the rail, with a boiler and a cab on either side, one for the driver and one for the fireman who should, ideally, be of equal poundage. Likewise, the passengers and cargo had to be distributed evenly, by weight, inside the carriages. It was a complicated, indeed delicate business boarding the train, and offence was quite frequently given – and taken. The carriages rolled alarmingly and the journey took 40 minutes, which was quite long enough to get queasy.

Nonetheless, the monorail became a tourist attraction itself, and happily

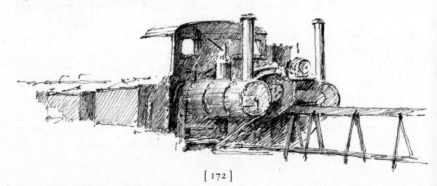

carried freight, passengers and cattle between Listowel and Ballybunion for 36 years. It received considerable damage during the Civil War and had to close in 1924.

The Lartigue monorail has now been fully restored and is once again offering a unique travel experience for visitors to Co. Kerry.

Four miles (6.5 km) north-west of Listowel is GUNSBOROUGH LODGE, birthplace of 1ST EARL KITCHENER OF KHARTOUM (1850–1916), whose face was on the memorable World War One recruitment poster, *Your Country Needs You!*

Banna Strand

Beached

Just up the coast from Ardfert are the glorious golden sands of BANNA STRAND. On the morning of Good Friday 21 April 1916 the diplomat and Irish nationalist SIR ROGER CASEMENT came ashore here from the German U-boat *Aud*, carrying rifles from Berlin for the Easter Rising. He was arrested almost as soon as he landed and tried for treason. Casement was executed on 3 August 1916, even though some people believe that he may have come to try and discourage the rebellion. There is a monument at the spot where he was captured.

Banna Strand was also one of the locations for the 1970 film *Ryan's Daughter*, starring ROBERT MITCHUM, SARAH MILES, TREVOR HOWARD and JOHN MILLS. Director DAVID LEAN

had a whole village built on the hillside behind DUNQUIN, right at the tip of the Dingle Peninsula. The cobbled main street is still there, as are the stone foundations of some of the houses.

Apparently Robert Mitchum found the remote west coast of Ireland a little too quiet for his liking. He drank too much whiskey, grew cannabis in the back garden of Milltown House, where he and his family were staying, and got became embroiled in frequent brawls at the local bars. On one occasion he received a black eye which meant that he couldn't do any close-ups for a month.

St Brendan

A Land of Promise

Although buried at Clonfert in Co. Galway, ST BRENDAN THE NAVIGATOR is also closely associated with Co. Kerry. He was born at FENIT, on Tralee Bay, in AD 483 and founded the cathedral at nearby ARDFERT in the 6th century. The remains of a 13th-century cathedral, which loom impressively over the coastal sands, contain a magnificent Irish Romanesque west door, a remarkable survival considering the corrosive, salt-laden winds that blast across these flatlands.

On the summit of MOUNT BRANDON, on the north coast of the Dingle Peninsula, there is a small beehive chapel, with far-reaching views from where St Brendan is said

Ardfert Cathedral

to have glimpsed the LAND OF PROMISE (*see* Co. Galway, page 5). He began his seven-year voyage of exploration from the beach at the foot of the mountain. Mount Brandon is 3,127 feet (953 m) high, THE HIGHEST MOUNTAIN IN IRELAND OUTSIDE MACGILLYCUDDY'S REEKS, and used to be a venue for celebrating the Celtic summer festival of Lughnasa.

Tom the Pole

Antarctic Hero

The SOUTH POLE INN at ANNASCAUL village on the Dingle Peninsula was opened by TOM CREAN (1877–1938) when he returned home from serving in World War One. He was known as 'TOM THE POLE', having taken part in THREE ANTARCTIC EXPEDITIONS, two with ROBERT FALCON SCOTT and one with ERNEST SHACKLETON. Crean was a member of Scott's tragic expedition of 1912 but was not part

of the team that made the final leg to the South Pole, never to return. He was awarded the ALBERT MEDAL for helping his own ailing companions back to base camp, and then led the search party that found Scott's body later that year. He was also one of the four men who accompanied Shackleton on his rescue mission from Elephant Island to South Georgia in 1916 (*see* Co. Kildare, page 67).

Valentia Island

The Olde World

For a small, barren island on Europe's western extremity, VALENTIA ISLAND has had a remarkable influence on the world.

To begin with, THE OLDEST FOOTPRINTS IN THE NORTHERN HEMISPHERE, 385 MILLION YEARS OLD, give or take a day or two, were found on the island's sea cliffs in 1992 by the Swiss geologist DR IVAN STOSSEL.

They are thought to have belonged to a salamander-like amphibian creature of about 3 feet (90 cm) in length.

In the 19th century, slate from the island's quarry was exported all over the world, 25 miles (40 km) of it for shelving at the LONDON PUBLIC RECORD OFFICE. Valentia slate can also be found in the roofs of the PARIS OPERA HOUSE, LONDON'S HOUSES OF PARLIAMENT, railway stations all over Britain and even railway stations in SAN SALVADOR, South America.

Valentia Island is the first place in Europe to experience weather conditions coming in from the Atlantic, and so one of Europe's FIRST WEATHER FORECASTING STATIONS was set up here in 1860 by VICE-ADMIRAL ROBERT FITZROY. He was an experienced weatherman, having been the first to use the new BEAUFORT WIND SCALE (*see* Co. Meath, page 105) on his ship HMS *Beagle*, during the voyage that inspired CHARLES DARWIN to espouse his THEORY OF EVOLUTION (of which Fitzroy strongly disapproved).

Valentia Island was THE FIRST PLACE IN THE OLD WORLD TO BE PHYSICALLY LINKED TO THE NEW WORLD when THE FIRST TRANSATLANTIC CABLE was landed here in August 1858. That line quickly burned out, but in 1865 they tried again with a new cable designed by WILLIAM THOMSON, later LORD KELVIN (*see* Belfast, page 211). The cable was laid by the *Great Eastern*, the BIGGEST SHIP IN THE WORLD at the time, captained by ROBERT HALPIN (*see* Co. Wicklow, page 138) and the only vessel capable of handling the weight of 2,000 miles (3,200 km) of heavy cable. The cable snapped in mid-ocean but another was laid in 1866 and was an instant success, linking Valentia Island to HEART'S CONTENT in NEWFOUND-LAND. It came ashore on the south-west tip of the island and THE FIRST COMMERCIAL MESSAGE was sent by QUEEN VICTORIA to the AMERICAN PRESIDENT ANDREW JOHNSON: *'Glory to God in the Highest, on earth peace, good will to men.'*

County Kerry soon had three transatlantic cable stations at VALENTIA, WATERVILLE and BALLINSKELLIGS, making it the hub of the world's international communications. All the stations are now closed and used for other purposes, but are marked by commemorative plaques.

Cable Station

One of the first messages sent from VALENTIA RADIO STATION, set up by the Royal Navy at the end of 1914, was to the *Lusitania*, warning of submarine activity in the area. It turned out to be all too prescient when the ship was torpedoed by a German submarine, off Kinsale Head, in 1915 (*see* Co. Cork, page 158). Valentia was THE LAST RADIO STATION IN IRELAND TO STOP USING MORSE CODE, sending its final message in this form on 1 February 1999. The station continues today as an important coordination centre for air and sea rescue services.

Daniel O'Connell

The Liberator

The IVERAGH PENINSULA in Co. Kerry was the home territory of DANIEL O'CONNELL (1775–1847), known as 'THE LIBERATOR'. He was born into a Catholic family and spent his early years at CARHAN HOUSE, a humble cottage, and for many years a romantic ivy-covered ruin on the water near CAHIRCIVEEN. O'Connell later inherited DERRYNANE HOUSE, a few miles to the south, from an uncle who had made his money by smuggling from Spain and France.

O'Connell was a hot-headed young man and in 1815 killed a man in a pistol duel, an action that turned him against violence for the rest of his life – he often wore a black glove in remembrance. He became a barrister and in 1823 formed the CATHOLIC  ASSOCIATION to campaign for Catholic emancipation, staging 'MONSTER RALLIES' of up to a million people all over the country.

In 1828 O'Connell was elected to Parliament as member for Co. Clare, but wasn't allowed to take his seat because of laws banning Catholics. When he was re-elected the following

Carhan House

Derrynane House

year Parliament was forced to repeal the legislation with the CATHOLIC EMANCIPATION ACT of 1829. It was this success that earned O'Connell his name of 'The Liberator'.

In 1967 Derrynane House opened as a museum in his memory.

In the middle of Cahirciveen stands the DANIEL O'CONNELL MEMORIAL CHURCH, THE ONLY CHURCH IN IRELAND DEDICATED TO SOMEONE OTHER THAN A SAINT.

O'CONNELL STREET in the centre of Dublin, THE WIDEST STREET IN IRELAND, is named after him.

CASTLEISLAND, east of Tralee, has THE SECOND-WIDEST MAIN STREET IN IRELAND.

The Lakes of Killarney

The most beautiful tract in the British Isles
Macaulay

There is a scenic stopping point on the N71 between Kenmare and Killarney called 'LADIES VIEW', from where Queen Victoria and her ladies-in-waiting famously admired the scenery.

SIR WALTER SCOTT called the landscape of mountain, lake and river around Killarney 'THE GRANDEST SIGHT I HAVE EVER SEEN'.

LOUGH LEANE is the largest of the Lakes of Killarney and home to the KILLARNEY SHAD, A TYPE OF FISH FOUND NOWHERE ELSE IN THE WORLD.

INNISFALLEN, the largest island on Lough Leane, was a notable centre of learning, the site of an abbey founded in the 6th century by ST FINLAN THE LEPER. The famed *Annals of Innisfallen*, a history of Ireland, were written here between the 12th and 15th centuries. The island is also famed for its luxuriant vegetation, especially evergreens, including what may have been THE BIGGEST HOLLY TREE IN IRELAND.

On ROSS ISLAND, on Lough Leane, is THE OLDEST MINE IN IRELAND, a copper mine that was worked during the Bronze Age, some 4,500 years ago.

Somewhere in the undergrowth of a small tree-lined churchyard overlooking the Lakes of Killarney, on Killeaghy Hill near Muckross, is the grave of RUDOLPH ERICH RASPE (1737–94), the creator of BARON MUNCHAUSEN. Raspe, born in Hanover, was a talented geologist, but possessed many of the characteristics of his rackety creation, including grand ideas allied to an acute shortage of money. He had to leave Germany in a hurry after pawning his employer's antique coin collection, and went as a surveyor to Scotland. Here, he 'salted the mine' by planting the land he was surveying with rich ore samples and left for Ireland with his reward before he could be rumbled. He got a job managing a copper mine in Killarney, but died within a year from typhoid fever.

Well, I never knew this
ABOUT
COUNTY KERRY

Tearaght Island lighthouse

GARRAUN POINT, on DUNMORE HEAD, at the tip of the Dingle Peninsula, is THE WESTERNMOST POINT ON THE IRISH MAINLAND.

The lighthouse on TEARAGHT ISLAND, off the Dingle Peninsula, is EUROPE'S MOST WESTERLY LIGHTHOUSE, and marks THE WESTERNMOST POINT OF IRELAND and THE WESTERNMOST POINT OF EUROPE. Also on the island are the remains of EUROPE'S MOST WESTERLY RAILWAY, built to transport provisions to the lighthouse. The lighthouse was automated in 1988.

DINGLE IS THE MOST WESTERLY TOWN IN EUROPE. DINGLE BAY has been the home, since 1983, of FUNGI THE DOLPHIN, who is always willing to show up and swim with sightseers.

GREAT BLASKET ISLAND, under the leadership of the Gaelic chief PIARAS FERRITER, was the VERY LAST PART OF IRELAND TO SURRENDER TO OLIVER CROMWELL.

GALLARUS OBSERVATORY is perhaps the most photographed and symbolic early Irish structure that exists. Simple, rugged and still almost perfect, it has sat here in the untamed wilds of the Dingle Peninsula for 1,200 years or more, a beacon shining through from the days when Ireland was a land of enlightenment and the rest of Europe was still groping in the dark. Today, the power of this remote and desolate location has been sadly diluted by too many sightseers and a visitor centre.

CARRANTUOHILL, 3,414 ft (1,040 m) high, in MACGILLYCUDDY'S REEKS, is THE HIGHEST MOUNTAIN IN IRELAND.

'Reeks' means 'Ridges', hence MacGillycuddy's Reeks means 'the ridges where the MacGillycuddy tribe took refuge'. The Irish name is Na Cruacha Dubha *– 'The black peaks'.*

BLACK LOUGH, high up in MACGILLYCUDDY'S REEKS, is said to have no fish in it because this is where ST PATRICK DROWNED IRELAND'S LAST SNAKE.

In the picturesque fishing village of WATERVILLE, on the Iveragh Peninsula, there is a monument to a famous visitor, CHARLIE CHAPLIN, who came here regularly with his family and stayed at the BUTLER ARMS HOTEL.

Gallarus Observatory

Approached from the coast road by a steep, narrow track, STAIGUE FORT, on the Iveragh Peninsula, is THE LARGEST AND BEST-PRESERVED PRE-CHRISTIAN STONE FORT IN IRELAND. It is over 2,000 years old and encompasses an area of 30 sq yards (25 sq m).

Close to the little resort village of GLENBEIGH on the Iveragh Peninsula are the grim remains of GLENBEIGH TOWERS, or 'WINN'S FOLLY'. Glenbeigh Towers was a formidable Victorian-medieval fortress built in 1867–71 for ROWLAND WINN, 4TH LORD HEADLEY, described as *'mad from start to finish'*. He envisaged setting up here as a kind of feudal baron and the Towers were designed to reflect this. Add the fact that the architect was EDWARD GODWIN, who was going through a messy affair with the actress ELLEN TERRY at the time, and you have all the ingredients for the extraordinary castrametation that arose at Glenbeigh. The house was inherited by the 5th Lord Headley who, no doubt frightened witless by the place, went off to Mecca and became a Muslim. Glenbeigh Towers was burned down in 1922.

KILLORGLIN is famous for its age-old PUCK FAIR, held in August, where the good people of the village go up into the mountains and catch a goat to crown as their KING PUCK for two days. The chosen monarch is borne through the streets amidst scenes of wild adulation and excitement, before a solemn coronation ceremony in the village square, to the accompaniment of pan pipes, fireworks and the occasional bleat. In the 17th century an exhausted mountain goat galloped into Killorglin to warn the villagers of the approach of Oliver Cromwell's marauding soldiers. This is their way of saying thank you – and celebrating the beginning of the harvest.

Glenbeigh Towers

There is nothing beyond SKELLIG ROCKS except America. LITTLE SKELLIG is stained white by THE WORLD'S SECOND-LARGEST GANNET COLONY. GREAT SKELLIG rises sheer out of the sea and was home from 1966 until 1992 to THE WORLD'S OLDEST-KNOWN STORMY PETREL. Before that it was a virtually inaccessible, early Christian anchorite settlement, perched 700 feet (215 m) above the sea and reached by a formidable climb of 600 rough-hewn steps. A pilgrimage to here was worth almost as much as a pilgrimage to Rome. There are remains of some steps, a number of clochans or stone huts, and an oratory similar to the Gallarus on the Dingle Peninsula.

IRELAND'S FIRST LARGE-SCALE SUSPENSION BRIDGE was built in 1841 across the Kenmare river at Kenmare. In 1932 it was replaced by the double-arched concrete OUR LADY'S BRIDGE.

The Nationalist leader ROBERT EMMET (*see* Co. Dublin, page 61) is thought to have been born at BALLYDOWNEY, near Killarney, where his mother Elizabeth lived in an elegant Georgian house belonging to her father, James Mason.

The five-storey windmill at the wee port of BLENNERVILLE, a short canal ride from Tralee, is THE MOST WESTERLY WINDMILL IN EUROPE. At 40 ft (12 m) high it is also THE TALLEST WINDMILL IN EUROPE, as well as THE BIGGEST WORKING WINDMILL IN IRELAND OR BRITAIN. It was built in 1800 by SIR ROLAND BLENNERHESSET of BALLYSEEDY HOUSE, after whom the port is named. A section of the Dingle light railway has been restored and steam train excursions are run to the windmill from Tralee.

The rare KERRY COW is THE OLDEST BREED OF CATTLE IN IRELAND, and was brought over from Central Asia by Celts more than 2,000 years ago.

The colourful spotted slug of Kerry – look for it when it comes out after rain – is found NOWHERE ELSE IN THE BRITISH ISLES.

COUNTY LIMERICK

COUNTY TOWN: LIMERICK

Luimneach – 'bare patch of ground'

St John's Cathedral, Limerick – Ireland's tallest spire

Limerick City

Treaty Town

LIMERICK, one of the first Norse towns, stands at the lowest fording point on the River Shannon and is now THE FOURTH-LARGEST CITY IN IRELAND.

ST MARY'S CATHEDRAL, built in 1178, is the oldest building in the city. Much restored, it retains a fine 12th-century Romanesque doorway and some wonderfully carved 15th-century

black oak misericords, THE ONLY CARVED MISERICORDS SURVIVING IN IRELAND.

In 1966 Mrs RITA HARRIS became VERGER OF ST MARY'S CATHEDRAL – THE FIRST LADY VERGER EVER TO BE APPOINTED IN THE BRITISH ISLES.

The spire of ST JOHN'S CATHEDRAL, built in 1861 and THE HIGHEST SPIRE IN IRELAND, is 308 ft (94 m) high.

KING JOHN'S CASTLE, in Limerick's ENGLISHTOWN, was built around 1200 and is unusual for a Norman castle in NOT HAVING A KEEP.

Limerick was the setting for FRANK McCOURT's best-selling novel *Angela's Ashes*. The movie of the book was filmed in Limerick in 1998/9.

In July 2005 DOLORES McNAMARA, from Limerick, won a record-breaking €113 MILLION on the Euro-Millions Lottery.

Sitting atop a pedestal on the river bank, across the Thomond Bridge from King John's Castle, is the TREATY STONE, an irregular block of limestone on which the TREATY OF LIMERICK was signed in 1691, finally ending the war between the supporters of William of Orange and James II.

After the BATTLE OF THE BOYNE in 1690 the rump of James II's defeated army retired to Limerick under the command of PATRICK SARSFIELD, 1ST EARL OF LUCAN, where they held out under siege for over a year. When they surrendered, they were given the option of safe passage to France with their wives and families. Most of the soldiers took up this option and marched south to Cork, along with Sarsfield, where they embarked for France in what became known as THE FLIGHT OF THE WILD GEESE. Once in France they formed the IRISH BRIGADE in the French army.

Ever since, men who have left Ireland to fight for foreign armies in Europe or America have been called WILD GEESE (*see* Co. Carlow, page 54).

Treaty Stone

BORN IN LIMERICK

Television presenter and radio broadcaster SIR TERRY WOGAN was born in Limerick in 1938. Between 1984 and 1993 Terry fronted a ground-breaking thrice-weekly talk show on BBC Television. His radio show on BBC Radio Two, *Wake up to Wogan*, is THE MOST POPULAR RADIO SHOW EVER ON BRITISH RADIO, with a regular audience of over eight million listeners.

Racehorse owner J.P. McMANUS was born in Limerick in 1951. Known as 'THE SUNDANCE KID', he came to prominence during the fight in 2004 with Manchester United manager SIR ALEX FERGUSON over ownership of the racehorse ROCK OF GIBRALTAR. Along with his partner JOHN MAGNIER, he sold his shares in Manchester United, the world's biggest football club, to MALCOLM GLAZER, enabling the American tycoon to acquire the club. In 2005 his personal fortune was estimated in the *Sunday Time*s Rich List at £400 MILLION, making him THE 14TH-RICHEST MAN IN IRELAND.

Hell-raising actor RICHARD HARRIS (1930–2002) was born in Limerick. He starred in many blockbusting films such as *Camelot* (1967), *A Man Called Horse* (1970) and *The Field* (1990). He found a new audience as DUMBLEDORE, the Headmaster of Hogwarts School in the HARRY POTTER films. Although best known as a film actor, he also had a hit single with Jimmy Webb's song 'MacArthur Park', which sold five million copies worldwide.

All four members of the pop group THE CRANBERRIES were born in, or near, Limerick.

MARY JANE KELLY (1863–88), the fifth and final victim of JACK THE RIPPER, was born in Limerick.

Foynes

Flying Firsts

On 9 July 1939, just 20 years after Alcock and Brown had nosedived into the bogs of Connemara, Pan Am's *Yankee Clipper* BOEING B-314 flying boat, the most luxurious aircraft in the sky, landed on the River Shannon at FOYNES having completed THE FIRST-EVER DIRECT COMMERCIAL PASSENGER FLIGHT FROM AMERICA TO EUROPE.

For the next few years this modest estuary village was THE MOST IMPORTANT CIVILIAN AND COMMERCIAL AIRPORT IN THE WORLD, as the European terminus for transatlantic

The Boeing B-314 flying boat

air services. Pan Am, Imperial Airways, Air France and BOAC all flew out of Foynes.

The seaplane of choice for those with the money was the Boeing B-314, as used by Pan Am. It could carry up to 36 passengers in complete luxury, along with solicitous flight attendants, a dining room that could seat 14, specially cooked meals, beds, and even a honeymoon suite. Passengers could stretch their legs by strolling around on the indoor promenade. Cruising speed was 183 mph (294 kph), at a cruising height of 13,000 ft (4,000 m). It had only one design flaw – if the landing was rough and a wing dipped into the sea, the dining room would fill with water.

Because Ireland remained neutral during the war, the airlines were able to continue using Foynes, with transatlantic flights terminating here, and passengers transferring to Sunderland flying boats for the short hop to Poole Harbour. Countless political leaders, military personnel and celebrities passed through, including Humphrey Bogart, John F. Kennedy, Douglas Fairbanks Snr, Yehudi Menuhin and Ernest Hemingway. In 1942 Eleanor Roosevelt sneaked through as 'Mrs Smith'.

Also in 1942, Captain Charles Blair made the first non-stop passenger flight from Foynes to New York in 23 hours and 40 minutes – previously flights had needed to land in Newfoundland for refuelling.

It was Captain Blair who made the last flight out of Foynes as well, in 1945. On arriving in New York, he then flew the first landplane back to the new airport at Rineanna, in Co. Clare, which later became Shannon International Airport. Captain Blair later married the actress Maureen O'Hara (*see* Co. Mayo, page 20).

Flying Boat Museum

The famous terminal building at Foynes is now occupied by the Foynes Flying Boat Museum.

It was at Foynes, in 1942, that Irish Coffee was invented. A flight that had just left Foynes, bound for New York, was forced to turn back due to bad weather. Joe Sheridan, who was serving in the airport restaurant at the time, knew that the returning passengers would be cold, miserable and disgruntled and might appreciate a little drop of something warming to cheer them up – so he added a dash of Irish whiskey to their coffee. A pleasantly surprised American passenger asked, 'Is this Brazilian coffee?' to which Joe replied, 'No, it's Irish coffee.' The legend was born.

The Limerick

A flea and a fly in a flue
Were caught, so what could they do?
'Let us fly,' said the flea.
'Let us flee,' said the fly.
So they flew through a flaw in the flue.
ANONYMOUS

This well-known example of a LIMERICK sometimes takes different forms and is also an effective tongue-twister, so is often used by English teachers to help their students with the subtleties of the language.

A limerick is a short, humorous poem of five lines where the first, second and fifth lines rhyme with each other, as do the third and fourth. There are many theories as to the origins of this form of poem – some think that it was dreamed up by soldiers returning to Limerick from France, others that it comes from the chorus *'Will you come up to Limerick?'*, sung at the end of improvised songs at Irish parties.

The people of CROOM, on the River Maigue in Co. Limerick, *know* that the limerick was initiated in their own home town. In the 18th century, the poets of the Maigue valley would hold meets and festivals at Croom, during which they would amuse themselves and their friends by concocting light, funny and often bawdy verses, which eventually became known as 'poems from Limerick' or 'limericks'.

Glin Castle
Good Knight

In the days of flying boats, passengers approaching Foynes would have been able to look down upon one of the loveliest houses in Co. Limerick, shining like a white jewel on the banks of the Shannon. This is GLIN CASTLE, home of the romantically titled KNIGHTS OF GLIN, a branch of the Fitzgerald family who have lived in these parts for over 700 years. The castle is said to have a window for every day of the year, and inside there is a very rare and beautiful double flying staircase.

The Knights of Glin have had a pretty torrid time trying to hold on to their possessions. During the 16th-century wars against the Elizabethan English, the son and heir of the then Knight was hanged, drawn and quartered in Limerick. His mother, clasping the severed head of her son to her bosom, drank from his flowing blood and then carried the mutilated body away to be buried at Lislaughtin Abbey.

In July 1600, the old Castle Glin,

Glin Castle

now a ruin in the village, was besieged by SIR GEORGE CAREW, who tied the Knight's six-year-old son to the mouth of a cannon and threatened to spatter him across the castle walls, unless the castle was surrendered. The Knight shrugged and gestured towards his beautiful wife. 'My wife is strong and I am virile – it will be easy to produce another heir.' This would appear to have been no idle boast – the castle at the time was being defended by a score of the Knight's illegitimate children.

There has been quite a colourful procession of knights through the years, including the wild 'KNIGHT OF THE WOMEN', so named for obvious reasons, and the eccentric 'CRACKED KNIGHT', never quite recovered from falling off his horse, who burnt the family archives and publicly horsewhipped LORD KITCHENER'S FATHER for evicting his tenants. On one occasion, when displeased with the beef at dinner he flung it, along with its silver dish and cover, the full length of the dining room and out of the window. Small wonder that his son, 'THE BIG KNIGHT', took solace in whiskey.

Anyone who wishes to experience this fairy-tale place for themselves can now do so, as it is run as a stylish hotel by the present (29th) Knight of Glin, president of the Irish Georgian Society, and his wife Olga FitzGerald, the garden writer.

Well, I never knew this
ABOUT
COUNTY LIMERICK

The GRANGE STONE CIRCLE near LOUGH GUR dates from around 2000 BC. It is made up of 113 stones and is THE LARGEST PREHISTORIC STONE CIRCLE IN IRELAND.

MATRIX CASTLE, near Adare, was built in 1400, and is one of several places in the country where SIR WALTER RALEIGH is said to have planted THE FIRST POTATO IN IRELAND.

Adare

ADARE, on the River Maigue, is a picturesque collection of thatched cottages, medieval ruins, antique shops and castles, and is often called IRELAND'S PRETTIEST VILLAGE. Although it dates back to before the Norman Conquest, the village owes its present-day appearance to the 3RD EARL OF DUNRAVEN. In the 1830s, while everyone else was rebuilding their estates with slate, he decided to rebuild with thatch, making Adare one of Ireland's few thatched villages.

Incorporated within Holy Trinity Church in ADARE are the remains of the WHITE MONASTERY, founded in 1230, and THE ONLY HOUSE OF THE TRINITARIAN ORDER IN IRELAND.

TOM FITZGERALD from BRUFF, south of Limerick, emigrated to Boston in America in around 1850. His son, JOHN FRANCIS FITZGERALD, known as HONEY FITZ, became Mayor of Boston in 1906, THE FIRST MAYOR IN UNITED STATES HISTORY TO HAVE PARENTS BORN IN IRELAND. In 1889 Honey Fitz married MARY HANNAN, daughter of Michael Hannan from Lough Gur, Co. Limerick. Michael Hannan had emigrated along with Honey Fitz's father, Tom Fitzgerald, in 1850. In 1890, Honey Fitz and Mary Hannan gave birth to their first-born, ROSE, the mother of PRESIDENT JOHN FITZGERALD KENNEDY.

THE FIRST POLO MATCH IN EUROPE was played near LIMERICK CITY in 1868. Members of the British Cavalry Regiment the 10TH HUSSARS, arranged a practice match against the local gentry, before leaving for England to take part in the first officially recorded polo match, on Hounslow Heath in London in 1869.

The longest-serving of Ireland's 20th-century politicians, EAMON DE VALERA (1882–1975) was born in New

York, but was brought up and went to school in the Limerick village of BRUREE. He worked alongside MICHAEL COLLINS in the Nationalist movement and took part in the EASTER RISING of 1916, for which he was sentenced to death. This sentence was commuted and he was released because, being born in New York, de Valera could have been considered an American. His opposition to the ANGLO-IRISH TREATY of 1921 provoked the CIVIL WAR. In 1926 he founded FIANNA FAIL, which won power in the IRISH FREE STATE in 1932, and he was largely responsible for drawing up the constitution of the new REPUBLIC OF IRELAND or EIRE. De Valera was three times TAOISEACH (Prime Minister) and twice PRESIDENT OF IRELAND. His boyhood

cottage at Bruree is now a National Monument.

THE INDEPENDENT SOVIET REPUBLIC OF LIMERICK was founded, along with its own currency and newspaper, in 1919 by workers objecting to British rule. They applied to join the Soviet Union but their form was never returned. The fledgling state was wound up after two weeks, but not before the would-be commissars had achieved worldwide publicity.

SOPHIE PIERCE (1896–1939), born in NEWCASTLE WEST, Co. Limerick, was THE FIRST WOMAN TO LOOP THE LOOP, THE FIRST WOMAN TO MAKE A PARACHUTE JUMP and THE FIRST PERSON IN THE WORLD TO FLY SOLO FROM CAPE TOWN TO LONDON. She was also THE FIRST WOMAN IN IRELAND AND BRITAIN TO GAIN A COMMERCIAL PILOT'S LICENCE. She was not so agile on land, however, and at the young age of 44 she fell out of a tram and was killed. In accordance with her last wishes her ashes were scattered over Newcastle West from an aeroplane.

COUNTY TIPPERARY

Cormac's Chapel on the Rock of Cashel – Ireland's finest Romanesque building

Clonmel

Transport Hub

CLONMEL, the county town of Tipperary, was once the beating heart of a vast transport network that covered most of Ireland, the 19th-century equivalent of the chariot roads from the Hill of Tara (*see* Co. Meath, page 105). It was all the brainchild of a young Italian pedlar, who built up IRELAND'S FIRST PUBLIC TRANSPORT SYSTEM and became known as THE KING OF THE IRISH ROADS. His name was CHARLES BIANCONI.

Charles Bianconi was born in Italy, near Lake Como, on 24 September 1786, the son of a farmer. At the age of 16 he was sent away, possibly because of an entanglement with a girl already promised to a local landowner, and in 1802 he ended up in Dublin as apprentice to a dealer in prints and small items. As he travelled around the country selling his wares, he found himself pondering on the need for some sort of cheap and efficient form of transport. The roads were bad and frequently dangerous. There were only a few mail wagons or expensive stagecoaches for the very rich and most people had to walk everywhere, which was slow and not much fun.

By 1815 Bianconi had settled in Clonmel. The war against Napoleon in Europe had come to an end after the Battle of Waterloo, and there was suddenly a glut of unwanted army horses on the market. Bianconi saw his chance. He purchased a two-wheeled wagon and some horses, and on 6 July 1815 the first Bianconi coach left CLONMEL for CAHIR, 11 miles (18 km) away. There were six passengers.

The enterprise was an instant success, with people clamouring for tickets at a farthing apiece. Bianconi bought more coaches and more horses and extended the service to Tipperary and Limerick. Before long he was covering much of the south and west of Ireland, Kilkenny, Waterford, Cork and Wexford.

He started to build his own coaches, the famous Bianconi 'LONG CARS', four-wheeled, with room for 15 passengers and their luggage. 'BIANS', as they were known, became a familiar sight on roads throughout Ireland.

He bought premises in the towns his coaches served, sub-letting them as hotels and 'eating houses', and opened up parts of Ireland that others had always considered remote and inaccessible, bringing, in the words of a writer of the time, 'civilisation and letters into some of the wildest haunts of the rudest races of Erin's Isle'.

When the railways arrived in the 1830s Bianconi saw them as a fresh opportunity and he adapted his network to service the new railway stations. At one time his vehicles were making daily journeys of over 4,000 miles (6,500 km) in 22 different counties, with Clonmel right at the

centre of IRELAND'S FIRST INTEGRATED PUBLIC TRANSPORT SYSTEM. Today, many Irish towns still possess a distinctive 'Bianconi' terminus building, or even a Bianconi Hotel. HEARN'S HOTEL in Clonmel, named after Bianconi's agent and friend DAN HEARN, was the first Bianconi terminus – the clock that was used to time departures is still there.

Eventually Bianconi sold off his coaches and retired into politics, becoming Mayor of Clonmel and buying himself the LONGFIELD estate near Cashel, where he died peacefully at the age of 89 in 1875. He is buried in a small mortuary chapel he built himself, beside the parish church in the little village of BOHERLAHAN.

Charles Bianconi was a great friend and admirer of DANIEL O'CONNELL and was thrilled when his daughter MARY ANNE married The Liberator's nephew, MORGAN JOHN O'CONNELL.

The celebrated novelist and vicar LAURENCE STERNE (1713–68) was born, the son of an army officer, in Clonmel, his mother's home town. When he was seven years old he survived falling into a millrace at ANNAMOE (*see* Co. Wicklow, page 138). He went on to write one of the great novels of English literature, *The Life and Opinions of Tristram Shandy*, full of humour and insight and considered to have paved the way for the modern novel. It was hugely popular, partly because no one knew quite what to make of it. As Sterne himself said, 'every man turned the story to what was swimming uppermost in his own brain'. He is thought to have been the first person to coin the word 'sentimental'.

Laurence Sterne was somewhat unhappily married to ELIZABETH LUMLEY, a cousin of the original 'bluestocking' ELIZABETH MONTAGUE. Never in the best of health, he died of pleurisy at the age of 54.

Another writer with connections to Clonmel was ANTHONY TROLLOPE (1815–82), who worked here in the 1840s as a Post Office Inspector. Trollope, best known for his Barchester Chronicles, is credited with introducing the PILLAR BOX into the British Isles and also with inventing the POSTCARD.

Cashel

Rock of Ages

The first view of the ROCK OF CASHEL is one of the few such views in life that actually exceed expectations. Nothing can prepare you for the breathtaking and dramatic tableau of cathedrals and towers, chapels and crosses that seems to grow out of the very rock it so magnificently crowns, THE MOST IMPRESSIVE GROUP OF MEDIEVAL STRUCTURES IN IRELAND.

The Rock of Cashel was one of the many places where ST PATRICK was said to have used a shamrock to explain the Trinity, and for 500 years it was the seat of the KINGS OF MUNSTER. They handed it over to the Church in 1101. In 1495 the EARL OF KILDARE set fire to the cathedral because he 'thought the Archbishop was in it'. This seemed a valid enough

reason to HENRY VII, who, in reply to the Bishop of Meath's complaint that 'All Ireland cannot rule this man,' replied, 'Then let him rule all Ireland,' and made Kildare Lord Lieutenant. The building was burned down again, this time with 3,000 people inside, by MURROUGH O'BRIEN, in 1647 during the Cromwellian wars.

Cormac's Chapel, interior

In many people's minds THE LOVELI-EST BUILDING IN IRELAND, CORMAC'S CHAPEL, is 12th-century, and THE LARGEST AND MOST COMPLETE EXAM-

PLE OF ROMANESQUE ARCHITECTURE IN THE COUNTRY. Known as the JEWEL OF CASHEL, it has one of the earliest known stone roofs, still in remarkably good condition, two fine towers, a wonderful barrel-vaulted roof inside, and a sublime carved doorway that was once the main entrance but is now boxed in by the wall of the newer cathedral.

The views from the Rock are glorious, and if you look north on a fine day you can see across Tipperary's Golden Vale to the place where Cashel came from, DEVIL'S BIT MOUNTAIN. There is a great scoop torn out of the mountain-top, visible for miles, where the Devil chewed off a mouthful of rock but found it disagreeable and spat it out here, thus creating the unforgettable Rock of Cashel.

The Song

It's a long way to Tipperary, it's a long way to go;
It's a long way to Tipperary, to the sweetest girl I know!
Goodbye Piccadilly, farewell, Leicester Square,
It's a long, long way to Tipperary, but my heart's right there!

The song that made TIPPERARY famous across the world was written in 1912 by JACK JUDGE (1878–1938) and HARRY WILLIAMS (1874–1924). It had in fact been composed, and then put aside, three years earlier, as

'It's a long way to Connemara' – Jack's family were from Co. Mayo, and although neither man had been to Ireland, this was their attempt to write an Irish ballad to appeal to the emigrant Irish who were missing their homeland. When, on that night in 1912, Jack was bet that he couldn't write a song in 24 hours, he fished out 'Connemara', rewrote it as a marching song, replaced Connemara with Tipperary, and the most famous song of World War One was born.

It was first recorded by the Irish tenor COUNT JOHN MCCORMACK (*see* Co. Westmeath, page 120) in 1914, and then sung by the CONNAUGHT RANGERS, an Irish Regiment of the British Army, as they marched through Boulogne on 13 August 1914, and reported by GEORGE CURNOCK of the *Daily Mail*. The song soon became popular with soldiers on both sides. 'It's a Long Way to Tipperary' gained a new audience when it featured in the musical *Oh What a Lovely War* in 1963.

With his proceeds from the song, co-writer Harry Williams bought his parents' old pub in Kenilworth, England, and renamed it THE TIPPERARY INN. He died in 1924 and is buried nearby at Temple Balsall, where the inscription on his tomb reads:

Author of It's a Long Way to Tipperary
Give me the making of the songs
of a nation
And let who will make its laws.

Well, I never knew this
ABOUT
COUNTY TIPPERARY

Mona Incha

TIPPERARY IS IRELAND'S LARGEST INLAND COUNTY.

A Tipperary man from EMLY, EDWARD RYAN, who boarded the *Titanic* at COBH, was in THE LAST LIFEBOAT TO LEAVE THE STRICKEN LINER as it sank in the middle of the Atlantic Ocean. He was rescued by the *Carpathia* and landed safely in New York.

ATHASSEL PRIORY, founded in 1192 on the west bank of the River Suir near Cashel, was THE LARGEST MEDIEVAL PRIORY IN IRELAND. It was burned down in 1447.

JAMES O'NEILL, father of the American playwright EUGENE O'NEILL, was born on a farm outside the town of Tipperary.

In deep, quiet country not far from ROSCREA, a long walk down a pinewood track takes you to the lost abbey of MONA INCHA. This used to be a great site of pilgrimage, but only if you were a man – legend and GERALD CAMBRENSIS say that 'no woman or animal of the female sex could enter the island without dying immediately'. Apparently, 'this has been put to the test many times by means of cats, dogs and other animals of that sex which have often been brought to it as a test, and have died at once'. The remains are perched rather forlornly on a round, stone-walled islet in the middle of what was once LOUGH CRE but is now green, marshy pasture. There is a lovely small church here, with a richly sculptured doorway, and part of an ancient Celtic cross. This is one of those places that Ireland does so well, an exquisite architectural gem abandoned, but somehow still loved, and set in emerald seclusion. In Ireland you can experience the past, undisturbed, like nowhere else.

US PRESIDENT RONALD REAGAN'S great-grandparents came from Co. Tipperary. MICHAEL O'REAGAN was born in BALLYPOREEN, the Knock-mealdown Mountains, in 1829, the same year as his wife-to-be CATHERINE, who was also born in Co. Tipperary. They emigrated to Illinois in 1858.

The castle at NENAGH is unusual for a Norman castle in having a round castle keep – THE BIGGEST ROUND CASTLE KEEP IN IRELAND.

The famous 'MULBERRY' floating harbours used by the Allied troops immediately after the D-DAY LAND-INGS in 1944 were designed by JOHN DESMOND BERNAL (1901–71), who was born in NENAGH, Co. Tipperary.

The magnificently gabled stone house added to the 15th-century towers of ORMOND CASTLE at CARRICK-ON-SUIR was built some time after 1565 and is THE FINEST TUDOR MANOR HOUSE IN IRELAND.

The ancient stone bridge across the Suir at Carrick, strategically impor-tant as the first bridge across the estuary, was built in 1447 and is one of THE OLDEST BRIDGES IN IRELAND STILL IN USE. In 1799 a barge was swept against the bridge by flood-waters and over 100 people drowned in the Suir.

MITCHELSTOWN CAVES in the GALTEE MOUNTAINS are THE FINEST LIMESTONE CAVES IN IRELAND. They were discovered in 1833 by a local

Nenagh Castle

Ormond Castle

farmer who was breaking stones and lost his crowbar down a crack in the rocks. While digging to find it, he opened up the entrance to the cave, which is still used as an entrance today. Mitchelstown was THE FIRST CAVE IN IRELAND TO BE LIT WITH ELECTRICITY. The most spectacular feature in the cave is a 30 ft (9 m) high column called the TOWER OF BABEL.

Nearby is the DESMOND CAVE, where on 29 May 1601 the last EARL OF DESMOND, the so-called 'EARL OF STRAW', whose family had been dispossessed of THE MOST EXTENSIVE ESTATES EVER HELD IN IRELAND, hid

from the English. He was found and betrayed by his kinsman, the WHITE KNIGHT.

THE COOLMORE STUD, owned and run by JOHN MAGNIER and acknowledged as THE WORLD'S LEADING STUD, is located in Co. Tipperary's GOLDEN VALE.

The 13th-century CAHIR CASTLE, THE FINEST AND BEST-PRESERVED EXAMPLE OF A LATE MEDIEVAL CASTLE

Cahir Castle

The Swiss Cottage

IN IRELAND, occupies a rocky island in the middle of the River Suir. It was used in the 1981 film *Excalibur* to portray a castle from the Dark Ages. The Castle belonged to the BUTLER family until 1964. On a completely different scale, just down the road is the SWISS COTTAGE, a rustic folly or *cottage orné* built for Lady Butler by JOHN NASH in 1810.

To the north-east of Clonmel is SLIEVENAMON, 2,368 ft (722 m) high, THE MOUNTAIN OF THE FAIR WOMEN OF FEIMHINN, scene of a legendary romantic contest. FINN McCOOL, the chap who built the GIANT'S CAUSEWAY (*see* Co. Antrim, page 221), was unable to decide on a wife, so he perched himself on the summit of Slievenamon and invited all the hopeful young lovelies who were vying to be his bride to race each other to the top. The lucky, and energetic, winner was GRAINE, the daughter of CORMAC, King of Ireland.

COUNTY WATERFORD

COUNTY TOWN: DUNGARVAN

Vadrefjord (Viking word) – 'wether inlet'

19th-century gateway at Ballysaggartmore Towers

Waterford Town

Flying the Flag

WATERFORD is a bustling seaport with Viking origins. The Viking name is VADREFJORD, meaning the inlet where wethers – castrated sheep – are loaded onto boats. Waterford is also where STRONGBOW first landed in support of the deposed King of Leinster, DIARMAIT MACMURROUGH, in 1170.

Throughout the Anglo-Norman period Waterford was IRELAND'S SECOND CITY after Dublin. THE EARLIEST USE OF ENGLISH IN OFFICIAL IRISH DOCUMENTS can be found in Waterford's GREAT PARCHMENT BOOK of 1360–1649.

Sitting solid on the waterfront where the mile-long Quay meets the wide, attractive Mall is REGINALD'S TOWER, Waterford's most distinctive building. It is an impregnable round Norman edifice that replaced a Viking tower of 1003 and is THE

FIRST BUILDING IN IRELAND TO BE CONSTRUCTED WITH MORTAR, a mixture of fur, blood, lime and sea mud.

In 1171 Strongbow was married in the Tower to EVA, Diarmait MacMurrough's daughter, thus becoming heir to the King of Leinster. Later that same year HENRY II became THE FIRST ENGLISH KING TO SET FOOT IN IRELAND, landing at Waterford backed by a large fleet in case Strongbow should need dissuading from attempting to set up a rival Norman kingdom.

Reginald's Tower has been a fortress, an arsenal, a prison and a mint. It now houses Waterford's CIVIC MUSEUM and is THE OLDEST URBAN CIVIC BUILDING IN IRELAND.

Waterford's motto is *Urbs Intacta Manet Waterfordia*, or loosely translated, 'WATERFORD THE UNCONQUERED CITY'. This accolade was bestowed by HENRY VII after the city had defied LAMBERT SIMNEL, PRETENDER TO THE THRONE, and survived a 12-day siege at the hands of the EARL OF DESMOND and PERKIN WARBECK, another pretender.

The product that has done most to make Waterford a name known around the world is WATERFORD CRYSTAL. The original glass factory was set up in 1783 by two Quakers, uncle and nephew, GEORGE AND WILLIAM PENROSE, who chose Waterford because it was Ireland's premier export gateway and also because

Irish glass was exempted from British taxes. They were soon producing the finest lead crystal in Europe, but the sudden imposition of heavy taxes forced the closure of the works in 1851, ironically while Waterford Crystal was the toast of the GREAT EXHIBITION at the CRYSTAL PALACE in London. A century later the Irish government revived the industry, recruiting glass-makers from Europe to train local apprentices. Today Waterford Crystal is part of the WEDGWOOD group and THE BIGGEST PRODUCER OF HANDMADE CRYSTAL IN THE WORLD.

Waterford has also given to the world the BACON RASHER, invented in 1820 by a local butcher, HENRY DENNY. Until that time, pork had been cured by soaking great chunks of meat in barrels full of brine. Denny decided to sandwich long, flat pieces of meat between two layers of dry salt and found that this helped the bacon to last much longer. His discovery revolutionised the meat industry and Denny successfully exported his idea to other countries, such as Denmark.

In 1885 the CREAM CRACKER was invented by a Quaker, W.R. JACOBS, at his bakery in Bridge Street. Jacobs went on to create the FIG ROLL in 1903.

THOMAS FRANCIS MEAGHER (1823–67), DESIGNER OF THE NATIONAL FLAG OF IRELAND, was born in Waterford, son of the city's Member of Parliament. Fired up by DANIEL O'CONNELL's speech-making, he was a founder member of the YOUNG

IRELAND group which eventually split from O'Connell's Repeal Party, favouring more aggressive tactics. In 1848 Meagher introduced his new flag, similar to the present-day flag, except that the orange was placed nearest the flagstaff and the white middle was decorated with the Red Hand of Ulster. This flag was first flown by Meagher during the Waterford by-election, above the headquarters of his WOLFE TONE CONFEDERATE CLUB at 33 The Mall, Waterford, on 1 March 1848. Meagher's explanation for the design states that 'the white in the centre signifies a lasting truce between the "Orange" and the "Green", and I trust that beneath its folds the hands of the Irish Protestant and the Irish Catholic may be clasped in generous and heroic brotherhood'.

Meagher was arrested shortly afterwards and sentenced to deportation to Australia. His 'SPEECH FROM THE DOCK' ('Stigmatise the sword? Never!') stands second only to ROBERT EMMET's pre-execution speech (*see* Co. Dublin, page 61) in the annals of Irish nationalist eloquence.

After many adventures Meagher escaped from Tasmania to America. During the American Civil War he rose to become a general in the Union army and fought at THE FIRST BATTLE OF BULL RUN in 1861. He also organised the IRISH BRIGADE OF NEW YORK. He went on to become temporary GOVERNOR OF MONTANA TERRITORY in 1866.

Blackwater Valley

Irish Rhine

The BLACKWATER RIVER IS THE SECOND-LONGEST RIVER IN IRELAND. Often called the 'IRISH RHINE', it wends its way past woods and rocky cliffs crowned with abbeys, fairy-tale castles and grand houses, all redolent with stories.

On an islet in the river, a little north of YOUGHAL, are the ruins of MOLANA ABBEY, founded in the 6th century as an anchorite settlement by an Abbot of Lismore. RAYMOND LE GROS, friend and companion-in-arms of STRONGBOW, is thought to be buried here.

Molana Abbey was the home for a while of the mathematician and astronomer THOMAS HARIOT (1560–1621), a friend of SIR WALTER RALEIGH and scientific adviser on Raleigh's second expedition to Virginia. While he was living at Molana Abbey, Hariot wrote *A Briefe and True Report of the New Found Land of Virginia*, based on notes he had made during his stay in the colony. This was THE FIRST SURVEY OF THE NEW WORLD WRITTEN IN ENGLISH and is still widely referred to. Hariot was fascinated by astronomy and invented a TELESCOPE with which he made a map of the moon, observed the comet that would later be known as HALLEY'S COMET, and discovered

Ballynatray House

SUNSPOTS. He also devised the mathematical symbols for 'is more than' (>) and 'is less than' (<).

Molana Abbey lies within the grounds of the BALLYNATRAY estate and is reached by means of a causeway put here in 1806 by GRICE SMYTH, a descendant of the 1ST EARL OF CORK who owned much of the property along the Blackwater. Smyth also built BALLYNATRAY HOUSE, beautifully positioned on the riverbank, in 1795, on the site of an earlier castle. His second daughter PENELOPE was one of the great beauties of her day and caused an international incident in 1836 when she eloped to Gretna Green in Scotland and married the PRINCE OF CAPUA, brother of KING FERDINAND II OF THE TWO SICILIES, without the King's permission.

Further north, in a romantic situation above the river, is STRANCALLY CASTLE, a Gothic pile built around 1830 by GEORGE AND JAMES PAINE. Close by are the ivy-clad remains of the old castle of the EARLS OF DESMOND, seemingly growing straight up from the rock. Underneath it there is a great cavern, with a drop to the river – the infamous 'MURDERING HOLE', scene in medieval times of many dark deeds. The Desmonds

Strancally Castle

would invite their prosperous neigh-
bours to dinner at the castle, get
them drunk, butcher them and then
hurl the bodies through the hole and
into the river. They would then lay
claim to the abandoned lands of their
victims, and so swiftly built up their
own holdings, THE MOST EXTENSIVE
IRELAND HAS EVER SEEN. Their
dastardly doings were eventually
uncovered when a victim escaped his
doom and raised the alarm. Retribution was swift. The Desmonds
were driven out and the castle blown
up.

A little south of CAPPOQUIN, on a
thickly wooded bluff above one of
the loveliest stretches of the Blackwater, is DROMANA, a vast edifice
that, over the centuries,
has grown organically
out of an ancient

At the entrance to Dromana is a
delightful Hindu-Gothic gateway,
THE ONLY ONE OF ITS KIND IN
IRELAND. It was originally constructed
out of papier mâché in 1826 for

Dromana

Fitzgerald fortress. Here was born
the remarkable CATHERINE, COUNT-
ESS OF DESMOND, and here she lived
through the entire 16th century and
more, for she is said to have reached
the great age of 140 YEARS OLD. She
acquired a new set of teeth in her
later years and died by falling out of
IRELAND'S FIRST CHERRY TREE, trying
to reach the fruit. The tree was one
of a number brought back from the
CANARY ISLANDS by SIR WALTER
RALEIGH and planted at AFFANE.

HENRY VILLIERS-STUART and his
bride, to welcome them home to
Dromana from their honeymoon.
They liked it so much that they had it
made into a permanent structure.

Just the other side of LISMORE
are the exotic BALLYSAGGARTMORE
TOWERS, two 19th-century Gothic
follies, one of them a turreted gateway, the other a castellated bridge
over a stream. This was intended
to be the gateway to a castle to be
constructed by ARTHUR KEILY, at the

Irish estates, including Lismore, to RICHARD BOYLE, later the 1ST EARL OF CORK, for £1,500. Such

Bridge at Ballysaggartmore

instigation of his wife, who was envious of her brother-in-law's castle at Strancally. However, the money ran out and the place was never built.

Lismore Castle

Lady of the Dance

The most magnificent of all the castles beside the Irish Rhine is LISMORE CASTLE, its fawn-grey towers rising high above the Blackwater, perched on tree-dressed cliffs, for all the world like Camelot come true. A monastery was founded at Lismore by ST CARTHAGE in the 7th century and was a rare place of civilisation and learning through the Dark Ages. KING JOHN built a castle by the river at the end of the 12th century and this was granted to SIR WALTER RALEIGH in 1589. When he fell on hard times, Raleigh sold all his

manoeuvres made Boyle, who had arrived in Ireland as an impoverished legal clerk, THE RICHEST MAN IN IRELAND, and he restored Lismore to be his home.

ROBERT BOYLE (1627–91), the FATHER OF MODERN CHEMISTRY, was born at Lismore, youngest of the Earl of Cork's 14 children. Using wisely the time and money available to him, Robert Boyle pursued a life of scientific discovery and experiment. He developed THE FIRST EFFECTIVE VACUUM PUMP and with this was able to prove that sound, a candle flame, and life, all need air to exist. He gave his name to BOYLE'S LAW, which addresses the relationship of the pressure and volume of a gas, and in 1662, along with a group of like-minded friends, he established the ROYAL SOCIETY, which still exists today as THE OLDEST SCIENTIFIC

infatuation with the flamboyant LORD BYRON who was, in her own words, 'mad, bad and dangerous to know'.

Lismore Castle

SOCIETY IN THE WORLD. Perhaps his greatest legacy was the fact that he was the first to write down and make public his findings for the benefit of all, at a time when science and alchemy were still shrouded in secrecy.

Lismore was sacked by a Confederate army in 1645 but made habitable again by the 2nd Earl after the Restoration. In 1689, JAMES II stayed for a night before the BATTLE OF THE BOYNE, and almost died of fright when he strolled over to the oriel window in the dining room and was taken aback by the dizzying drop to the river far below.

Eventually the castle passed by marriage to the DUKES OF DEVONSHIRE. In 1812 the 6TH DUKE, known as THE BACHELOR DUKE, brought his tempestuous cousin LADY CAROLINE LAMB to Lismore in the hope that she would get over her

Lismore as we see it today is largely the work of the Bachelor Duke's great friend SIR JOSEPH PAXTON, the man responsible for the CRYSTAL PALACE, home of the GREAT EXHIBITION of 1851.

Lismore Castle remains the holiday home of the Cavendish family and is not open to the public, but it is let out on an occasional basis, complete with staff and a butler. One unexpected delight is the colourful bathroom celebrating the magic of the Hollywood dance legend FRED ASTAIRE and his older sister ADELE. They started out together on Broadway as a brother and sister act, with Adele the bigger star, but she then fell in love with and married LORD CHARLES CAVENDISH, younger son of the 9th Duke of Devonshire, and came to live at Lismore as a hugely energetic and popular chatelaine from 1932 to 1944.

The gardens are open to the public between April and October and are THE OLDEST FORMAL GARDENS IN IRELAND, retaining much of their original Jacobean layout. There is a noble YEW WALK where EDMUND SPENSER spent the long summer days writing his poem *The Faerie Queene*.

Well, I never knew this
ABOUT
COUNTY WATERFORD

ERNEST WALTON (1903–95), THE MAN WHO SPLIT THE ATOM, was born in DUNGARVAN. He described the moment in 1932 that ushered in the Nuclear Age as 'a wonderful sight, lots of scintillations, looking just like stars'. Walton was awarded the NOBEL PRIZE FOR PHYSICS in 1951, becoming one of five Irishmen to be awarded the honour. The other four were all for LITERATURE – WILLIAM BUTLER YEATS (1923), GEORGE BERNARD SHAW (1925), SAMUEL BECKETT (1969) and SEAMUS HEANEY (1995).

The almost perfect Round Tower at ARDMORE, 98 ft (30 m) high, is late 12th century and the LATEST ROUND TOWER IN IRELAND. It is also unusual in having decorative bands on the exterior wall, indicating the position of each floor.

DUNGARVAN is reputed to have the 'SQUAREST TOWN CENTRE IN IRELAND', GRATTAN SQUARE.

CURRAGHMORE, the MARQUESS OF WATERFORD's seat near PORTLAW, is THE LARGEST DEMESNE IN IRELAND, with a boundary wall of 10 miles (16 km) round.

A little to the north of CAPPOQUIN is the celebrated TRAPPIST MONASTERY of MOUNT MELLERAY. It was founded here in 1833 by monks expelled from France. Trappists take a vow of silence and devote their lives to seclusion and to working the land. To see the beautiful gardens they have carved out of the wilderness is a moving experience. You can visit the monastery and be shown around. Free accommodation and food is provided,

The Round Tower at Ardmore

Curraghmore

although donations are gratefully accepted. There is a guest-house for ladies outside the walls of the monastery.

Curraghmore features in one of Ireland's most famous ghost stories. The 2nd Earl of Tyrone, a predecessor of the Marquesses of Waterford, made a childhood pact with his best friend Nicola Hamilton that whichever of them died first should 'visit' the other, in ghostly form, on the night of their decease. The Earl died horribly young at the age of 29 in 1693, and sure enough he appeared to Nicola and made a number of predictions about her life, informing her of how many children she was going to have, how one of them would marry his niece and heir, and that she would die on her 47th birthday. Nicola reached

out in sorrow to touch her friend and brushed his hand with her wrist, which burned and shrivelled up, leaving a gruesome scar. For the rest of her life she wore a black riband about her wrist. And the Earl's predictions came true. Nicola *did* die on her 47th birthday, although she deliberately confused her age in an effort to deny her fate, and her son Marcus *did* marry the Earl's niece, Catherine, heiress to Curraghmore.

The spirited 3rd Marquess of Waterford, from Curraghmore, gave rise to the phrase 'painting the town red' when he and his hunting companions, after an evening of binge drinking, rode through Melton Mowbray in Leicestershire, England, daubing the buildings with red paint.

Ulster

BELFAST

Beal Feirste – 'the approach to the sandy crossing'
(of the Farset)

Belfast City Hall, built in 1906

Belfast Shipyard

The Biggest and the Best

The shipyard at Belfast was once THE BIGGEST SHIPYARD IN THE WORLD, employing over 35,000 people.

The first sizeable shipyard on the RIVER LAGAN was opened in 1791 by HUGH AND WILLIAM RITCHIE. They were soon joined by COATES and YOUNG, who launched IRELAND'S FIRST IRON STEAMBOAT, the *Countess of Caledon*, in 1838.

In the 1840s a new yard was built on QUEEN'S ISLAND, which had been constructed by WILLIAM DARGAN (*see* CO. Laois, page 84) using material dredged from the river. In 1854, EDWARD HARLAND (1830–95) arrived to manage the yard, which he bought in 1858. In 1861 he was joined by GUSTAV WOLFF (1834–1913).

Harland and Wolff grew into THE BIGGEST SHIPBUILDING COMPANY IN THE WORLD, building THE BIGGEST SHIPS IN THE WORLD.

In 1889 the *Majestic* was launched, in 1899 the *Oceanic*, and in 1901 the *Celtic*, all for the WHITE STAR LINE. Each ship was THE BIGGEST IN THE WORLD when she was launched.

Titanic

The *Majestic* was just over 10,000 tonnes. Some twenty years later Harland and Wolff launched THE MOST FAMOUS SHIP EVER BUILT, the *Titanic*, and its sister ship the *Olympic*, each over 77,000 tonnes.

In 1936 SHORT BROS, THE WORLD'S OLDEST AIRCRAFT COMPANY, who built aircraft for the Wright brothers, set up a factory on Queen's Island in a joint venture with Harland and Wolff, in time to make fighter aircraft, bombers and ships for World War Two. During the conflict Belfast was a hive of industries contributing to the war effort. Torpedoes, artillery shells and uniforms were manufactured in a number of different workshops around the city. GALLAGHER'S TOBACCO FACTORY, at that time THE LARGEST IN THE WORLD, produced cigarettes for the troops. All of this made the city a target

for the Luftwaffe, and Belfast was bombed twice during 1941; the shipyards suffered extensive damage. After the war, Harland and Wolff carried on shipbuilding while Shorts continued to make aircraft at their Belfast works, including, in 1957, the SHORTS SC 1, THE WORLD'S FIRST VERTICAL TAKE-OFF AND LANDING AEROPLANE.

In 1960 the P&O liner SS *Canberra* was launched, the last passenger cruise liner to be built by Harland and Wolff. *Canberra* became famous when she was used as a troopship during the FALKLANDS WAR in 1982 and was nicknamed the GREAT WHITE WHALE.

The last ship of any kind to be built by Harland and Wolff was the *Anvil Point*, a roll-on, roll-off ferry, which sailed out of Belfast on 22 March 2003.

SS Canberra

Harland and Wolff, now owned by Olsen Energy, remains in business tendering for ship repair work and other civil engineering projects.

It is still possible to see many evocative sites associated with the historic shipyard, such as the former HARLAND AND WOLFF OFFICE BUILD-ING where *Titanic* was conceived and designed, the Thompson Graving Dock, 880 ft (270 m) long, THE LARGEST BUILDING DOCK IN THE WORLD, and SAMSON AND GOLIATH, the two giant yellow cranes that are such a distinctive part of the Belfast skyline.

Also berthed here is HMS *Caroline*, the only vessel still surviving from the BATTLE OF JUTLAND in 1916. Launched in 1914, she is THE SECOND-OLDEST COMMISSIONED SHIP IN THE ROYAL NAVY, after HMS *Victory*.

THE BELFAST ROPEWORK COMPANY was founded in 1873 by WILLIAM SMILES, and for many years it owned THE BIGGEST ROPE FACTORY IN THE WORLD, supplying rope for the Harland and Wolff shipyard and for the celebrated French tightrope walker BLONDIN. The Company closed in 1970, a victim of competition from synthetic yarns and new adhesives.

The area is now being developed as a housing and entertainment complex called the TITANIC QUARTER. The historic sites are being preserved.

Crown Liquor Saloon

Victoriana

The CROWN LIQUOR SALOON, in the centre of Belfast opposite the Europa Hotel, was THE FIRST PUB TO BE OWNED BY THE NATIONAL TRUST. It originally opened in 1826 as the Railway Tavern, celebrating the arrival of the railway in Belfast. In the 1880s it was transformed into a high-Victorian drinking palace, with a dazzling façade of brightly coloured tiles and rows of engraved stained-glass windows. The opulent interior is full of marbling, mirrors and mosaics, with swing doors, wooden floors, private booths and atmospheric gas lighting, more reminiscent perhaps of a Wild West saloon than a city pub. Upstairs are some sumptuous panels made for the *Titanic*'s sister ship *Britannic*, but never used – the outbreak of World War One meant that *Britannic* was fitted out as a hospital ship instead. The

Crown shrugged off some 42 bomb attacks during the 'Troubles' to remain THE FINEST SURVIVING EXAMPLE OF A LATE VICTORIAN PUB IN BRITAIN.

Belfast Inventors

Temperatures, Tyres and Tea-leaves

THOMAS ANDREWS (1813–85), Professor of Chemistry at the Belfast Academical Institution (known as 'Inst'), was born in Donegall Square South, Belfast. He discovered that any gas could be turned into liquid under pressure and below a certain temperature, and this discovery enabled him to produce the first LIQUID GAS, a product we use today for cooking and refrigeration, as well as rocket fuel.

WILLIAM THOMSON, LORD KELVIN (1824–1907), was born at 21 College Square East, opposite the Belfast Academical Institution, where his father was professor of mathematics. His birthplace was subsequently the site of BELFAST'S FIRST CINEMA, appropriately enough named the KELVIN. He introduced the ABSOLUTE SCALE OF TEMPERATURE, named 'Kelvin' after him, with ABSOLUTE ZERO reached at −273 DEGREES CENTIGRADE. His greatest commercial success was the invention of equipment that enabled telegraphic signals to be sent along lengthy submarine cables, and he was present on the *Great Eastern* as the first transatlantic cable was laid from VALENTIA

ISLAND to NEWFOUND-LAND in 1865–6 (*see* Co. Kerry, page 171).

JOHN BOYD DUNLOP (1840–1921) was a veterinary surgeon from Ayrshire in Scotland. His practice, based in Gloucester Street near Belfast City Hall, was THE LARGEST VETERINARY PRACTICE IN IRELAND.

In 1887 Dunlop's small son JOHNNIE asked his father if there was anything he could do to make riding his bike less painful. In those days wheels were solid and road surfaces cobbled or uneven, making cycling a most uncomfortable experience. Dunlop decided that what was needed were cushioned wheels, and his first thought was to use rubber tubing filled with water. However, his son's football gave him the idea of using air instead, so he inflated a rubber tube with a football pump and then tacked it on to a wheel rim and tried it out in the yard. He was delighted to find that the rubber-clad wheel was not only much more comfortable but enabled the bike to travel faster.

For the next few months John Dunlop and his son rode round and round in his yard perfecting what he termed his 'pneumatic' tyre, and in December 1888 his idea was granted a patent. In May 1889, local cyclist WILLIE HUME put pneumatic tyres on to the wheels of his racing bike

> *The first 'air tyre' was invented by the Scotsman* ROBERT THOMPSON *in 1845 and used on carriage wheels, but it was never commercialised.*

and won every race at a Belfast cycling event, earning huge publicity for Dunlop's invention. In the crowd that day was HARVEY DU CROS, father of the Irish cycling champion who had been soundly beaten into second place by Willie Hume. Du Cros bought a share of Dunlop's patent and together they set up THE WORLD'S FIRST PNEUMATIC TYRE FACTORY, in Dublin. Within 10 years Dunlop's invention had almost entirely replaced solid wheels.

In 1913 Dunlop opened JAPAN'S FIRST-EVER TYRE PLANT in Kobe.

The Dunlop Company provided tyres for many successful speed trials, including SIR MALCOLM CAMPBELL'S 1935 LAND SPEED RECORD in *Bluebird*.

During the 1950s the Dunlop Company was the major supplier of tyres for FORMULA 1 GRAND PRIX RACING, achieving 66 wins with eight world champions.

The Dunlop Company is now owned by Goodyear Tyres.

The yard where John Dunlop experimented with his invention no longer exists, but the site is marked with a blue plaque. Two cobbled stones from the yard, showing grooves worn by the world's first pneumatic tyres, can be seen at the STRAFFAN STEAM MUSEUM in Co. Kildare.

SIR SAMUEL DAVIDSON (1846–1921) was born in the family mill in Belfast. Sent to work on an Indian tea plantation, he invented a machine for drying tea-leaves and went on to develop THE WORLD'S FIRST FORWARD-BLADED CENTRIFUGAL FAN, calling it a SCIROCCO. In 1879 he built the SCIROCCO FAN FACTORY on Short Strand in Belfast. Davidson designed and installed a revolutionary air-conditioning system in Belfast's new ROYAL VICTORIA HOSPITAL, which opened in 1903, ONE OF THE FIRST BUILDINGS IN THE WORLD TO CONTAIN INTEGRAL AIR-CONDITIONING. The Scirocco Fan Company was sold to the Howden Group in 1999 but the old factory site is being preserved.

Old Royal Victoria Hospital

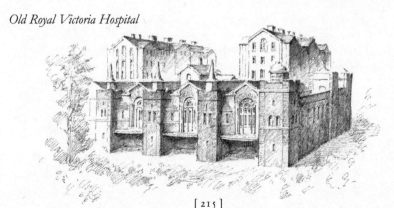

Lady Lavery

A Noted Beauty

The portrait painter SIR JOHN LAVERY was born at 47 NORTH QUEEN STREET, Belfast, in 1856. In 1909 he married the American socialite HAZEL MARTYN from Chicago, known as 'THE MOST BEAUTIFUL GIRL IN THE MIDWEST'. She was the daughter of Edward Martyn, who was descended from the Martins of Galway and so had Irish roots.

Hazel Lavery was passionate about Irish independence and developed a strong relationship with the nationalist hero MICHAEL COLLINS (*see* Co. Cork, page 158). She persuaded her husband to paint the portraits of the leading Anglo-Irish figures of the time at his studio in London, and while they were there she worked to convince them of the need for reconciliation between England and Ireland. These efforts came to fruition with the signing of the ANGLO-IRISH TREATY granting independence to Southern Ireland in December 1921.

The IRISH FREE STATE, which emerged from the IRISH CIVIL WAR, asked Lavery to paint a portrait of his wife to put on the new Irish banknotes. He portrayed her as a 'colleen', a representation of Irish feminine beauty, and her picture remained on Irish banknotes until the 1970s.

Well, I never knew this
ABOUT
BELFAST

BELFAST is not only THE SECOND-LARGEST CITY IN IRELAND but also IRELAND'S NEWEST CITY.

ST GEORGE'S CHURCH on the High Street occupies the site of one of the very first buildings to be put up in the area. THE CHAPEL OF THE FORD was built around 1306 as a place of prayer and thanksgiving for travellers crossing the RIVER FARSET. The name Belfast comes from *Beal Feirste*, meaning 'the approach to the sandy crossing' (of the Farset). The Farset now runs underneath the High Street in a tunnel big enough to hold a bus.

Belfast High Street was once home to THE ULSTER OVERCOAT COMPANY. The distinctive 'ULSTER' was famously worn by SHERLOCK HOLMES and also by BILLY CONNOLLY, when he was playing Queen Victoria's ghillie, JOHN BROWN, in the 1997 film *Mrs Brown*.

In Queen's Square is Belfast's OLDEST SURVIVING BUILDING, dating from 1715 and now occupied by MCHUGH'S BAR.

The ALBERT CLOCK MEMORIAL TOWER in Queen's Square was erected in 1865 in memory of Queen Victoria's late consort PRINCE ALBERT; 113 ft (34.5 m) high, it was built on soft, reclaimed land and now inclines 4 feet (1.2 m) from the vertical, earning it the name 'THE LEANING TOWER OF BELFAST'.

The UNITED IRISHMEN (*see* CO. Kildare, page 67) movement was founded in a tavern on CROWN ENTRY in the centre of Belfast in 1791.

The author ANTHONY TROLLOPE wrote *The Warden*, the first of his BARSETSHIRE novels, while he was working at the BELFAST CUSTOM HOUSE as Surveyor for the northern half of Ireland, in 1853.

The flamboyant GRAND OPERA HOUSE, opened in 1894, suffered considerable collateral damage from the bombings of the Europa Hotel next door, but has continued on gamely as a major venue for concerts and plays. In 1984 the Belfast-born singer VAN MORRISON recorded a live album there.

Grand Opera House

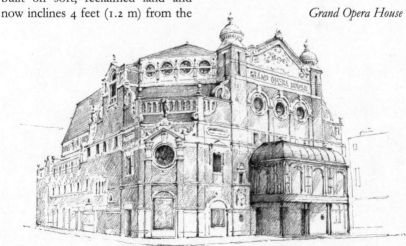

In 1896 JOHN BROWN of Longhurst, Belfast, imported THE FIRST CAR INTO IRELAND, a SERPOLLET STEAM CAR from France.

There is a piece of stone FROM EVERY ONE OF IRELAND'S 32 COUNTIES in the structure of ST ANNE'S CATHEDRAL in Donegall Street. Buried in the south aisle of the cathedral is the barrister Edward Carson (1854–1935), leading opponent of Irish Home Rule and the man who defended the 9th MARQUESS OF QUEENSBERRY against OSCAR WILDE's libel charge, an action that eventually led to Wilde's downfall and imprisonment. Carson and Wilde were fellow undergraduates at Trinity College, Dublin.

At one time Belfast was THE WORLD'S LEADING LINEN PRODUCER.

The dome of Belfast's exuberant CITY HALL was inspired by the dome of ST PAUL'S CATHEDRAL in London, and like St Paul's, contains a 'WHISPERING GALLERY'.

Belfast was home to THE FIRST MUNICIPAL AERODROME IN THE BRITISH ISLES. It operated at MALONE, on the outskirts of the city, in the mid-1920s.

In 1942 Belfast was THE FIRST PLACE IN EUROPE TO RECEIVE AMERICAN TROOPS, on their way to fight in World War Two.

St Anne's Cathedral

The Europa Hotel

The EUROPA HOTEL in Belfast is THE MOST BOMBED HOTEL IN THE WORLD.

The SHERIDAN IMAX cinema in Belfast is IRELAND'S ONLY 3D CINEMA.

Belfast boasts IRELAND'S BIGGEST CHINATOWN.

BORN IN BELFAST

DR WILLIAM DRENNAN (1754–1820), patriot, radical and poet, was born in Rosemary Street, Belfast. He was THE FIRST PRESIDENT OF THE UNITED IRISHMEN and a co-founder in 1810 of the famous BELFAST ACADEMICAL INSTITUTION ('Inst') in College Square. In his poem 'When Erin First Rose', Drennan described Ireland for the first time as 'THE EMERALD ISLE'.

GEORGE BEST (1946–2005), MANCHESTER UNITED FOOTBALLER, EUROPEAN PLAYER OF THE YEAR IN 1968, PELE'S FAVOURITE PLAYER, and for many people THE MOST TALENTED FOOTBALLER THE WORLD HAS EVER SEEN, was born, and is buried, in Belfast.

ALEX 'HURRICANE' HIGGINS, snooker player, was born in Belfast in 1949.

CHAIM HERZOG (1918–97), PRESIDENT OF ISRAEL FROM 1983 TO 1993, was born, the son of the Chief Rabbi of Ireland, at 2 Norman Villas, off Cliftonville Road, Belfast.

JAMES GALWAY, flautist, was born in Belfast in 1939.

VAN MORRISON, singer and musician, was born in Belfast, the son of a shipbuilder, in 1945.

In 1843 SIR HENRY POTTINGER (1789–1856) became THE FIRST GOVERNOR OF HONG KONG. He was born in MOUNT POTTINGER, east Belfast.

Little Lea

SIR SAMUEL FERGUSON (1810–86), poet and antiquarian, was born at 23 High Street, Belfast.

KENNETH BRANAGH, actor and director, was born in Belfast in 1960.

CLIVE STAPLES LEWIS (1898–1963), author and critic, was born in DUNDELA AVENUE, STRANDTOWN, BELFAST. He tutored at both Oxford and Cambridge and published a number of books on Christianity (*The Screwtape Letters, The Problem of Pain*). The romanticised story of his love affair and marriage to the American JOY GRESHAM was told in the 1993 film *Shadowlands*, starring ANTHONY HOPKINS and DEBRA WINGER. Lewis is celebrated today for his much-loved books for children, THE NARNIA CHRONICLES, the first of which was filmed by WALT DISNEY in 2005. When he was seven years old Lewis went to live in LITTLE LEA, a house on the outskirts of Belfast which his father had built. This house contained the original 'Wardrobe' of *The Lion, the Witch and the Wardrobe*. The MOUNTAINS OF MOURNE in Co. Down are said to have inspired the land of NARNIA. Little Lea still stands, but is a private house and is not open to the public. C.S. Lewis died on the same day as John F. Kennedy, 22 November 1963.

COUNTY ANTRIM

COUNTY TOWN: ANTRIM

Aon Troim – 'solitary place'

Gateway to Glenarm Castle, home of the Earls of Antrim

Ballymoney

The Lost Princess

In 1689, while on his way to the siege of Derry, KING JAMES II spent a night in BALLYMONEY with a local farmer's daughter. The result of this encounter was a child called DOROTHEA, who was brought up a Protestant and married a wealthy merchant from Coleraine. She died in her early twenties and is buried in the ruined churchyard at BALLYWILLAN, just outside Portrush. Her gravestone, marked with a fleur de lys and the Stuart coat of arms, was erected by Dorothea's half-sister ANNE, QUEEN OF ENGLAND. As a Protestant, had Dorothea lived longer and survived

William III and Queen Anne, she might have had a sound claim to the throne of England and changed the course of history for both Ireland and Britain.

The great-grandmother of the American writer EDGAR ALLEN POE (1809–49) (*Murders in the Rue Morgue*) was born in Ballymoney, the daughter of a Presbyterian Minister.

Ballymoney was the hometown of ONE OF THE GREATEST MOTORCYCLE RACERS OF ALL TIME, JOEY DUNLOP (1952–2000). He won 26 ISLE OF MAN TT RACES and five FORMULA ONE WORLD TITLES, although his favourite race was the NORTH WEST 200, IRELAND'S BIGGEST BIKE-RACING FESTIVAL and THE FASTEST MOTORBIKE RACE ON PUBLIC ROADS IN THE WORLD. Held in May, the race is run between Coleraine, Portrush and Portstewart. Joey Dunlop was appointed an MBE for services to sport and an OBE for his humanitarian aid to the orphans of Romania. He was killed racing in Estonia and there is a memorial to him in Ballymoney.

Ballymena

Shopping news

BALLYMENA was the birthplace in 1834 of the department store pioneer TIM EATON. In 1854 he emigrated to Canada and opened a shop in Toronto, which quickly became famous for a number of innovations. First, goods were sold for cash at the marked price only, thus doing away with the need for bartering. Second, Eaton's introduced the first 'SATISFACTION GUARANTEED OR MONEY REFUNDED' system, which was soon adopted around the world. Eaton's was ONE OF THE FIRST TRUE DEPARTMENT STORES and its famous catalogue was the FIRST DEPARTMENT STORE MAIL-ORDER CATALOGUE. Eaton's was bought by Sears in 1999.

The *Belfast News-Letter*, THE OLDEST NEWSPAPER IN THE ENGLISH-SPEAKING WORLD, was founded in Ballymena by paper manufacturer FRANCIS JOY in 1737. It was later moved to RANDALSTOWN before finally settling at premises on JOY'S ENTRY in Belfast.

In 1776 the *News-Letter* claimed the FIRST WORLD EXCLUSIVE when it published THE FIRST COPY OF THE AMERICAN DECLARATION OF INDEPENDENCE SEEN OUTSIDE AMERICA. The boat carrying a copy of the Declaration for the English King George III, which was the first copy to leave America, was caught in a storm off the north coast of Ireland and put into harbour at Derry. The precious document was taken on horseback to Belfast to be put on another ship for England. Somehow the editor managed to get access to the Declaration, which duly appeared on the front page of the *News-Letter* on 23 August 1776.

In 1871 the *Belfast News-Letter* began printing THE WORLD'S FIRST REGULAR NEWS FEATURE FOR WOMEN. It was contributed by CATHERINE DREW.

Film actor LIAM NEESON was born in Ballymena in 1952.

Dunluce

A Treasured Family Home

Spectacular DUNLUCE CASTLE became the seat of the MCDONNELLS when it was captured from the English in 1584 by SORLEY BOY MCDONNELL, whose descendants became the EARLS OF ANTRIM. The castle stands in a breathtaking location on a detached rock and could only be reached by a drawbridge. Sorley Boy is reputed to have infiltrated one of his men into the castle, who then hauled his leader and comrades up the cliff in a basket.

In 1588 a treasure ship from the Spanish Armada, the *Girona*, was wrecked off the Giant's Causeway and the McDonnells used some of their share of the booty to restore Dunluce, but in 1639 the kitchens fell into the sea during a storm, along with a number of the domestic staff. Later improvements were made to the castle by the wife of the 2nd Earl of Antrim, widow of the Duke of Buckingham murdered in Portsmouth, but at the end of the 17th century Dunluce was left to decay when the family moved their main residence down the coast to Glenarm.

Dunluce Castle was used as a location for the 1995 BBC television production of *The Buccaneers*, based on the novel by EDITH WHARTON.

Bushmills

Water of Life

The BUSHMILLS DISTILLERY is THE OLDEST LICENSED WHISKEY DISTILL- ERY IN THE WORLD and THE ONLY *working* IRISH WHISKEY DISTILLERY OPEN TO THE PUBLIC. It was granted a licence in 1608 by King James I, although whiskey has been made here since at least the 13th century.

The word WHISKEY comes from the Gaelic *uisce beatha* meaning 'water of life'. It was first produced in Ireland over 1,000 years ago by monks who had learnt the art of distilling during their travels in Asia. On their return they invented their own method of distilling, using a pot still. Irish whiskey (spelt with an 'e') is an older product than Scotch whisky and is also a somewhat different brew, being distilled three times, whereas Scotch is distilled twice (and Canadian bourbon once). Irish whiskey has suffered many

setbacks. In the 17th century a tax on whiskey was introduced that forced production underground, and the TEMPERANCE MOVEMENT of the 19th century succeeded in halving the consumption of whiskey. Scotch whisky makers marketed their product vigorously, particularly in foreign markets, with the result that Scotch has a much higher profile. Today Irish whiskey is regaining its popularity.

The WORLD'S FIRST HYDROELEC- TRIC TRAMWAY, which was also THE FIRST ELECTRIFIED RAILWAY IN IRELAND OR BRITAIN, ran FROM BUSHMILLS village to PORTRUSH. It was invented by local man WILLIAM TRAILL (1844–1933) and opened in 1882. It was then extended to the Giant's Causeway in 1887 and contin- ued to run until 1949. It was powered by a small generating station on the Bush river that supplied power through a conducting rail. In 1900 this was changed to overhead power lines. The line was restored in 2001 and today narrow-gauge steam trains run along the route.

Giant's Causeway

World Heritage Site

THE GIANT'S CAUSEWAY on the north Antrim coast is IRELAND'S FIRST WORLD HERITAGE SITE. Legend says that it was built by the Irish giant FINN McCOOL as a way of getting to the island of Staffa in Scotland, where his lady love lived. The causeway consists of some 40,000 polygonal columns of basalt formed by cooled lava. Most of the columns are six-sided but a happy time can be spent looking for those rare columns with a different number of sides. For instance there is only one column with three sides and one with eight sides – called the KEYSTONE because some people

think that if it was removed the whole causeway would collapse! Some of the columns mark out interesting formations like the 'WISHING CHAIR'. If you sit here and make three wishes they will come true.

A little way to the east of the Giant's Causeway, jutting out from the cliffs, there are some isolated columns known as the CHIMNEY TOPS, standing 300 feet (91 m) above the sea. In 1588 ships from the Spanish Armada fired on them, thinking they were shooting at Dunluce Castle.

Ballycastle

Early Waves

Down by the harbour at BALLY-CASTLE there is a memorial to the radio pioneer GUGLIELMO MARCONI (*see* Co. Galway, page 5). For the

MOYLE DISTRICT COUNCIL
Marconi Memorial
Unveiled by
Princess Elettra Marconi Giovanelli
Daughter of Guglielmo Marconi
on 24th July 1998
To Commemorate The Centenary Of The
World's First Commercial Radio Signal
From Rathlin Island To Ballycastle
on 6th July 1898

FIRST-EVER COMMERCIAL APPLICA-
TION OF RADIO, Marconi had been
invited by LLOYDS OF LONDON to set
up an experimental wireless link
between RATHLIN ISLAND and
BALLYCASTLE. The idea was to see if
radio could be of help to the important shipping lanes between the coast
of Antrim and the Mull of Kintyre in
Scotland, used by vessels on their
way into and out of Liverpool. On
6 July 1898 some of THE WORLD'S
EARLIEST RADIO SIGNALS and some of
the FIRST RADIO SIGNALS EVER TO BE
TRANSMITTED ACROSS WATER were
sent from the east lighthouse on
Rathlin Island to the 'WHITE LODGE'
at Ballycastle Harbour. The work was
actually carried out by Marconi's
assistant GEORGE KEMP, although
Marconi himself stayed in Ballycastle
for four days in August that year,
checking the equipment and trans-
missions for himself. The White
Lodge is still there by the ferry terminal car park.

Ballycastle boasts IRELAND'S OLDEST
TRADITIONAL FAIR, THE OUL' LAMMAS
FAIR, which marks the end of summer
and the beginning of the harvest and
dates from the 17th century.

Just outside Ballycastle are the
ruins of BUNAMARGY FRIARY, burial
place of SORLEY BOY MCDONNELL
(*see* Dunluce, page 223), his son, THE
1ST EARL OF ANTRIM, and RANDAL,
2ND EARL OF ANTRIM.

Rathlin Island

Spiders, but no snakes . . .

RATHLIN ISLAND lies 6 miles (10 km)
north of Ballycastle and was THE
FIRST PART OF IRELAND TO BE PIL-
LAGED BY THE VIKINGS, in AD 795.

In his novel *Westward Ho!* CHARLES
KINGSLEY describes Rathlin Island as
looking like 'a drowned magpie'
because of its alternating black and
white cliffs.

Ownership of Rathlin was hotly
disputed between Scotland and
Ireland until 1617, when RANDAL
MCDONNELL, 1ST EARL OF ANTRIM,
pointed out that there were no snakes
on the island and therefore it must be
Irish, since Ireland was famous for
having no snakes (*see* Croagh Patrick,
Co. Mayo, page 20).

In 1306 ROBERT THE BRUCE
escaped from defeat at the BATTLE
OF METHVEN and took refuge on
Rathlin Island. At the eastern end of
the island is BRUCE'S CAVE, where the
Scottish King was inspired to 'try, try
and try again' by the perseverance of
a spider that was attempting to weave
its web across the entrance to the
cave.

In 1898, GUGLIELMO MARCONI'S
assistant GEORGE KEMP and a Trinity

College graduate called EDWARD GLANVILLE, with the help of John Cecil and some other islanders, erected an 80ft-high (24 m) aerial on the island's east lighthouse. On 6 July, from the lighthouse, Glanville transmitted some of the FIRST WIRELESS SIGNALS ACROSS WATER. They were received by Kemp at the 'WHITE LODGE' at BALLYCASTLE HARBOUR. Two weeks later Edward Granville stumbled over a cliff on Rathlin Island and fell 300 feet (91 m) to his death.

Some 30 families live on Rathlin Island today, and there is a daily boat service from Ballycastle.

Glenarm

Chalk it up

GLENARM, a delightful seaside village at the foot of the glen from which it takes its name, claims to be THE OLDEST TOWN IN ULSTER, having received its charter in the 12th century.

Since 1636 Glenarm Castle has been the seat of the MCDONNELLS, EARLS OF ANTRIM, formerly of Dunluce Castle. Many of the pathways and avenues on the estate are laid with distinctive, chalky, grey and white gravel from the beach – Glenarm is home to IRELAND'S BIGGEST CHALK QUARRY. The chalk from here is renowned for its purity and brilliant whiteness and is used in the white paint employed for road markings all over Europe.

Glenarm was the birthplace of the MACNEILL brothers, EOIN AND JAMES. PROFESSOR EOIN MACNEILL (1867–1945) was a historian and Irish scholar who co-founded the GAELIC LEAGUE with DOUGLAS HYDE (*see* Co. Roscommon, page 29) and became Commander-in-Chief of the IRISH VOLUNTEERS. He was Minister of Education for the Irish Free State from 1923 to 1926. James MacNeill (1869–1938) was THE FIRST IRISH HIGH COMMISSIONER IN LONDON and the SECOND GOVERNOR-GENERAL OF THE IRISH FREE STATE.

> *The Irish Volunteers were formed in 1913 to defend the principle of* HOME RULE FOR IRELAND. *They were the recipients of the guns smuggled into Ireland in 1914 by* ERSKINE CHILDERS *at* HOWTH *(see Co. Dublin, page 61).*

Carrickfergus

Of Witches and Kings

CARRICKFERGUS CASTLE is one of the most impressive Norman castles in Ireland. Begun in the 12th century, it was garrisoned for 750 years until 1928. Carrickfergus means 'ROCK OF FERGUS' and is named from the 6th-century King Fergus, founder of the Royal House of Scotland, who was drowned nearby.

Carrickfergus Castle

In 1210 KING JOHN captured the castle from the EARL OF ULSTER, HUGH DE LACY, and resided there for a while.

Carrickfergus Castle was THE ONLY PART OF ULSTER NOT TO FALL TO EDMUND BRUCE, holding out under siege for several months in 1315–16.

In 1689 the castle *did* fall, to William III's commander GENERAL SCHOMBERG. King William himself landed at the harbour on 14 June 1690, on his way to the BATTLE OF THE BOYNE (*see* Co. Meath, page 105).

In 1711 IRELAND'S LAST WITCH-CRAFT TRIAL took place at Carrickfergus when a number of women from Island Magee were accused of causing a young girl to have fits. They were found guilty and sentenced to 12 months' imprisonment and four appearances in the stocks in the square at Carrickfergus.

In 1760 the French Commodore THUROT took the town and castle in THE ONLY FRENCH VICTORY EVER ON BRITISH SOIL. Thurot's grandfather was an Irishman by the name of O'Farrell.

On 24 April 1778, THE FIRST-EVER ACTION IN EUROPEAN WATERS BY AN AMERICAN SHIP took place offshore of Carrickfergus Castle. The American pirate commander JOHN PAUL JONES in his ship *Ranger* attacked the British ship *Drake* and forced her to strike her colours.

Carrickfergus is the home of IRELAND'S ONLY GAS MUSEUM.

Hail to the Chief

From Antrim to the White House

SEVEN US PRESIDENTS have ancestral ties with Co. ANTRIM.

ANDREW JACKSON (1767–1845), 7TH US PRESIDENT. Andrew Jackson was born in South Carolina two years after his parents had emigrated from BONEYBEFORE, 1 mile (1.6 km) east of Carrickfergus, in 1765. A blue plaque 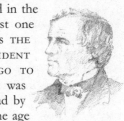 on a stone plinth marks the actual site of their cottage, which was demolished in the 1860s to make way for the railway, and the ANDREW JACKSON CENTRE stands nearby. The centre is designed as a single-storey thatched farmhouse with an open fireplace, similar to the original Jackson home.

Known as 'OLD HICKORY' and 'THE PEOPLE'S PRESIDENT', Andrew Jackson served two terms between 1829 and 1837. He was THE ONLY US PRESIDENT EVER TO BE HELD AS A PRISONER OF WAR – this during the Revolutionary War when he was aged just 13. He was also THE FIRST PRESIDENT TO RIDE ON A TRAIN, THE FIRST TO BE BORN IN A LOG CABIN and THE FIRST TO BE NOMINATED BY A POLITICAL PARTY – he was a Democrat. In 1835 he survived THE FIRST ATTEMPT TO ASSASSINATE AN AMERICAN PRESIDENT.

ANDREW JOHNSON (1808–75), 17TH US PRESIDENT (1865–9). Andrew Johnson's grandfather emigrated from MOUNTHILL, near Larne, in 1750 and settled in North Carolina. Andrew ran a successful tailor's business in Tennessee and was elected as ABRAHAM LINCOLN'S Vice-President in 1865, succeeding him as

President after Lincoln's assassination. Johnson was THE FIRST PRESIDENT TO BE IMPEACHED and was acquitted in the Senate by just one vote. He was THE ONLY PRESIDENT NEVER TO GO TO SCHOOL and was  taught to read by his wife at the age of 17. Under his presidency Alaska was bought from Russia for two cents per acre or $7.2 million.

CHESTER ARTHUR (1829–86), 21ST US PRESIDENT (1881–5). Chester Arthur's father, the REV. WILLIAM ARTHUR, left DREEN, CULLY- BACKEY, near Ballymena, in 1815 and sailed for America. His thatched farmhouse has been restored to its original 19th-century condition. From Cullybackey take the B96 towards Portglenone and turn right after a quarter mile. The cottage is signposted. 'Chet' Arthur was known

Arthur Cottage

as 'THE GENTLEMAN BOSS' and 'ELEGANT ARTHUR' because of his stylish dressing.

GROVER CLEVELAND (1837–1908), 22ND AND 24TH US PRESIDENT (1885–9 and 1893–7). Grover Cleveland's family emigrated to America from the BALLYMENA area of Co. Antrim. Cleveland was THE ONLY PRESIDENT TO HAVE BEEN ELECTED FOR TWO NON-CONSECUTIVE TERMS. He was also THE ONLY PRESIDENT TO BE MARRIED IN THE WHITE HOUSE and THE FIRST PRESIDENT TO HAVE A BABY BORN THERE.

WILLIAM MCKINLEY (1843–1901), 25TH PRESIDENT (1897–1901). McKinley's grandfather James McKinley was a farmer born at  CONAGHER, near Ballymoney, in 1783. McKinley was THE FIRST US PRESIDENT TO RIDE IN AN AUTOMOBILE. America's highest mountain, Mt McKinley in Alaska (20,320 ft/ 6,193 m) is named after him. He was assassinated by an anarchist in Buffalo on 6 September 1901.

THEODORE ROOSEVELT (1858–1919), 26TH US PRESIDENT (1901–9). Roosevelt's maternal ancestors emigrated from GLENOE, LARNE, in 1729. He was AMERICA'S YOUNGEST  PRESIDENT and THE FIRST AMERICAN TO WIN A NOBEL PRIZE. (He won the Nobel Peace Prize in 1906 for his role as peace maker in the Russian-Japanese War.) The 'TEDDY' BEAR was named after him.

RICHARD MILHOUS NIXON (1913–94), 37TH US PRESIDENT (1969–74). Milhous was Nixon's mother's maiden name and his Milhous kinsmen were a Quaker family from Carrickfergus. Nixon was THE ONLY US PRESIDENT TO RESIGN FROM OFFICE.

DeLorean

Back to the Future

The DELOREAN sports car, AMONG THE MOST FAMOUS CARS ON FILM, was built at DUNMURRY, near Lisburn in Co. Antrim. The DeLorean's futuristic looks, with its gull-wing doors and unpainted, stainless-steel skin, soon attracted the attention of Hollywood, and the producers of the *Back to the Future* films chose a DeLorean to play MICHAEL J. FOX's time machine.

THE DELOREAN CAR COMPANY was founded by American JOHN DELOREAN, a former General Motors executive, in 1981. The British government, keen to encourage 2,000 jobs in a time of unemployment, put up £80 million and a state-of-the-art factory was built on a brown-field site south of Belfast.

Although the car was innovative and well designed, it was a time of

was closed in 1982. The company was not helped when John DeLorean was arrested for drug-dealing and fraud, although he was later acquitted.

Because the design was unique and so few were made, the DeLorean has built up a cult following, and there are regular DeLorean conventions held in America and in Belfast. The original factory and test track in Dunmurry are still there, much visited by enthusiasts.

recession, and there was never enough demand for a car of this type. Only 9,000 were produced, most going to America, before the factory

Well, I never knew this
ABOUT
COUNTY ANTRIM

COUNTY ANTRIM IS THE COLDEST COUNTY IN IRELAND.

SLEMISH MOUNTAIN (1,437 ft, 438 m) near BALLYMENA is traditionally where Ireland's patron saint ST PATRICK tended swine and underwent his spritual awakening. He was 16 and living in Scotland when he was captured by Irish pirates, brought to Ireland and sold as a slave to the Irish chieftain Miliucc.

WALLACE PARK in LISBURN commemorates local MP SIR RICHARD WALLACE Bt. (1818–90), who lived in Castle Street where the Technical College now stands. Wallace's magnificent collection of paintings was left to the British nation by his widow and can be seen at the

WALLACE COLLECTION, located in Hertford House, their old home in Manchester Square, London.

HILDEN BREWERY in LISBURN, founded in 1981, is THE OLDEST INDEPENDENT BREWERY IN IRELAND.

LILIAN BLAND (1878–1971), THE FIRST WOMAN IN THE WORLD TO DESIGN, BUILD AND FLY AN AIRPLANE, was born and grew up at TOBARCOORAN HOUSE in CARNMONEY, north of Belfast. She was the grand-daughter of a Dean of Belfast and was inspired by Louis Blériot's flight across the English Channel in 1909 to try and create her own piece of aviation history. In 1910 her biplane, the *Mayfly*, took off from CARNMONEY HILL and flew for a quarter of a mile, with Lilian feeding the engine whiskey through her aunt's old ear trumpet.

Most of the little seaside village of CUSHENDUN was built in the 1920s by CLOUGH WILLIAMS-ELLIS, architect of the famous showcase village of Portmeirion in North Wales.

TORR HEAD, near Cushendun, is a mere 13 miles (21 km) from the Mull of Kintyre in Scotland and is THE CLOSEST POINT IN IRELAND TO SCOTLAND.

ONE OF IRELAND'S MOST UNUSUAL AND HEART-STOPPING ATTRACTIONS is the CARRICK-A-REDE ROPE BRIDGE, near Ballintoy. Suspended 84 feet (26 m) above the sea and spanning a chasm of 60 feet (18 m), and recently remade with the wooden planks hung from wires, the bridge rocks and sways as you step on to it, enough to test the steadiest of nerves. The bridge leads to a small rock island and was originally put up to provide access to a salmon fishery. It is taken down in the winter months.

KILROOT, near Carrickfergus, can boast THE ONLY SALT MINE IN IRELAND. DEAN SWIFT held his first living at Kilroot in 1694–6.

In the ruins of TEMPLECORRAN CHURCH at BALLYCARRY, near Carrickfergus, there is a memorial to REV. EDWARD BRICE, who in 1613 became THE FIRST PRESBYTERIAN MINISTER ORDAINED TO PREACH IN IRELAND.

Carrick-a-Rede

St Gobhan's church at Portbrad-dan, near Ballycastle, is THE SMALL-EST CHURCH IN IRELAND and ONE OF THE SMALLEST CHURCHES IN THE WORLD. It measures 12 ft (3.7 m) by 6 ft (1.8 m).

The profile of Cave Hill, looming above Belfast, is said to have given Jonathan Swift the idea for the giants in *Gulliver's Travels*. From some angles it can look very like a sleeping giant.

It was amongst the remains of MacArt's Fort on Cave Hill that Wolfe Tone and the United Irishmen (*see* Co. Kildare, page 67) met in 1795 in order to plan their rebellion.

The little seaside resort of Portballintrae was THE ONLY PLACE IN IRELAND TO BE SHELLED FROM THE SEA DURING World War One.

Drumalis, a rambling Edwardian mansion on the edge of Larne, is thought to have been where the 1914 gun-running operation for the Ulster Volunteer Force was master-minded. On the night of Friday 24 April 1914 Larne was suddenly sealed off from the outside world. While the authorities looked on helplessly, 20,000 guns for the UVF were landed from the collier SS *Clyde Valley*, to assist in the campaign against Irish Home Rule led by Edward Carson (*see* Belfast, page 218). Carson was a long-standing friend of the owner of Drumalis, Lady Smiley, widow of Sir Hugh Houston Smiley. The Smileys' second son married Ernest Simpson's sister. Ernest Simpson was the first husband of Wallis Simpson, the cause of King Edward VIII's abdication from the throne of England. Wallis Simpson and Edward VIII later married and became the Duke and Duchess of Windsor. Drumalis is now run as a religious retreat.

County Armagh

St Patrick's Protestant Cathedral

Armagh City

'My Sweet Hill'

In AD 445 St Patrick built a 'great stone church' inside a ring-fort on a hill called Druimsailech, granted to him for the purpose by a local chieftain, 'a certain rich and honourable man named Daire'. St Patrick described the place as 'my sweet hill' and ordained that this church should have pre-eminence over all other churches in Ireland. Hence, Armagh is the ecclesiastical capital of Ireland. It is the seat of two archbishops and has two magnificent St Patrick's Cathedrals facing each other across the town from rival hilltops. Both the Protestant and the Roman Catholic archbishops are entitled to call themselves Primate of All Ireland.

The older, Protestant, cathedral is built on the site of St Patrick's original church. The rings of the old hill-fort can still be traced, but the cathedral itself is a 19th-century restoration of a medieval building of about 1268. The first King of All Ireland, Brian Boru, was brought here to be buried, along with his son, after the Battle of Clontarf in 1014. A tablet on the outer face of the west wall of the north transept marks the actual site of his grave, and nearby in the churchyard there are fragments of a stone cross from his monument.

St Patrick's Catholic Cathedral

The more spectacular of the two cathedrals is the lofty neo-Gothic Catholic building whose twin spires are notable Armagh landmarks. It was begun in 1840 but not finished until 1873 because of a pause in construction during the Great Famine. A unique feature of the cathedral are the CARDINAL'S HATS that can be seen hanging above the Sanctuary. On the death of a Cardinal his hat would be hung there and left to decay, symbolising the end of all earthly glory. This practice is no longer followed, since new Cardinals are now presented with a biretta rather than a hat when they are created.

Cricket is played in summer on Armagh's lovely, oval, tree-ringed Mall, which is surrounded by some elegant Georgian houses, many of them the work of Armagh's own architect FRANCIS JOHNSTON (1760–1829), born in the city. He is remembered for designing the GENERAL POST OFFICE and NELSON'S PILLAR in Dublin's O'Connell Street, and the CHAPEL ROYAL in DUBLIN CASTLE. Johnston endowed his hometown of Armagh with the ARCHBISHOP'S PALACE, the CLASSICAL COURTHOUSE, the ROYAL SCHOOL and the OBSERVATORY.

Archbishop's Palace

Armagh Observatory, built in 1790, was the SECOND OBSERVATORY TO BE ESTABLISHED IN IRELAND after DUNSINK near Dublin (1785). Weather is of great importance to astronomers who rely on forecasts of clear or cloudy skies, and since 1795 they have taken weather statistics at Armagh Observatory – THE OLDEST CONTINUOUS WEATHER RECORDS IN IRELAND. THOMAS ROMNEY ROBINSON (1792–1882), the third Director of the Observatory, invented the CUP ANEMOMETER to measure wind speeds, a device still used all over the world. Robinson was married to MARIA EDGEWORTH's sister LUCY and is believed to have got the idea for the anemometer from Lucy's father, RICHARD LOVELL EDGEWORTH (*see* Co. Longford, page 90). The Observatory's telescope was installed in 1795 and is THE OLDEST TELESCOPE STILL IN ITS ORIGINAL DOME IN THE WORLD.

Armagh has THE ONLY PLANETARIUM IN IRELAND.

Loughgall

Apples and Oranges

County Armagh is known as THE ORCHARD COUNTY. The rich fruit-growing country to the north-east of Armagh, based around the beautiful village of LOUGHGALL, is known as the ORCHARD OF IRELAND. APPLE BLOSSOM SUNDAY, when the trees are a riot of white and pink flowers, is in late May. In the 17th century, many settlers came here from Worcestershire in England and laid out orchards along the same lines as those in the Vale of Evesham.

In 1795 the ORANGE ORDER was founded by Protestant farmers at SLOANE'S BAR in LOUGHGALL. This was a response to the Catholic secret society known as the DEFENDERS, after a skirmish between the Protestant PEEP O' DAY BOYS and the DEFENDERS at the sectarian BATTLE OF THE DIAMOND, outside the village. The first embryonic meeting of the Orange Order was at DAN WINTER'S COTTAGE near the Diamond crossroads, known as THE BIRTHPLACE OF ORANGEISM. Dan Winter's Cottage can be visited.

The Order is a revival of the ORANGE INSTITUTION of 1688 formed to support WILLIAM OF ORANGE, victor over the Catholic JAMES II at the BATTLE OF THE BOYNE in 1690, and is organised with a system of Lodges rather like freemasonry. The Orange Order's marches through the Catholic areas of DRUMCREE near Portadown have often sparked violent confrontations.

Dan Winter's Cottage

Brownlow House

Lurgan

Tunnel of Love

BROWNLOW HOUSE in Lurgan is an extraordinary Elizabethan-Revival house built in 1837 by WILLIAM PLAYFAIR for CHARLES BROWNLOW, 1ST LORD LURGAN. His family founded Lurgan in the 17th century. There are rumours of a secret tunnel running from Brownlow House up to Castle Lane in Lurgan, built by a Lord Lurgan who was forbidden by his wife to leave the castle after dark. He would slip out through the tunnel, unnoticed and defiant, to seek solace with an understanding local lass and then return to the castle in time for an innocent breakfast the next morning. The house is now THE LARGEST ORANGE HALL IN THE WORLD and the grounds have been turned into a public park.

JAMES LOGAN (1674–1751), A FOUNDING FATHER OF PENNSYLVANIA, was born in Lurgan. As secretary to WILLIAM PENN, Logan sailed with Penn on his second voyage to America in 1699 and was entrusted with administering the colony on Penn's return to England. He served as MAYOR OF PHILADELPHIA in 1723 and as CHIEF JUSTICE in the PHILADELPHIA SUPREME COURT from 1731 to 1739.

GEORGE W. RUSSELL (1867–1935), journalist, poet and painter better known as 'Æ', was born in WILLIAM STREET, LURGAN. He was a passionate nationalist, a co-founder of the ABBEY THEATRE and a leading figure, along with W.B. YEATS, in the Irish Literary revival of the late 19th and early 20th centuries. His initials are on the AUTOGRAPH TREE at COOLE (*see* Co. Galway, page 5).

THE FIRST 'SETTLED MEETING' OF QUAKERS IN IRELAND was held in Lurgan in 1654.

Well, I never knew this
ABOUT
COUNTY ARMAGH

Two miles (3 km) west of Armagh is NAVAN FORT, an 18-acre (7.2 ha) hillfort commanding extensive views over the surrounding countryside, which for 700 years was the royal capital of Ulster. In legend this was the site of EAMHAIN MACHA, palace of the mythical QUEEN MACHA who gives her name to Armagh. It was also the palace of KING CONCHOBAR, founder of the RED BRANCH KNIGHTS OF ULSTER. CUCHULAIN rode out from here to single-handedly confront the army of QUEEN MAEVE when she came to steal the BROWN BULL OF COOLEY (*see* Co. Louth, page 98).

The RED HAND OF ULSTER, which appears on the Ulster flag, is said to originate from a race between two clan chieftains, DERMOT and O'NEILL, who were fighting over which of them should be King of Ulster. They took their dispute to the High King, who suggested a horse race from Tara to Ulster. 'WHOEVER PUTS HIS HAND ON ULSTER FIRST SHALL BE KING,' he declared. The race was neck and neck until the two rivals reached the river that formed the border with Ulster. Dermot jumped in and began to swim, but O'Neill took out his sword and cut off his right hand, which he then flung across the river so that it landed on the opposite bank before Dermot could get there. O'Neill had put his hand on Ulster first, and hence became King. His red, bloodstained hand has been a symbol of Ulster ever since.

New York's famous CONEY ISLAND is named after the CONEY ISLAND 1 mile (1.6 km) out in LOUGH NEAGH, off Maghery.

WAUGH'S FARM, THE BIRCHES, near Portadown, was the birthplace of THOMAS JACKSON, grandfather of the great American Confederate GENERAL 'STONEWALL' JACKSON.

At EDENAPPA, just south of Jonesborough, is the 7-ft-high (2.1 m) KILNASAGGART STONE, the OLDEST DATABLE STONE MONUMENT IN IRELAND. On the south face is an inscription that reads '*This place did Ternoc son of Ciaran bequeath under the protection of Peter the Apostle*'. Ternoc died in 716.

Gosford Castle

GOSFORD CASTLE, a monumental granite pile near MARKETHILL, was designed for ARCHIBALD ACHESON, 2ND EARL OF GOSFORD, by THOMAS HOPPER and completed in 1839 as THE FIRST NORMAN-REVIVAL BUILDING IN IRELAND OR BRITAIN. Gosford Castle was bought by the Forestry Com-mission after World War Two and is being administered by a Trust who aim to raise money for its preservation. ANTHONY POWELL, who was stationed here during World War Two, based Castlemallock in *A Dance to the Music of Time* on Gosford.

Bessbrook is a model village founded in 1855 by a Quaker linen maker, JOHN GRUBB RICHARDSON. He believed in abstinence and the village has no pub, pawn shop or police station.

Near Bessbrook is the 18-arch CRAIGMORE VIADUCT, opened in 1852 and carrying the Belfast-to-Dublin railway line for a quarter of a mile across the Camlough river valley. This is THE HIGHEST VIADUCT IN IRELAND, with one lofty arch 126 ft (38 m) high. It is constructed from local granite.

CHARLES DAVIS LUCAS, Lieutenant of the Royal Navy, THE FIRST MAN TO WIN A VICTORIA CROSS, was born in DRUMARGOLE, Co. Armagh. He received his medal, the highest award

Craigmore Viaduct

for gallantry a British or Common-wealth serviceman can achieve, for picking up a live shell and throwing it overboard while serving on board HMS *Hecla* as it was bombarding Bomarsund, a fort on the Aland Islands in the Gulf of Bothnia, during the CRIMEAN WAR. He was presented with his medal by Queen Victoria on 26 June 1857.

Armagh is one of the five counties to border LOUGH NEAGH, at 153 square miles (400 sq km) THE BIGGEST FRESHWATER LAKE IN IRELAND OR BRITAIN. Tradition has it that Lough Neagh was created by FINN MCCOOL, builder of the Giant's Causeway, when he picked up a clod of turf and hurled it into the Irish Sea, thus forming at one stroke Lough Neagh and the Isle of Man.

Just outside BESSBROOK is DERRY-MORE HOUSE, an 18th-century thatched cottage *orné* built for SIR ISAAC CORRY, MP for Newry and last Chancellor of the Irish Exchequer. THE ACT OF UNION OF 1801 was drafted in the drawing room here. The house is now owned by the National Trust.

COUNTY CAVAN

COUNTY TOWN: CAVAN

Cabhan – 'the hollow place'

Bellamount Forest, Cootehill – Ireland's finest Palladian villa

Shannon Pot

A Fishy Tale

High up on the barren slopes of bleak CUILCAGH MOUNTAIN in little County Cavan, there lies a deep, silent, brown pool, wrapped in swirling mists and legend. A few sad trees dip their branches in the water, descendants perhaps of the hazel trees into which the Druids gathered all their knowledge. All is quiet and drowsy. Nothing stirs. We are at the mystical source of Ireland's majestic RIVER SHANNON, the liquid silver

thread that runs through the heart and the history of Ireland.

Shannon Pot

In the ancient days at the dawn of time this pool was home to the

SALMON OF WISDOM. Only the Druids were allowed to consult and have discourse with the Salmon, but one day there came a proud young woman of great beauty and high demeanour, SIONNAN, DAUGHTER OF LODAN, who wished to learn the secrets of the world for herself. So she waited until the Druids were gone and then she crept up to the side of the pool and started to sing softly, in the hope of luring the Salmon to the surface. But the Salmon of Wisdom was angered at such impertinence and caused the pool to overflow in a raging torrent that swept Sionnan into the sea, and so created the river that bears her name to this day.

That may seem an unlikely story, but somehow, standing there beside that murky pool with just the mountains and possibly a cow for company, it seems to make a certain sense. How else could this humble pond feed such a mighty river, if not through magic? A feeble stream trickles away through the cow pasture and it is almost impossible to conceive of how this dribble of water can become Ireland's great highway, THE LONGEST RIVER IN IRELAND AND BRITAIN.

The SHANNON POT is a mere 344 ft (105 m) above sea level and is a natural well that collects the waters of several small streams running off the mountainside. They disappear into the limestone bedrock and break through to the surface here, forming the spring that is the acknowledged source of the river. From here the Shannon flows for 240 miles (386 km) to the Atlantic Ocean, including the estuary, which is 68 miles (109 km) long and begins just downstream from Limerick. The river drains ONE FIFTH OF ALL IRELAND and historically divides the east and west of the country, forming the border between the provinces of Connacht and Leinster.

The Shannon is languid as it meanders through the Midlands, forming a series of great lakes, bogs and water meadows, home to otters, herons, swans and geese and myriad varieties of plantlife. In the 100 miles (160 km) between LOUGH ALLEN and KILLALOE it drops a mere 56 ft (17 m) before tumbling towards Limerick in a series of rapids that power the Arnacrusha hydroelectricity station.

The River Shannon is still a formidable barrier to some – the grey squirrel, which was introduced into Ireland in the early years of the last century, has yet to cross the river into the west.

And, of course, the Shannon is still famous for the fish that started it all – the Salmon.

Kilmore

The Cathedral in the Country

KILMORE CATHEDRAL, seat of the Church of Ireland Bishop of Kilmore with Elphin and Ardagh, stands proud and alone on a sylvan green hill above the road running south from Cavan Town. To come across such a 'great church' (*Cell Mor*) in this pleasant rural setting is quite a surprise. It is a restrained modern-Gothic building of 1860 with lovely proportions, and incorporates a Romanesque doorway which was rescued from a monastery on Trinity Island in Lough Oughter. The stones have not all been reset in the right place, which gives it an endearing quality.

In the nearby graveyard is the tomb of BISHOP WILLIAM BEDELL (1571–1642) who FIRST TRANSLATED THE BIBLE INTO IRISH.

> *Eoghan Rua O'Neill was a leader
> of the Catholic Confederate forces
> who achieved a notable victory at the
> BATTLE OF BENBURB against the
> Scottish Covenanters under ROBERT
> MUNRO in 1646.*

sons, in a 'cold, wet and windy room
almost at the top of the tower'.

The Confederate hero EOGHAN
RUA O'NEILL died here in 1649.
Cloghoughter was THE LAST STRONG-
HOLD IN IRELAND TO FALL TO
CROMWELL'S ARMY, not surrendering
until 1653.

Cloghoughter Castle

Last Stand

Somewhat hidden away on an island
in Lough Oughter is CLOGHOUGHTER
CASTLE, the BEST-PRESERVED EXAM-
PLE OF A NATIVE IRISH ROUND TOWER
CASTLE LEFT IN IRELAND.

Bishop William Bedell was imprisoned here by the CONFEDERATE
CATHOLICS in 1641–2 with his two

> *The Confederate Catholics were an
> alliance of Old English and Gaelic
> Irish Catholics who joined forces in
> 1641 in an attempt to rule Ireland
> until a settlement could be reached
> with the English KING CHARLES I.
> However, they were unable to preserve
> a united front and were crushed by
> Oliver Cromwell in his campaign
> of 1649–51.*

Virginia

Lilliput's Cradle

VIRGINIA is a pleasant, flower-strewn
market town on the north shore of
lovely LOUGH RAMOR, which dates
from the Ulster Plantations and is
named after Queen Elizabeth I, the
'Virgin Queen'.

It was here, to CUILCAGH HOUSE,
that DEAN JONATHAN SWIFT would
come and stay with his old friend
REV. THOMAS SHERIDAN (1687–
1738), and it was here that Swift
wrote most of his memorable work
Gulliver's Travels, which he completed
in 1725. His giant Brobdingnagian
farmer was modelled on an extra
ordinarily large local man called Mr
Doughty.

The Rev. Thomas Sheridan was the
father of the actor THOMAS SHERIDAN

Gulliver's Travels *is one of the most popular novels ever written in the English language and has rarely been out of print.* George Orwell *reckoned it to be amongst the six most indispensable books in world literature. The term* Yahoo, *now the name of an Internet search engine, originates from* Gulliver's Travels *and was the name of a race of base, hideously deformed human creatures.*

(1719–88), lexicographer and manager of Dublin's Smock Alley Theatre. He was also grandfather of Richard Brinsley Sheridan (1751–1816) the playwright. Richard Sheridan loved it at Cuilcagh House and spent a large part of his boyhood here, returning as often as he was able.

Well, I never knew this
ABOUT
County Cavan

The noted American Civil War General Philip Sheridan (1831–88) was born in Geagh near Bailieborough. The remains of the small cottage in which he was born can still be seen.

Bellamont Forest, at Cootehill, built by Edward Lovett Pearce in 1730, was inspired by Palladio's Villa Rotonda at Vicenza in Italy and is considered to be the finest example of a Palladian villa in Ireland. Cootehill was named after the Coote family who settled here in the 17th century. A descendant, Richard Coote, became Governor of New York and Massachusetts.

The history of milling in Cavan Town can be traced back to early medieval times. In the centre of the town, the Lifeforce Mill, which closed in 1950, has recently been fully restored and now mills wheat for wholemeal flour and bread. The present building was erected in 1846. It contains the only known working McAdam Water Turbine in the world and is the oldest operating water turbine mill in Ireland.

Swanlinbar, in the Cavan hills, was named after the four men who built a water mill there in the 17th century to process the local iron ore. They were called *Sw*ift, *San*ders, *Dar*ling and *Bar*ry. In the 18th century Swanlinbar was one of Ireland's most popular spa towns, noted for the sulphur and magnesium in its waters. You can still drink from a well at DRUMBROCHAS half a mile outside the town, where the water is said to cure rheumatism. Or, if you have a stomach ache, you may prefer the magnesium-rich water from the URAGH well near where the old spa hotel stood. Today the only spa town left in Ireland is Lisdoonvarna in Co. Clare.

The historic plain of MAGH SLECHT in Co. Cavan has been occupied for 6,000 years and contains THE DENSEST GROUPING OF PRE-CHRISTIAN AND EARLY CHRISTIAN MONUMENTS IN IRELAND. Within 3 square miles (8 sq km) there are at least nine megalithic tombs, seven barrows, three stone circles, nine standing stones, six crannogs, 33 raths, the remains of three early Christian churches, two holy wells and two medieval castles.

BALLYHAISE HOUSE on the Analee River was built by Richard Castle in 1733 and contains THE EARLIEST SURVIVING OVAL ROOM IN IRELAND AND BRITAIN.

MARCUS DALY (1841–1900), from BALLYJAMESDUFF in Co. Cavan, emigrated in 1856 to work in the mines of Nevada and California. He turned out to have a talent for discovering rich seams and in 1880 he bought a silver mine in Montana. This developed into THE WORLD'S LARGEST COPPER MINE, supplying conductors for the rapidly emerging electrical industry. To service his mines Daly built the city of COPPEROPOLIS in Montana, now called ANACONDA. He never forgot Ballyjamesduff and provided money for the local church. There is a plaque on the ruins of his boyhood home. Ballyjamesduff was featured in a song by PERCY FRENCH, 'Come back, Paddy Reilly, to Ballyjamesduff!'

SHANE CONNAUGHTON, script-writer for plays, films and television, was born in Co. Cavan in 1946. In 1989

Ballyhaise House

he was nominated for an Oscar for Best Adapted Screenplay for the film *My Left Foot*, about the crippled artist CHRISTY BROWN, starring DANIEL DAY-LEWIS (*see* Co. Wicklow, page 138).

CAVAN CRYSTAL has been hand-blown and cut in the traditional way in Cavan since 1969 and is THE OLDEST IRISH CRYSTAL after Waterford.

St Mary's Church in the little village of KINGSCOURT on the River Navan has four outstanding stained-glass windows by EVIE HONE (1894–1955). Evie was severely disabled by polio, but was an accomplished modernist and abstract painter who moved on to working with glass. She received commissions from all over Britain, her biggest being for an 18-light window for Eton College chapel. It is generally accepted that her finest work is here at Kingscourt, her favourite window of all being

The Ascension

The Ascension, completed in 1948, perhaps THE FINEST EXAMPLE OF CONTEMPORARY IRISH GLASS IN THE COUNTRY.

County Derry

Derry Guildhall

City of Derry

Within these Walls

Derry is a delightful discovery, THE MOST COMPLETE WALLED CITY IN IRELAND OR BRITAIN, set on a steep hill above the Foyle estuary, with narrow, bustling streets and wide views across to the hills of Donegal.

Derry was founded in AD 546 when St Columba established a monastery amongst the oak trees on the hill, and called it 'Daire', the Gaelic for 'oak grove'. The saint thought it a special place where 'the angels of God sang in the glades of Derry and every leaf held its angel'.

In the early 17th century King James I of England invited

merchants from the City of London to take responsibility for the development and settlement of Derry, and the prefix 'London' was added to the name. LONDONDERRY is still the official title of the city, but today it is more usually called Derry.

In 1613–18 the city walls, THE LAST CITY WALLS TO BE BUILT IN EUROPE, were constructed to defend the new Plantation town from the marauding chiefs of Donegal. The walls are just over 1 mile (1.7 km) in circumference, rise to a height of 26 ft (8 m), and in some places are 30 ft (9 m) thick. THEY HAVE NEVER BEEN BREACHED. Today it is possible to make a complete circuit of the walls on foot. On the Double Bastion at

the south-west corner of the walls is 'ROARING MEG', a cannon that got its name from the loud noise it made when fired during the Siege of Derry.

The Siege

The SIEGE OF DERRY in 1688–9 was THE LAST SIEGE IN IRISH OR BRITISH HISTORY. The city of Derry was one of the few Protestant enclaves at a time when most of Ireland supported the Catholic James II against William of Orange, in the dispute that was to be settled at the BATTLE

Ferryquay Gate

OF THE BOYNE in 1690 (*see* Co. Meath, page 105). When a Catholic army tried to enter the city on 7 December 1688, 13 young APPRENTICE BOYS closed the FERRYQUAY GATE against them, and thus began a siege that was to last 105 days – THE LONGEST SIEGE IN IRISH OR BRITISH HISTORY.

A boom was thrown across the River Foyle by the besiegers to prevent supply ships from reaching the town, and some 8,000 people within the city walls died of starvation and disease. The townspeople were inspired to hold out by the fervour of one of their Governors, the REV. GEORGE WALKER, whose statue now sits atop a 90-ft (27-m) column near BUTCHER'S GATE. At one point during the siege the Catholic General Hamilton had a shell hurled over the walls into the city, containing his terms of capitulation. The blunt answer 'NO SURRENDER' is now the city motto. The shell can be seen in the vestibule of ST COLUMB'S CATHEDRAL at the top of the town – completed in 1633, this was THE FIRST CATHEDRAL TO BE BUILT IN WESTERN EUROPE AFTER THE REFORMATION.

Finally, on the evening of 28 July three ships sent by William's General Schomberg sailed up the Foyle and broke the boom, relieving the siege. CAPTAIN BROWNING of the lead ship, the *Mountjoy*, died in the attack.

St Columb's Cathedral

The site of the boom is marked by BOOM HALL, a fine classical house built in 1779 on the west bank of the River Foyle where the boom came ashore. The house suffered a fire in the 1970s and is now derelict. It can be found at the west end of the new Foyle Bridge.

On 14 May 1945 the German submarine fleet surrendered to ADMIRAL SIR MAX HORTON on the River Foyle at Derry.

Today the old walled city lies at the centre of one of Ireland's biggest and fastest-growing conurbations. SHIPQUAY STREET, within the walls, is THE STEEPEST COMMERCIAL STREET IN IRELAND OR BRITAIN.

On the tower of Derry's Neo-Gothic GUILDHALL, built in 1890, is one of THE LARGEST FOUR-FACED CLOCKS IN IRELAND OR BRITAIN.

In 1958 the American firm DU PONT opened its FIRST-EVER EUROPEAN PRODUCTION FACILITY at MAYDOWN, just outside Derry.

Every year in October Derry holds IRELAND'S OLDEST HALLOWE'EN CARNIVAL, which is also THE LARGEST STREET PARTY IN IRELAND.

To the west of the city walls is an area reclaimed from marshy land called BOGSIDE, a Catholic enclave at the entrance to which is a huge mural announcing that 'You are now entering Free Derry'. In 1972, FREE DERRY CORNER was the scene of 'BLOODY SUNDAY', when 13 people were killed in one of the most notorious incidents of the modern 'Troubles'.

BORN IN DERRY

The novelist JOYCE CARY (1888–1957) was born at BANK HOUSE on the corner of Shipquay Street and Bank Place. Two of his novels were made into films, *The Horse's Mouth*, starring ALEC GUINNESS, in 1958, and *Mister Johnson* in 1990.

The tenor JOSEF LOCKE (1917–99) was born in CREGGAN TERRACE on St Patrick's Day. A popular performer throughout Ireland and Britain in the 1940s and 50s, he also served in the British Army in World War Two as THE YOUNGEST SERGEANT TO PARTICIPATE IN THE NORTH AFRICAN CAMPAIGN. He became a household name for a new audience when his life story was told in the 1992 film *Hear My Song*, starring NED BEATTY as Locke, alongside TARA FITZGERALD and ADRIAN DUNBAR.

AMANDA BURTON, the actress best known for her role as a forensic pathologist in the BBC television series *Silent Witness*, was born in BALLOUGHRY, Derry, in 1956.

GEORGE FARQUHAR (1678–1707), the Restoration playwright (*The Recruiting Officer*, *The Beaux' Stratagem*), was born in Shipquay Street.

BURIED IN DERRY

WILLIAM COPPIN (1805–95) is buried in ST AUGUSTINE'S CHURCH in Derry. Born in Kinsale, Co. Cork, he studied shipbuilding in Canada and in 1831 settled in Derry and took over the shipyard there, turning it into one of the biggest and most important in Ireland. In 1842 he gave Derry a moment of supreme glory when he launched from the shipyard the stupendous *Great Northern*, THE BIGGEST SCREW-PROPELLED SHIP THE WORLD HAD EVER SEEN. Unfortunately, he couldn't find a buyer and the ship had to be scrapped at a loss, but Coppin continued to provide employment throughout most of the 19th century, building transatlantic sailing ships, steamships and salvage vessels.

RICHARD BRANSON and his colleague PER LINDSTRAND landed near LIMAVADY in the *Virgin Atlantic Flyer*, having achieved THE FIRST ATLANTIC CROSSING BY HOT-AIR BALLOON. Their flight from MAINE took 31 hours and 41 minutes.

Down in Derry

A Good Place to Land

On 20 May 1932 AMELIA EARHART swooped out of the sky and touched down gingerly in a cow pasture near BALLYARNET, a few miles north of Derry. Clambering out of her Lockheed Vega, she asked a startled farm hand, 'Where am I?' 'In Gallagher's pasture,' he replied. This surprised her because she had in fact been heading for Paris, but nothing could take away from the fact that she had just completed THE FIRST SOLO TRANSATLANTIC FLIGHT BY A WOMAN, and only the second solo flight since CHARLES LINDBERGH, exactly five years earlier in 1927. It had taken her just under 15 hours to reach Ireland from HARBOUR GRACE in NEWFOUNDLAND, having been blown way off course during a very stormy crossing. A sculpture marks the spot where she landed and there is an exhibition dedicated to her memory in a cottage on the edge of the field.

One of the great aviation pioneers, Amelia disappeared over the Pacific Ocean in 1937 while attempting to circumnavigate the globe.

On 3 July 1987, a few miles away across the Foyle estuary, Virgin boss

The Mitred Earl

Bristol Fashion

In the late 18th century a great sporting event was held on the sands of DOWNHILL, near Portstewart. The competitors were clergymen and they were racing each other for the glittering prize of a benefice or a curacy. The mastermind behind this new kind of steeplechase was FREDERICK AUGUSTUS HERVEY, the eccentric BISHOP OF DERRY and 4TH EARL OF BRISTOL, known as 'THE MITRED EARL'.

The Mitred Earl was a great collector, and in 1775 he built himself a vast palace on the bleak uplands of Downhill, which he filled with books, frescoes and paintings. Alas, the house was destroyed by fire in 1851 and is now just a gaunt ruin, but the magnificent grounds survive in part and provide exhilarating clifftop walks.

Still in excellent condition and perched dramatically above the Atlantic Ocean is the exquisite MUSSENDEN TEMPLE, one of Co. Derry's most recognisable landmarks. It was built by the Earl in 1785, in honour of his cousin MRS

Downhill

FRIDESWIDE MUSSENDEN, who died at the age of 22. The design of the temple is based on the TEMPLE OF VESTA at Tivoli outside Rome. It is now maintained by the National Trust and is open to the public.

Mussenden Temple

The Mitred Earl also started to build himself another great pile at MAGHERA called BALLYSCULLION HOUSE. The design of this was modelled on his home at Ickworth, in Suffolk, England, and consisted of a huge central dome flanked by long, curving wings. There was a window for every day of the year, but this was the time of the window tax and the house became uneconomical and was never finished. It was eventually dismantled by the Earl's descendants and the central portico now adorns ST GEORGE'S CHURCH in Belfast High Street (*see* Belfast, page 211). Across the fields from Ballyscullion, on the inaccessible Church Island, there is an elegant spire without a church, known as HERVEY'S FOLLY, which the Mitred Earl had put up as a vista from Ballyscullion House.

The Mitred Earl was a well-known traveller on the Continent and many Bristol Hotels around the world are named after him.

Well, I never knew this
ABOUT
COUNTY DERRY

MAGILLIGAN STRAND, running for 6 miles (10 km) from the mouth of Lough Foyle towards Portstewart, is THE LONGEST BEACH IN IRELAND.

Nobel Prize-winning writer SEAMUS HEANEY was born in 'MOSSBAWN', his family's farmhouse near CASTLEDAWSON, in 1939.

In 1851 MISS JANE ROSS stood in the doorway of her house in LIMAVADY and listened to a haunting tune being played by an itinerant fiddler, probably blind JIMMY MCCURRY, in the market opposite. She was so taken with the melody that she wrote it down, and it was published in 1855 in a book called *The Ancient Music of Ireland* by GEORGE PETRIE. The tune became known as 'The Londonderry Air', and is ONE OF THE MOST WIDELY PLAYED AND RECOGNISED PIECES OF MUSIC ANYWHERE IN THE WORLD. The words of the popular song 'Danny Boy' were put to the tune of the Londonderry Air by an English lawyer called FRED WEATHERLY in 1913.

WILLIAM MASSEY (1856–1925), PRIME MINISTER OF NEW ZEALAND 1912–25, was born in LIMAVADY, the son of a farmer. He emigrated to New Zealand with his family at the age of 14.

SIR JAMES MURRAY (1788–1871), the inventor of MILK OF MAGNESIA, was born in CULNADY, Co. Derry. He moved to Belfast to become an apothecary and was on hand to comfort the Lord Lieutenant, the 1ST MARQUESS OF ANGLESEY, when he went down with a bad stomach upset. Murray gave him some of the medicine he had been developing from liquid magnesium at his dispensary, which he called MURRAY'S FLUID MAGNESIA. It proved so effective that in 1831 Murray was made resident physician to the Lord Lieutenant in Dublin, and was knighted in 1833.

The WILLIAM CLARKE & SONS factory in UPPERLANDS near Maghera, established in 1726, is THE OLDEST LINEN FACTORY IN IRELAND.

CHARLES THOMSON (1730–1824), permanent secretary of the Continental Congress of America, was born in UPPERLANDS, Co. Derry, and emigrated to America with his brothers when he was 11 years old. In 1782 he designed the GREAT SEAL OF AMERICA and he also wrote, and signed, the first draft of the DECLARATION OF INDEPENDENCE, before it was refined by Thomas Jefferson.

It turns out that DRACULA may have been an Irishman. In a field just outside SLAUGHTAVERTY, near GARVAGH, there is a monument known as ABHARTACH'S SEPULCHRE, marking the tomb of an evil and tyrannical chieftain, ABHARTACH. His put-upon people appealed to the great warrior CATHRAIN to rid them of this monster and Abhartach was duly dispatched and buried, standing up. Two days later he emerged from his grave to seek out his treacherous subjects and drink their blood. Cathrain slew him again, but again he returned and drank of their blood. This went on until Cathrain eventually consulted a local religious man who informed him that Abhartach had joined the *neamh-mairbh* or undead. He could not be killed, but he could be restrained by running him through with a wooden sword and then burying him upside-down, surrounded by thorn trees. Cathrain followed these instructions and the people were freed at last from their wicked overlord – although there have been tales of spine-chilling cries in the night and animals disappearing in the neighbourhood. Abhartach is believed by some to be the inspiration behind Dublin-born writer BRAM STOKER'S creation COUNT DRACULA.

County Donegal

Ruins of Donegal Castle, begun in 1505 by Donegal's ruling family the O'Donnells

Lough Swilly

Comings and Goings

Lough Swilly is a gloriously desolate and scenic sea lough, some 30 miles (50 km) long, that separates the Inishowen Peninsula from the rest of Donegal. The lough is deep enough to allow for quite large vessels and this, allied to its remoteness, has made it the perfect place for smuggling goods or people in and out of the country. Consequently, Lough Swilly has seen more than its fair share of intrigue and adventure and has played host to some pivotal events in Ireland's turbulent history.

Red Hugh

In 1587 at RATHMULLAN, a small port on the western shore of Lough Swilly, a cruel trick was played upon 15-year-old RED HUGH O'DONNELL, heir to the O'Donnell titles, which led to years of bitter warfare ended only by the FLIGHT OF THE EARLS in 1607.

The Lord Deputy of Ireland, SIR JOHN PERROTT, had became alarmed at talk of an alliance between two great Ulster clans, the O'Donnells and the O'Neills, and devised a plan to put a stop to it.

Red Hugh O'Donnell was staying with the MacSweenys in their castle down on the beach at Rathmullan, when a merchant ship dropped anchor offshore. The ship was loaded with Spanish wine and began a brisk trade with the townsfolk. Word reached the castle about the excellent quality of the wine, and quite naturally the MacSweenys put in a large order. The captain of the vessel was delighted, and invited the family and their guests on board for dinner and the chance to sample some of the cargo. The hospitality was generous, so generous in fact, that, to a man, the visitors all fell asleep. The hatches were battened down, the ship slipped anchor, and the next thing Red Hugh O'Donnell knew, he was waking up with a headache, anchored in Dublin Bay. He was hauled off to imprisonment in Dublin Castle, where he languished and plotted his revenge.

In 1592 he managed to escape and the next year, succeeding to the title of LORD OF TYRCONNELL, he joined forces with fellow Ulster chief HUGH O'NEILL, EARL OF TYRONE, and declared open rebellion against the English. There followed the NINE YEARS WAR, which saw the Ulster forces achieve some considerable successes. However, after defeat at the BATTLE OF KINSALE in 1601, Red Hugh fled to Spain, where he died in 1602.

Flight of the Earls

On 4 September 1607 little Rathmullan was again the scene of notable events, this time the mysterious FLIGHT OF THE EARLS. The EARL OF TYRONE and Red Hugh's successor the EARL OF TYRCONNELL, along with their families and a significant number of the northern Gaelic nobility, arrived in the town in some disarray, boarded a ship and departed for Spain, never again to see Ireland. Such was their haste that the Earl of Tyrone left his young son Con behind, while the Earl of Tyrconnell sailed without his pregnant wife.

To this day no one quite knows why they left in such haste. After the Nine Years War had been brought to an uneasy conclusion by the TREATY OF MELLIFONT in 1603, relations between Catholics and Protestants were strained. Hostilities seemed likely to break out at any moment, and eventually something caused the Ulster Earls to flee, whether to try and raise support in Spain for a further rebellion or because they were in fear of their lives, no one knows. They never made it to Spain but were forced by bad weather to land in France and eventually ended their days in Rome. By apparently abandoning their estates, the Ulster Earls opened the way for the ULSTER PLANTATIONS of 1609, whereby their vacant lands were granted to immigrant Protestant families, mostly from Scotland.

There is a heritage centre in Rathmullan that tells the story of the Flight of the Earls.

in 1683. He founded THE FIRST PRESBYTERIAN COMMUNITY IN AMERICA at SNOW HILL in Maryland, where there is now a Makemie Memorial Presbyterian Church. Later, Makemie founded a church at REHOBETH in Maryland, which stands to this day as AMERICA'S OLDEST PRESBYTERIAN CHURCH.

JAMES BUCHANAN, father of the 15TH (and only bachelor) PRESIDENT OF THE UNITED STATES OF AMERICA, JAMES BUCHANAN, was born in Ramelton in 1761.

Ramelton

RAMELTON, a small port on Lough Swilly with wide tree-lined streets and some fine Georgian buildings, is home to THE OLDEST PRESBYTERIAN CHURCH, OR MEETING HOUSE, IN IRELAND. It was built in 1680. Ramelton was the birthplace of FRANCIS MAKEMIE (1658–1708), known as THE FATHER OF AMERICAN PRESBYTERIANISM, who worshipped at the Old Meeting House before being sent to America as a missionary

Wolfe Tone

In 1798 the captive WOLFE TONE was imprisoned in a small castle near BUNCRANA on the eastern shore of Lough Swilly, after his abortive attempt to land in Donegal with French troops in support of the 1798 REBELLION. Tone was captured aboard the French warship *Hoche* in a fierce fight against an English fleet off Lough Swilly. From Buncrana he was taken to Dublin, where he was sentenced to be hanged but slit his

The Meeting House, Ramelton

own throat before he could be executed (*see* Co. Kildare, page 67). The ruins of the castle where Wolfe Tone was held can still be seen by the shore, a little to the north-west of Buncrana.

Lough Derg

The Entrance to the Underworld

Lurking in the bleak hills and heathery bogland east of Donegal Town is grey, chill, rain-swept LOUGH DERG. On an island in the middle of the lough is a small, dark cave. Be afraid, for here is the ENTRANCE TO THE UNDERWORLD.

In more simple times it was believed that the souls of those about to die flew towards the dying embers of the sun as it set in the west, and there they would enter the UNDERWORLD for the FINAL JUDGEMENT. And in those days the UTMOST WEST was Ireland, where the sun sank into the sea, almost beyond the known world. So this must be where the entrance lay. Here, if a man had the courage, he could enter the cave, experience PURGATORY, have his soul purged of sin and then return to life, obviating the need to revisit Purgatory after death.

Only the most virtuous, such as St Patrick, survived. Ireland's Patron Saint is said to have spent many days in Purgatory on the island during which time he slew a huge dragon, which stained the waters of the lough red with its blood – hence the name Derg,

from the Irish *dearg* meaning 'red'.

STATION ISLAND, the site of the cave, has become ONE OF THE MOST FAMOUS SITES OF PILGRIMAGE IN ALL OF EUROPE. Every summer for over 800 years, thousands of Catholics have come here between June and August for THE PILGRIMAGE OF ST PATRICK'S PURGATORY. In 1152, TIERNAN O'ROURKE, Prince of Breffni, came here, only to return home to find his wife DEVORGILLA gone (*see* Co. Leitrim, page 16), an event that rewrote Ireland's destiny.

The cave has long since been blocked off and the island is now completely covered by a complex of hostels and religious buildings, including a vast basilica built in 1921. Only pilgrims may visit the island, where they must survive for three days with only one meal of bread and tea a day. Even for those not making the pilgrimage, the atmosphere of this desolate location is at once exciting, powerful and daunting.

Tory Island

Keep Off

TORY ISLAND is a tiny speck of rock off the north-west tip of Co. Donegal, often cut off for days at a time by bad weather. The island is home to a small community of artists who run an art gallery in the main village of West Town. The inhabitants mostly speak Gaelic and have a strong sense of independence, even electing their own KING OF TORY, whose job is to promote and protect the interests of the Tory islanders.

In 1884 a gunboat, the *Wasp*, was sent to collect taxes from the islanders but was wrecked on rocks near the lighthouse and broke up with the loss of 52 lives. In the 1970s the Irish government tried to evacuate the islanders to council houses on the mainland, so that they could use the island as an artillery firing range, but the islanders refused to move and stayed put. On Friday 13th in June 2003 a boat full of contestants for a new RTE reality television show called *Cabin Fever* hit the rocks off Tory Island and sank, with no loss of life but causing the show to be postponed for some considerable time.

TORY was a word for Irish bandits who robbed and plundered in the north-west of Ireland during the 17th-century English Civil War between Parliament and the King. They purported to be on the side of the Crown, and hence the name was subsequently applied to those who upheld the prerogatives of the Crown. In time the name was given to those who resisted change and protected the old order, or conservatives, which is why the modern-day Conservative Party in British politics is known as the 'Tory' Party.

Well, I never knew this
ABOUT
COUNTY DONEGAL

INISHTRAHULL ISLAND, 4 miles (7 km) north of the Inishowen Peninsula, is THE NORTHERNMOST POINT OF IRELAND.

A headland 1 mile (1.6 km) from MALIN HEAD is THE NORTHERNMOST POINT OF MAINLAND IRELAND.

All SPOT HEIGHTS recorded on Ordnance Survey of Ireland maps are measured from the mean sea level at MALIN HEAD.

The greatest of Ireland's 'Annals' or histories, *The Annals of the Four Masters*, was compiled in Co. Donegal between 1630 and 1636 by MICHAEL O'CLEARY, a Franciscan friar of Donegal Abbey. He was assisted by PEREGRINE O'CLEARY, PEREGRINE DUIGNAN and FEARFEASA O'MUL-CONRY. The *Annals*, written in Irish, were mainly a compilation of earlier annals, with some original material added, and cover Irish history from around AD 550 until 1636.

LETTERKENNY, the largest town in Co. Donegal, has THE LONGEST MAIN STREET IN IRELAND. The town is dominated by the 215 ft-high (65 m) spire of ST EUNAN'S, CO. DONEGAL'S ONLY CATHEDRAL.

The cliffs at SLIEVE LEAGUE, drop-

St Eunan's Cathedral,
Letterkenny

ping 1,972 ft (601 m) to the sea, are THE SECOND-HIGHEST SEA CLIFFS IN EUROPE, after those on Achill Island.

ARRANMORE IS THE SECOND-LARGEST ISLAND OFF IRELAND.

ARRANMORE UNITED are THE ONLY ISLAND FOOTBALL TEAM TO PLAY IN AN IRISH MAINLAND LEAGUE.

The singer ENYA was born in GWEEDORE, Co. Donegal, in 1961. One of nine children, she spent most of her childhood in Gweedore. In 1980 Enya fronted the Irish folk music group CLANNAD, which was made up of members of her family. In 1982 she embarked upon a solo career and has become ONE OF IRELAND'S MOST SUCCESSFUL INTER-NATIONAL ARTISTS.

CAVANACOR HOUSE is a pleasant early 17th-century house near Lifford. It was the birthplace in 1634 of MAGDALENE TASKER, who grew up to marry a fellow native of Co. Donegal, ROBERT POLLOCK. They and their children emigrated to America and settled in Maryland. They shortened their name to Polk, and in 1845 Magdalene's great-great-great-grandson JAMES KNOX POLK became the 11TH PRESIDENT OF THE UNITED STATES OF AMERICA. Polk was a quiet, unassuming man, of short stature, and when he walked into a room no-one took any notice of him at all. This enraged his spirited wife Sarah and she ordained thereafter that the song 'Hail to the Chief' be played whenever her husband made an entrance – a tradition honoured by all Presidents to this day.

West of Dunfanaghy at the north end of Tramore Strand is MACSWEENEY'S GUN, a massive blow-hole. In stormy weather the sea rushes in with a bang that they say can be heard in Derry.

BLOODY FORELAND is at the north-west tip of Co. Donegal and gets its name from the red hue of the rocks, particularly when lit up by the sunset.

County Donegal has IRELAND'S LARGEST GAELTACHT. A Gaeltacht is an area where Gaelic is spoken as the primary language.

ST COLUMBA, one of Ireland's most celebrated saints, was a native of Co. Donegal. He was born near GARTAN LOUGH, north-west of Letterkenny, in AD 521. There is a flagstone at LACKNACOO, on the west shore of the lough, which marks the exact spot. About 1 mile (1.6 km) north of here, in Churchtown, there are two stone crosses marking the site of his first foundation. St Columba later established the famous abbey on the Scottish island of IONA, as penance for his part in the BATTLE OF THE BOOKS (*see* Co. Sligo, page 36).

In the 1930s HENRY MCILHENNY, the Irish-American art connoiseur and owner of GLENVEAGH CASTLE, Co. Donegal, created THE LARGEST HEATED SWIMMING POOL EVER SEEN when he installed steam pipes in the lake near his home to heat the water for a pool party of visiting Hollywood guests.

COUNTY DOWN

an Dun – 'fort'

Stormont, completed in 1932, is the headquarters of government in Northern Ireland

Hillsborough

The Birthplace of the United States of America

The course of history was changed at HILLSBOROUGH, an elegant show-piece Georgian town 12 miles (19 km) south of Belfast. It takes its name from SIR ARTHUR HILL, builder of HILLSBOROUGH FORT in 1650. In October 1771 BENJAMIN FRANKLIN, on a diplomatic mission to Britain as the American Colonial Envoy, stayed at Hillsborough as a guest of WILLS HILL, 1ST MARQUESS OF DOWNSHIRE, Colonial Secretary for KING GEORGE III. Hill and Franklin sat down to try and find an amicable solution to the problems between Britain and her American colonies, but they loathed each other on sight. Franklin described Wills Hill thus: *'his character is conceit, wrong-headedness, obstinacy and passion.'* Franklin went back to America and

Hillsborough Fort

told the anxious colonists that there was no alternative but revolution, and in 1776 they issued THE DECLARATION OF INDEPENDENCE. George III ever after blamed Wills Hill for losing the American colonies.

HILLSBOROUGH CASTLE, completed in 1797, sits back from the road behind magnificent wrought-iron gates and is now the Monarch's official residence in Ireland and seat of the Secretary of State for Northern Ireland.

It was also at Hillsborough that HARRY FERGUSON (1884–1960), the 'MAD MECHANIC', became THE FIRST IRISHMAN TO FLY. Ferguson was born on the family farm at GROWELL, some 3 miles (5 km) outside Hillsborough. He didn't take to farming and instead joined his brother's car and cycle repair business in Belfast. He was inspired to fly by Blériot's cross-Channel flight in January 1909, and in that same year he built his own monoplane, with which he made IRELAND'S FIRST POWERED FLIGHT on 31 December 1909 – flying 390 ft (119 m) at a height of 12 ft (3.7 m) above Hillsborough Park.

Ferguson went on to build the lightweight grey-painted tractors

affectionately known as 'Fergies' for which he is famous, and also to design the FERGUSON SYSTEM, which allowed the tractor driver to operate any machinery he was towing from the safety of the driver's seat, with a system of hydraulics. His inventions were responsible for helping to transform and modernise agriculture all over the world.

Another of Ferguson's creations was an early form of four-wheel drive known as the FERGUSON FORMULA, employed in one of the world's most stylish and exciting classic cars, the JENSEN FF.

Castle Ward

A Tale of Two Houses

CASTLE WARD, set resplendently above Strangford Lough, is one of the most extraordinary and intriguing houses in Ireland. It is really two houses in one, one Strawberry Hill Gothic, one Classical – a monument to the different tastes of husband and wife.

On the outside it looks as though the husband, BERNARD WARD, later 1ST VISCOUNT BANGOR, got the better of the deal, with a Classical

Castle Ward garden front

entrance front and two Classical sides. However, his wife, LADY ANNE WARD, got the garden front, which can be seen from the lough, and of course she could sit inside and look at the gorgeous view framed in her beloved Gothic windows.

The conundrum continues inside, and here Lady Anne prevails, with some sumptuous Gothic interiors on the garden side that defy description – her boudoir resembles nothing so much as a huge raspberry and meringue pudding. Wandering through the house from Gothic to Classical and then back to Gothic again is a strange but entertaining experience. It can leave the visitor a little dazed, and certainly in no fit state to confront Castle Ward's

Castle Ward entrance front

supreme challenge – the SQUIRRELS' BOXING MATCH. Installed in Victorian times in the Morning Room, it is a tableau of stuffed squirrels dressed in bloomers and wearing boxing gloves, competing in an unnervingly realistic, choreographed boxing match – a sight to make the strongest quail.

A revivifying stroll in the glorious grounds is recommended. Castle Ward is now a National Trust property.

Helen's Tower

A Symbol of Ulster
Helen's Tower, here I stand,
Dominant over sea and land.
Son's love built me and I hold
Mother's love in letter'd gold.
TENNYSON

HELEN'S TOWER stands proudly on a hilltop, at the edge of the Marchioness of Dufferin and Ava's CLANDEBOYE estate on the southern shores of Belfast Lough. A turreted folly, it was erected in 1862 in honour of the 1st Marquess's mother HELEN, composer of the ballad 'THE LAMENT OF THE IRISH EMIGRANT', and granddaughter of the playwright RICHARD BRINSLEY SHERIDAN.

The tower is not just a prominent landmark but something of a symbol of Ulster. In 1921 a replica known as the ULSTER TOWER was built close to the site of the BATTLE OF THE SOMME in France, as a memorial to the soldiers of the ULSTER DIVISION who fought and died there. They had done their training on the Clandeboye estate, and Helen's Tower would have been almost the last thing in Ulster they saw as they sailed for France – some 5,000 soldiers of the Ulster Division died on the first day of the Battle of the Somme in July 1916.

Thomas Andrews Jr

He went down with his ship

THOMAS ANDREWS JR, Managing Director and Chief Naval Architect of Harland and Wolff, the man responsible for overseeing the design of the *Titanic*, was born in ARDARA HOUSE, COMBER, in 1873. His father owned the Andrews Linen Mill in Comber, which operated until 1997.

Andrews Jr always went along on the maiden voyage of the ships in his charge and was one of more than 1,500 people who went down with *Titanic* when it struck an iceburg and sank on 15 April 1912. The first man to realise that the ship was doomed, Andrews spent his last moments checking as many cabins and staterooms as he could, urging passengers to put on their lifejackets and make for the lifeboats.

In the hugely successful Oscar-winning 1997 film *Titanic*, starring LEONARDO DI CAPRIO and KATE WINSLET, Andrews was sympathetically portrayed by the actor VICTOR GARBER.

The Belfast house where Andrews lived with his wife HELEN, in WINDSOR AVENUE, is now the head-quarters of the IRISH FOOTBALL ASSOCIATION.

In 1914 the THOMAS ANDREWS JR MEMORIAL HALL was built in Comber, the foundation stones laid by his daughter Elba and mother Eliza.

Killyleagh

A Family Feud, a Frenchman and Drinking Chocolate

KILLYLEAGH CASTLE, dominating the attractive little port of KILLYLEAGH, on Strangford Lough, is one of THE OLDEST INHABITED CASTLES IN IRELAND. It dates from 1180 and is the only one of the series of castles built by the Norman knight JOHN DE COURCY that is still lived in and not a ruin.

Killyleagh Castle

In the 17th century the castle was owned by HENRY HAMILTON, 2ND EARL OF CLANBRASSIL, who was poisoned by his wife after changing his will in her favour – disinheriting his Hamilton cousins, the rightful heirs. The cousins contested the will, and after a court case that lasted for two generations it was ruled that the property should be divided. The castle went to Gawn Hamilton, and the huge bawn and gatehouse to his cousin Anne, and hence by inheritance to the BLACKWOOD family. For over 100 years the feuding camps confronted each other from opposite ends of the bawn. The Blackwoods, who were to become the LORDS DUFFERIN, provocatively built the gatehouse up into a splendid Georgian residence, even though their main residence was at CLANDEBOYE (*see* Helen's Tower, page 266).

Eventually the 5th Lord Dufferin fell in love with, and married, the daughter of the Hamiltons in the cas-

tle, and agreed to give the gatehouse and bawn back to his in-laws in return for a pair of silver spurs and a golden rose, on alternate years. He also rebuilt the gatehouse in a more suitable Baronial style, while his father-in-law enlarged and embellished the castle into the romantic jumble of turrets and spires that we see today.

In the Middle Ages the Castle was owned by a number of prominent Co. Down families, mainly the WHITES and the McCARTANS. French President CHARLES DE GAULLE (1890–1970) was descended, on his mother's side, from the McCARTANS of Co. Down.

The man who gave us DRINKING CHOCOLATE and the BRITISH MUSEUM, SIR HANS SLOANE, 1ST BT. (1660–1753), was born in Killyleagh. Hans Sloane

The Gatehouse at Killyleagh Castle

trained as a physician and in 1687 he was appointed Surgeon to the West Indies fleet. During his time in the Caribbean he became particularly fond of the local cocoa drink and discovered that adding milk rendered it more palatable to European tastes. On his return to England he began to sell his 'MILK CHOCOLATE' as a health remedy. In the 19th century JOHN CADBURY picked up on the recipe and built a chocolate empire on the strength of it – Hans Sloane's drinking chocolate was the first chocolate product Cadbury's ever made.

When Hans Sloane settled in London, he started to build up a collection of books, antiquities and plants from all over the world, funded by his successful physician's practice, his Caribbean investments and his wife's fortune. He left this collection to the nation and it formed the nucleus of the new British Museum at Montague House in Bloomsbury.

There is a memorial to Hans Sloane, mounted on a boulder, that stands close to Killyleagh Castle, and a new statue of him has been erected down by the harbour.

Well, I never knew this
ABOUT
COUNTY DOWN

BIG BOW MEEL ISLAND, half a mile (800 m) off the Ards Peninsula, is IRELAND'S MOST EASTERLY POINT.

BURR POINT, 1 mile (1.6 km) south of the village of BALLYHALBERT on the Ards Pensinsula, is THE MOST EASTERLY POINT ON THE MAINLAND OF IRELAND.

The ROYAL BELFAST GOLF CLUB, founded in 1881 and now based at CRAIGAVAD, is IRELAND'S OLDEST GOLF CLUB.

The important fishing town of ARDGLASS possesses MORE MEDIEVAL TOWER HOUSES THAN ANY OTHER TOWN IN IRELAND, with a total of four.

The BALLYCOPELAND WINDMILL near Millisle, built around 1780, IS THE LAST WORKING WINDMILL IN ULSTER.

On the main street in HOLYWOOD you can find THE ONLY MAYPOLE IN IRELAND.

The prosperous town of BANBRIDGE boasts IRELAND'S FIRST UNDERPASS. Known as THE CUT, it was constructed in 1834 to help horses negotiate the steep main street.

The marina at BANGOR is THE LARGEST MARINA IN IRELAND.

STRANGFORD LOUGH is THE LARGEST INLET IN IRELAND OR BRITAIN.

The former Ferrari Formula One motor-racing driver EDDIE IRVINE was born in NEWTOWNARDS in 1965.

The NEWRY CANAL, linking Lough Neagh with Newry, opened in 1741 and is THE OLDEST SUMMIT CANAL IN IRELAND OR BRITAIN. A series of six locks takes the canal from the River Bann at Portadown up to the summit at POYNTZPASS, 82 ft (25 m) above sea level, from where another nine locks descend into Newry. The canal was last used commercially in 1937 but remains in a good state of repair. Many of the locks, quays, and docks associated with the canal survive and can be visited along the towpath, which is part of the Ulster Way.

ST PATRICK'S CHURCH in NEWRY, dating from 1578, is THE FIRST CHURCH TO BE BUILT FOR THE PROTESTANT FAITH IN IRELAND.

SIR JAMES MARTIN (1893–1981), INVENTOR OF THE EJECTOR SEAT, was born in CROSSGAR, Co. Down. His ejector seat was first tested on a human in 1946 and within 12 months every new British military plane was fitted with one. Martin was motivated to find a way of enabling pilots to escape from doomed aircraft when his business partner, CAPTAIN VALENTINE BAKER, was killed during an emergency landing in 1942. The MARTIN-BAKER COMPANY still exists, making ejector seats and crash-resistant seats for passenger planes. The 3-ft high (1 m) James Martin Memorial Stone has been erected in his memory in Crossgar.

Built in 1611, GRACE NEILL'S BAR in DONAGHADEE on the Ards Peninsula is THE OLDEST PUB IN IRELAND.

At SAUL, just to the east of Downpatrick, there is the replica of a small early church with a round tower, signifying the place where ST PATRICK FIRST PREACHED IN IRELAND, in AD 432. He stepped

Down Cathedral

Mountains o' Mourne sweep down to the sea'.

In the late 1950s SHORTS produced the YORK NOBEL BUBBLE CAR under licence at their factory in NEWTOWNARDS. It was originally a three-wheeler but progressed to four wheels, with the two small back wheels placed very close together. It could be bought in kit form.

ashore, on his mission to convert the Irish to Christianity, where the Slaney River flows into Strangford Lough. St Patrick also died at Saul in AD 461 and is buried in the graveyard of DOWN CATHEDRAL in nearby DOWN-PATRICK, beneath an enormous rough block of granite inscribed with the word PATRIC in old Irish letters. ST BRIGID and ST COLUMBA are reputed to be buried here also.

PATRICK PRUNTY, later BRONTË, (1777–1861), the father of the three famous Brontë sisters ANNE, EMILY and CHARLOTTE, was born in a small cottage in EMDALE, near Banbridge. The ruins of the cottage are preserved and marked with a plaque.

There is a PERCY FRENCH MEMORIAL FOUNTAIN in NEWCASTLE where, in the words of his famous song, 'the

The family of JOHN HANCOCK, THE FIRST PERSON TO SIGN THE AMERICAN DECLARATION OF INDEPENDENCE, came from Co. Down.

MAJOR-GENERAL ROBERT ROSS from ROSTREVOR, Co. Down, commanded the British troops who set fire to the EXECUTIVE MANSION IN WASHINGTON DC on the night of 24 August 1814. PRESIDENT MADISON'S vivacious wife DOLLEY was so upset by the smoke-blackened walls that she insisted on having them painted white, the colour they have remained ever since. THEODORE ROOSEVELT, some of whose ancestors hailed from Co. Antrim, was the first President to officially use the name THE WHITE HOUSE.

COUNTY FERMANAGH

COUNTY TOWN: ENNISKILLEN

Fear Manach – 'Manach's men'

The Celtic 'Janus Idol'

Lough Erne

A Lusty Man

UPPER AND LOWER LOUGH ERNE COVER ONE THIRD OF COUNTY FERMANAGH and are home to something like 5 PER CENT OF THE WORLD'S WHOOPER SWANS. In early Christian days the loughs were an important highway from the sea at Ballyshannon to deep into the heart of Ireland. Monasteries sprang up on many of the hundreds of tiny islands and inlets that are scattered along the way, as ports of call and places where travellers could worship, rest and feed.

The most spectacular remains are on DEVENISH ISLAND, just north of Enniskillen, which was an important religious centre up until the 17th century. A monastery was founded here by ST MOLAISE in the 6th century but was constantly sacked by Viking raids, and the ruins are from a medieval monastery. The perfect 12th-century round tower is 82 ft (25 m) high and is THE BEST-PRESERVED ROUND TOWER IN IRELAND. All five floors can be reached by ladders inside. The roof is supported by a cornice with a human face carved above each of the four windows – A UNIQUE FEATURE FOUND ON NO OTHER ROUND TOWER IN IRELAND. There is a regular boat service to the island.

On WHITE ISLAND, off the eastern shore of Lower Lough Erne, are the remains of a delightful Romanesque church with a parade of eight EXTRAORDINARY AND UNIQUE CARVED STONE FIGURES set into one wall, dating from the 9th or 10th century.

In the ancient CALDRAGH CEMETERY on BOA ISLAND, at the northern end of Lough Erne, are the magical treasures of Co. Fermanagh, the JANUS IDOL and the LUSTY MAN. These are two of the most recognisable and photographed examples of 'Celtic' art in the world. The Janus Idol is, in fact, two figures carved back to back, the east side being only too obviously male and the west side female, with a protruding

tongue. The Lusty Man, considerably more weathered, was brought here from the nearby private Lusty More Island. This figure is clearly blind in one eye and may represent BADHBHA or the DIVINE HAG – the name Boa is an anglicisation of her name. They were both carved over 1,000 years ago in the 8th century and nobody quite knows what to make of them. What is undeniable is that there is nothing quite like them anywhere else, and it is well worth while making the effort to find them – no easy task in this remote and very distinctive part of Ireland.

Round Tower, Devenish Island

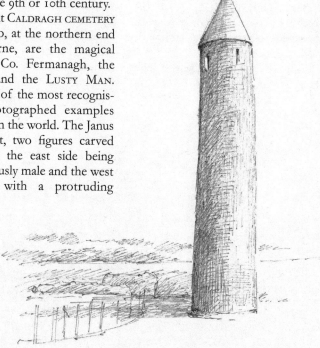

Crom

The Birds and the Trees

CROM CASTLE is a huge castellated pile on the shores of Upper Lough Erne, designed in the 1830s by EDWARD BLORE for the 3RD EARL OF ERNE. In the old plantation castle garden is a remarkable arborial citadel, two magnificent yew trees, well over 800 years old, that have grown together to create THE LARGEST YEW TREE IN IRELAND. The EARL OF TYRONE is said to have bade farewell to his lady love under this yew tree before embarking for Spain during the FLIGHT OF THE EARLS (*see* Co. Donegal, page 256).

On GAD ISLAND in the middle of Upper Lough Erne is CRICHTON TOWER, built in 1847 to provide work during the Great Famine and once used as an observatory.

Since 1987, 1,900 acres of the Crom estate, including ONE OF THE LARGEST SURVIVING AREAS OF OAK WOODLAND IN IRELAND and THE LARGEST HERONRY IN IRELAND, have been administered by the National Trust.

Noon's Hole

Revenge of the Ribbonmen

NOON'S HOLE, THE DEEPEST POTHOLE IN IRELAND, lies 3 miles (5 km) north-west of the village of BOHO, in the limestone hills west of Enniskillen. It is 250 ft (76 m) deep and gets its name from a notorious murder. DOMINICK NOON was a colourful character who arrived in the area from Co. Roscommon and supposedly earned his living as a highwayman. He was, more importantly, a member of the RIBBONMEN, an illegal secret organisation formed to defend Catholic farmers from the Orangemen.

Crom Castle

One day, out of the blue, several local men were arrested and tried, with one, John Maguire, being sentenced to transportation. Noon's colleagues began to suspect that he was an informer, so they lured him up into the hills one dark night in 1826 and bludgeoned him to death. Then they hurled his body down the pothole. Unfortunately for them the corpse got caught on a ledge and was recovered eight days later after a tip-off. Despite a thorough investigation none of his murderers was ever caught – although a number of local men suddenly emigrated to America around that time.

In 1912 four potholers made the first descent of Noon's Hole, using a rope ladder. They didn't find much at the bottom except a small 'dungeon-like' space, with a short passageway leading off it to a watery dead end.

Well, I never knew this

ABOUT

COUNTY FERMANAGH

The playwright and wit OSCAR WILDE, Nobel prize-winning playwright SAMUEL BECKETT and hymn writer HENRY FRANCIS LYTE ('Abide with Me') were all pupils at PORTORA ROYAL SCHOOL in ENNISKILLEN, founded in 1628 by KING JAMES I.

CASTLE COOLE, just south of Enniskillen, is regarded as THE FINEST CLASSICAL COUNTRY HOUSE IN IRELAND. It was built in 1790–8 and designed by JAMES WYATT for the 1ST EARL BELMORE. The house has no back door, a deliberate omission to discourage salesmen from calling. Lough Coole, overlooked by the house, is home to THE ONLY BREEDING COLONY OF GREY-LAG GEESE IN IRELAND. They were introduced in 1700 and it is said that if ever the geese leave, then the Belmores will leave too. The house is now owned by the National Trust.

Castle Coole

In the grounds of FLORENCE COURT, an 18th-century Palladian house built for the Cole family, Earls of Enniskillen, you can find THE MOTHER OF ALL IRISH YEW TREES. In 1740 a Fermanagh man called GEORGE WILLIS was walking on nearby Cuilcagh, the mountain Co. Fermanagh shares with Co. Cavan, when he came across two unusual yew seedlings which he took with him and transplanted, one in his own garden and one at Florence Court. The trees proved to be of a particularly elegant upright variety, and cuttings from this 'Irish' yew were, and still are, much sought after all over the world, since it can only be reproduced from these cuttings. Willis's tree died, but the original Florence Court tree survives and can still be seen on the edge of Cottage Wood, at the end of a woodland trail to the south-east of the house, now owned by the National Trust.

The tour of the MARBLE ARCH CAVES, in the Cuilcagh Mountain, is THE ONLY CAVE TOUR IN IRELAND THAT INCLUDES A BOAT RIDE. The 30 ft (9 m) limestone marble arch itself stands outside the cave system in the glen where the Cladagh river emerges from the mountainside.

The tiny riverside village of BELLEEK, in the far west of Co. Fermanagh, is the home of the world-famous BELLEEK POTTERY, which has been made here since 1857 and is IRELAND'S OLDEST POTTERY. The company is known for its distinctive pearl-white PARIAN china, which resembles the Parian marble of Ancient Greece. No two pieces are ever made alike and founder JOHN CALDWELL BLOOMFIELD stipulated that any item with even the slightest flaw should be destroyed, a policy that is applied today. Belleek pottery is particularly popular in America.

The REV. JAMES MACDONALD, from the quiet village of BALLINAMALLARD, north of Enniskillen, certainly left his mark on society. Two of his daughters married the painters SIR EDWARD BURNE-JONES and SIR EDWARD POYNTER, another became the mother of the author RUDYARD KIPLING and a fourth became the mother of British Prime Minister STANLEY BALDWIN.

In the middle of the 18th century John Armstrong emigrated to America from Co. Fermanagh. His great-great-great-grandson was THE FIRST MAN ON THE MOON, NEIL ARMSTRONG.

The family of US PRESIDENT BILL CLINTON hails from ROSLEA in Co. Fermanagh according to Clinton family legend.

BROOKEBOROUGH, east of Enniskillen, is the ancestral home of World War Two leader FIELD MARSHAL 1ST VISCOUNT ALANBROOKE (1883–1963). The ONLY DIAMOND EVER FOUND IN IRELAND was discovered early in the 19th century in the Colebrook river at Brookeborough and now belongs to the Brooke family, Lords Brookeborough.

JAMES GAMBLE, co-founder of the soap company PROCTOR AND GAMBLE, was born in 1802 to a travelling Methodist minister thought to have come from ENNISKILLEN. James Gamble emigrated to Cincinnati, Ohio, in 1819 and merged his soap company with William Proctor's candle-making business in 1837. In 1932 the Proctor and Gamble soap company became the first commercial backers of a daytime drama, sponsoring the *Puddle Family* radio show – THE FIRST 'SOAP' OPERA.

MICHAEL BARRETT, THE LAST MAN TO BE PUBLICLY HANGED IN IRELAND AND BRITAIN, was born near KESH in Co. Fermanagh. He was hanged outside Newgate prison in London on 26 May 1868, for his alleged part in an attempt to rescue two convicted Fenians, Burke and Casey, from Clerkenwell Prison. The operation involved exploding a keg of gunpowder next to the prison wall, and a young boy loitering in the vicinity was badly injured.

COUNTY MONAGHAN

COUNTY TOWN: MONAGHAN

Muineachain – 'place of small hills'

10th-century High Cross at Clones

Castle Leslie

Royal Retreat

Lost among the drumlins of little-known Co. Monaghan, not 60 miles (95 km) north of Dublin but some-how on a completely different planet, is glittering CASTLE LESLIE, a stone-grey Victorian pile set in glorious lacustrine landscape, and possessed of a guest book more full of celebrities than *Hello* magazine.

Castle Leslie has been the home

Castle Leslie

of the Leslies since 1665, when the remarkable 'FIGHTING' BISHOP OF CLOGHER, JOHN LESLIE, fell in love with the area and retired here. He married a much younger wife and started a family at the age of 67, eventually fathering five children. He died at the age of 100 in 1671 and is buried in Glaslough Church on the edge of the estate.

A later generation of Leslies were great friends with DEAN JONATHAN SWIFT, who became a regular visitor – and commentator:

> *Here I am in Castle Leslie,*
> *with rows and rows of books upon*
> *   the shelves,*
> *written by the Leslies,*
> *all about themselves.*

There has been plenty for the Leslies to write about down the years. CHARLES POWELL LESLIE, who took over the estate in 1743, was MP for Monaghan and was largely responsible for the education of his nephew by marriage, young ARTHUR WELLESLEY, the future Duke of Wellington, victor of the Battle of Waterloo in 1815.

Charles's grandson John, the 1ST BARONET OF GLASLOUGH, married CONSTANCE, the daughter of MINNIE SEYMOUR, GEORGE IV'S DAUGHTER by his morganatic marriage to MRS FITZHERBERT. Being of royal blood she was able to insist that her husband rebuild the house as a more comfortable place to live, and this is the Castle Leslie we see today. Its most striking feature is the delightful Italian Renaissance cloister copied from Michelangelo's cloister at SANTA MARIA DEGLI ANGELI in Rome. In her later years Constance invented a useful new table ornament, since adopted by fashionable hostesses everywhere, a huge floral display that she called '*un cache marie*' – 'a hide the husband'.

Their son John married the American beauty LEONIE JEROME, sister of WINSTON CHURCHILL'S MOTHER JENNIE JEROME, and

Winston would often come and visit his uncle and aunt at Castle Leslie, until he was banned by the former for espousing Home Rule. Churchill found a more sympathetic ear with his cousin the 3rd Baronet, who became a Catholic, was a passionate Irish nationalist and changed his name from John to the Irish SHANE.

SIR SHANE LESLIE was a prolific writer and poet, and in his day Castle Leslie was much frequented by leading Irish literary figures of the day such as GEORGE MOORE, WILLIAM BUTLER YEATS and OLIVER ST JOHN GOGARTY.

Yeats stayed in the RED BEDROOM, now haunted by Sir Shane's brother NORMAN, who fought THE LAST DUEL IN THE BRITISH ARMY and died heroically in World War One. As if being haunted were not scary enough, the Red Bedroom was at one time equipped with a trick witch who would leap out of the bathroom at unsuspecting guests, and on one occasion caused the French ambassador's wife to swoon clean away.

The huge, wonderfully deep, panelled bath in the Red Bedroom is thought to be THE FIRST BATH INSTALLED IN IRELAND.

Whilst in bed in the PRINT ROOM, the Poet Laureate SIR JOHN BETJEMAN wrote his controversial but oft-quoted lines, 'Come friendly bombs and rain on Slough . . .'

The MAUVE ROOM at Castle Leslie has played host to a stream of royal guests including the DUKE OF CONNAUGHT (Queen Victoria's youngest son) and his wife, and Grace Kelly's father-in-law PRINCE PIERRE OF MONACO. When QUEEN MARGARET OF SWEDEN was staying an infatuated neighbouring Earl hid himself in the wardrobe and then couldn't get out. He was eventually released in the middle of the night by the startled Queen, who had been rudely awoken by muffled bangs and curses emanating from her wardrobe. She was not amused.

Pop star MICK JAGGER stayed in the Mauve Room with MARIANNE FAITHFULL and was chased up the church tower in the village by a mob of reformatory girls who were picnicking in the park.

Castle Leslie is THE FIRST HOUSE IN IRELAND TO BOAST A LANDING SITE FOR UNIDENTIFIED FLYING OBJECTS. This was created by Sir Shane's son DESMOND LESLIE, a Spitfire pilot in World War Two and celebrated as the author of the seminal work *Flying Saucers Have Landed.* Leslie is also famed for having punched Bernard Levin on a television show.

One easily identified visitor was ex-Beatle PAUL McCARTNEY, who landed at Castle Leslie in 2002 for his wedding to model HEATHER MILLS. His guests included Elton John, Sting, Bono and Ringo Starr. McCartney was, in a way, coming home. His mother, MARY MOHAN, was a native of TULLY-NAMALROE near CASTLEBLAYNEY, Co. Monaghan.

Hope Castle

The Blues

In the 19th century, BLAYNEY CASTLE at CASTLEBLAYNEY was known as HOPE CASTLE and was the home of HENRY HOPE, owner of the infamous HOPE DIAMOND of 45.52 carats, THE WORLD'S LARGEST BLUE DIAMOND and THE MOST CURSED JEWEL IN HISTORY.

This magnificent gem, reputed to have been stolen from the eye of a statue of the Hindu goddess SITA, was brought to France from India in 1668 by a chap called TAVERNIER. When Tavernier returned to India he was torn apart by wild dogs. The diamond, which they named the FRENCH BLUE, became part of the French Crown Jewels and was worn by MARIE ANTOINETTE shortly before she went to the guillotine. Then it was stolen, along with the rest of the Crown Jewels, and disappeared, turning up in 1830 having been recut to its present size by a Dutch diamond cutter called WILHELM FALS. He died of a heart attack when the gem was pilfered by his son – who committed suicide not long afterwards.

At this point Henry Hope bought the jewel, naming it somewhat ironically the HOPE DIAMOND. The Hope family sold it again around the turn of the century and it passed through a number of unfortunate hands – an Eastern potentate gave it to a dancer at the Folies Bergère and shot her dead while she was on stage, a Greek owner and his family plunged over a cliff in their car and were killed, and a Turkish Sultan was deposed months after taking possession of the stone. Eventually, in 1958, after a further series of misfortunes, the Hope Diamond was given to the SMITHSONIAN INSTITUTION in Washington DC by New York jeweller HARRY WINSTON. It can be seen there today.

Hope (Blayney) Castle is undergoing renovation.

Hope Castle

Well, I never knew this
ABOUT
COUNTY MONAGHAN

Glaslough Railway Station

SIR JOHN BETJEMAN thought GLASLOUGH's tiny mock-Gothic railway station 'THE PRETTIEST STATION IN THE WORLD'.

The foremost Irish poet PATRICK KAVANAGH (1904–67) was born in Co. Monaghan in MUCKER, near INNISKEEN. His work was deeply coloured and influenced by his early experiences growing up in the moody Monaghan landscape, as the son of a shoemaker and small farmer. Many local places can be recognised from his poems and today the area is known as KAVANAGH COUNTRY. Perhaps his masterpiece was the long poem *The Great Hunger*, published in 1942, a grim and brutally realistic evocation of Irish rural life with all its suffering and deprivation. His poem 'RAGLAN ROAD' was set to music by VAN MORRISON in 1988. Kavanagh is buried in the church at Inniskeen and there is a Patrick Kavanagh Centre in the village.

The small town of CARRICKMACROSS is world-famous for its delicate LACE, first produced in 1816. It has been made here ever since by the Nuns of ST LOUIS CONVENT, from where it can still be purchased. THE SLEEVES OF PRINCESS DIANA'S WEDDING DRESS were trimmed with Carrickmacross Lace.

INNISKEEN was also the hometown of PETER RICE (1935–92), the engineer whose skills and ingenuity realised and made possible the designs of some of the world's most exciting and recognisable structures. These included SYDNEY OPERA HOUSE, the POMPIDOU CENTRE and LOUVRE PYRAMID in Paris, the LLOYD'S BUILDING in London and Japan's KANSAI INTERNATIONAL AIRPORT TERMINAL, THE LONGEST BUILDING IN THE WORLD, at just over 1 mile (1.6 km) in length, which emerged unscathed from the 1995 Kobe earthquake.

'THE HIDDEN IRELAND', a collection of historic private houses that offer accommodation and hospitality, was formed at HILTON PARK near Clones, home of the MADDEN family since the 18th century. The house is a magnificent pile restored in the 19th century after it was burned down in 1803 when a servant dropped a bucket of glowing coals after clearing out the grate. Present owner Lucy Madden is the author of *The Potato Year – 365 Ways of Cooking a Potato –* one for each day of the year.

SIR CHARLES GAVAN DUFFY (1816–1903) was born in the county town, MONAGHAN. A leading member of the YOUNG IRELAND movement with THOMAS MEAGHER (*see* Co. Waterford, page 199) and DANIEL O'CONNELL (*see* CO. Kerry, page 171), in 1842 he founded *The Nation*, IRELAND'S FIRST NATION-ALIST NEWSPAPER. Disillusioned about the prospects for reform in Ireland, he emigrated to Australia and became Prime Minister of Victoria in 1871–2. In 1891 he became the first president of the IRISH LITERARY SOCIETY.

JOHN ROBERT GREGG (1868–1948), inventor of the widely used GREGG SHORTHAND SYSTEM, was born at ROCKCORRY, near BALLYBAY in Co. Monaghan.

COUNTY TYRONE

Omagh – the County Town

Strabane

The Power of Print

STRABANE sits in a beautiful setting on the Mourne River close to the border with Co. Donegal. In Main Street is the double bow-fronted, 18th-century shop front of IRELAND'S OLDEST SURVIVING PRINT WORKSHOP, GRAY'S PRINTING PRESS, where THE MAN WHO PRINTED THE AMERICAN DECLARATION OF INDEPENDENCE, pioneer printer JOHN DUNLAP, worked his apprenticeship and learned his trade.

JOHN DUNLAP (1747–1812) emigrated to America in his teens and joined his uncle's printing business in PHILADELPHIA. One of his first enterprises when he took over the running of the business in 1771 was to publish the *Pennsylvania Packet*, which in 1784 became AMERICA'S FIRST DAILY NEWSPAPER.

In 1773 he was appointed printer to Congress and was responsible in 1776 for printing the 'DUNLAP BROADSIDES', the first copies of the DECLARATION OF INDEPENDENCE. This was signed by the President of the Congress JOHN HANCOCK, whose family hailed from Co. Down, and the Secretary of the Congress CHARLES THOMSON, born in Co. Derry

Eight of the 56 signatories of the finalised Declaration of Independence had Ulster roots:

JOHN HANCOCK, whose family came from Co. DOWN

THOMAS McKEAN, whose father came from BALLYMONEY in Co. ANTRIM

THOMAS NELSON, whose grandfather came from STRABANE

ROBERT PAINE, whose grandfather came from DUNGANNON

EDWARD RUTLEDGE, from an Ulster Presbyterian family

GEORGE TAYLOR, also from an Ulster Presbyterian family

MATTHEW THORNTON, who emigrated from DERRY, settling in New Hampshire in 1718

WILLIAM WHIPPLE, whose parents came from Co. ANTRIM

COLONEL JOHN NIXON, whose parents came from Ulster, delivered THE FIRST PUBLIC READING OF THE DOCUMENT, in Philadelphia on 8 July 1776.

JAMES WILSON, grandfather of PRESIDENT WOODROW WILSON, also worked at GRAY'S PRINTING PRESS before emigrating to America in 1807. His whitewashed thatched farmhouse cottage is practically unchanged since he lived there, and can be found at DERGALT, 2 miles

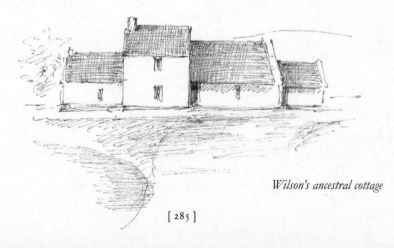

Wilson's ancestral cottage

(3 km) south-east of Strabane, on the slopes of the Sperrin Mountains. The Wilson family, who still live on the next-door farm, welcome visitors.

WOODROW WILSON (1856–1924) was 28TH US PRESIDENT and served two terms from 1913 to 1921. He led America through World War One and WAS THE FIRST US PRESIDENT TO TRAVEL TO EUROPE WHILE IN OFFICE. He was instrumental in setting up the LEAGUE OF NATIONS and won a NOBEL PEACE PRIZE in 1920.

Gray's Printing Press is now run by the National Trust.

In 1833 CECIL FRANCES HUMPHREYS (1818–95), later known as MRS CECIL FRANCES ALEXANDER, came to live at Milltown House in Strabane, now the Grammar School. In 1848, while residing in Strabane, she published her *Hymns for Little Children*, which contains some of the best-loved hymns in the English language, including 'ONCE IN ROYAL DAVID'S CITY', 'ALL THINGS BRIGHT AND BEAUTIFUL' and 'THERE IS A GREEN HILL FAR AWAY'. In 1850 she married the REV. WILLIAM ALEXANDER, and they later moved to Derry when he became Bishop of Derry. She is buried in the cemetery there.

Caledon

Six of the Best

Towards the end of the 19th century the grounds of CALEDON HOUSE, a splendid Georgian and Regency pile near Armagh, were inhabited by black bears and herds of wapiti (a kind of deer) brought here from the Wild West by the 4th Earl of Caledon.

Growing up there at the time, in what was his ancestral home, was the future FIELD MARSHAL EARL ALEXANDER OF TUNIS, born there in 1891, 3rd son of the 4th Earl. He was the youngest of six remarkable men of his generation from Ulster, three of them from Co. Tyrone, all of whom attained the rank of FIELD MARSHAL.

FIELD MARSHAL SIR ARCHIBALD MONTGOMERY-MASSINGBERD (1871–

Caledon House

1947) was wounded in the South Africa War, 1899–1902, and mentioned in despatches nine times during World War One. He was COMMANDER-IN-CHIEF SOUTHERN COMMAND, 1928–31, and CHIEF OF THE IMPERIAL GENERAL STAFF, 1933–6. His family home was BLESSINGBOURNE, near FIVEMILE-TOWN, CO. TYRONE.

FIELD MARSHAL SIR CLAUDE AUCHINLECK (1884–1981), nicknamed THE AUK, served as a General for longer than almost any other soldier in the British army. As COMMANDER-IN-CHIEF, SOUTHERN COMMAND, he prepared the way in the North Africa campaign for the triumphs of his fellow Ulsterman Montgomery and then became COMMANDER-IN-CHIEF, INDIA, being largely responsible for preparing the Indian and Pakistani armies for PARTITION in 1947. His ancestral home is CREEVENAGH HOUSE, outside OMAGH, CO. TYRONE.

FIELD MARSHAL SIR JOHN GREER DILL (1881–1944) is best remembered as the man who forged Britain's 'SPECIAL RELATIONSHIP' with the United States. Sent to Washington by Winston Churchill as CHIEF OF THE BRITISH JOINT STAFF MISSION, he established a strong rapport with GENERAL GEORGE

> *Winston Churchill coined the phrase 'special relationship' in his* 'SINEWS OF PEACE' *address in* FULTON, MISSOURI, *in 1946, where he also introduced the phrase* 'IRON CURTAIN'.

MARSHALL (of the Marshall Plan) and PRESIDENT ROOSEVELT, who described him as 'THE MOST IMPORTANT FIGURE IN THE REMARKABLE ACCORD WHICH HAS BEEN DEVELOPED IN THE COMBINED OPERATIONS OF OUR TWO COUNTRIES'. He was born in LURGAN, CO. ANTRIM, the son of a local bank manager, and is buried in ARLINGTON NATIONAL CEMETERY in Washington DC.

SIR ALAN FRANCIS BROOKE, 1ST VISCOUNT ALANBROOKE (1883–1963). At the outbreak of World War Two, Brooke was a commander in the British Expeditionary Force and played a leading role in the Dunkirk evacuation in 1940. From 1941 to 1946 he was made CHIEF OF THE IMPERIAL GENERAL STAFF and served as WINSTON CHURCHILL's foremost military adviser, responsible for the overall strategic direction of Britain's war effort. In 2001 his uncensored *War Diaries* were published, causing some lively controversy. His ancestral home is at BROOKEBOROUGH, near Enniskillen in Co. FERMANAGH, where the only diamond ever found in Ireland was discovered (*see* Co. Fermanagh, page 272).

FIELD MARSHAL VISCOUNT MONTGOMERY OF EL ALAMEIN (1887–1976) was known affectionately as 'MONTY'. He was made Commander of the British Eighth Army in North Africa on the recommendation of fellow Ulsterman ALAN BROOKE. Monty's greatest triumph was victory over Field Marshal Erwin Rommel at the BATTLE OF EL ALAMEIN in 1942. Winston Churchill said of the battle, *'This is not the end, it is not even the beginning of the end. But it is, perhaps, the end of the beginning.'* During the D-Day landings, Monty was in command of all the Allied British, American and Canadian ground forces. His father was a noted BISHOP OF TASMANIA and the Montgomery family came from MOVILLE in Co. DONEGAL.

FIELD MARSHAL 1ST EARL ALEXANDER OF TUNIS (1891–1969), born at Caledon House, was a Major-General of the BRITISH EXPEDITIONARY FORCE at the start of World War Two and controlled the DUNKIRK EVACUATION in 1940. He replaced his fellow Ulsterman AUCHINLECK as COMMANDER-IN-CHIEF SOUTHERN COMMAND and oversaw MONT-GOMERY's victory at El Alamein. After the war he was GOVERNOR-GENERAL OF CANADA from 1946 to 1952.

Well, I never knew this
ABOUT
COUNTY TYRONE

JOHN SIMPSON, the great-grandfather of PRESIDENT ULYSSES SIMPSON GRANT, was born at DERGINA, BALLYGAWLEY, in 1738. He emigrated to Pennsylvania in 1760.

Ulysses S. Grant

ULYSSES S. GRANT (1822–85) was 18TH US PRESIDENT and served two terms from 1869 to 1877. Before that he was a victorious Union General during the AMERICAN CIVIL WAR and took the surrender of Confederate Commander GENERAL ROBERT E. LEE at APPOMATTOX. The GRANT ANCESTRAL HOME, a small two-room cottage with mud floors, has been restored, and there is an adjoining visitor centre that tells the story of Ulysses S. Grant and his family.

The ULSTER AMERICAN FOLK PARK has grown up around a tiny white single-storey cottage from where the MELLON family went out to become THE RICHEST FAMILY IN THE WORLD. THOMAS MELLON emigrated to Pennsylvania with his family in 1818 when he was five years old and became a banker. His son ANDREW was Secretary of the US Treasury and Ambassador to London, and more or less built the steel town of PITTSBURGH. Mellon money funded San Francisco's GOLDEN GATE BRIDGE, the PANAMA CANAL, the

WALDORF ASTORIA HOTEL in New York – and the restoration of the

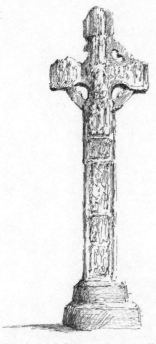

simple Irish home where it all began. The 10th-century ARDBOE HIGH CROSS, OLDEST AND TALLEST CROSS IN ULSTER and THIRD-TALLEST IN ALL IRELAND, stands at the entrance to the graveyard of ARDBOE ABBEY, founded on the shore of Lough Neagh by St Colman in the 6th century. Eighteen feet (5.6 m) high, the cross shows scenes from the Old Testament carved on one side, and from the New Testament on the other.

At CAVANACAW in the Sperrin Mountains there is THE FIRST NEW COMMERCIAL GOLD MINE IN IRELAND since the CROGHAN MOUNTAIN GOLD MINE first worked in 1795 (*see* Co. Wicklow, page 138).

The WELLBROOK BEETLING MILL at COOKSTOWN is an 18th-century water-powered linen hammer mill, ONE OF IRELAND'S LAST SURVIVING BEETLING MILLS. Beetling is the final stage of production where the linen is pounded for many hours with hammers to give it a sheen.

TYRONE CRYSTAL, one of Ireland's three great crystal makers along with Cavan and Waterford, is based at DUNGANNON.

Gazetteer

Interesting locations and places open to the public

International telephone codes are shown
For calling Republic of Ireland telephone numbers from within the
Republic of Ireland replace 353 with 0, so that for instance
+353 91 64743 becomes 091 64743
For calling Northern Ireland numbers from within the UK replace
44 with 0 – i.e. +44 28 9024 9476 becomes 028 9024 9476

NT = National Trust (*www.nationaltrust.org.uk*)

Connacht

Co. GALWAY

The Nora Barnacle House Museum,
 Bowling Green, Galway
 Tel +353 91 64743
Ballynahinch Castle (Hotel), Recess,
 Connemara
 Tel +353 95 31006
Alcock and Brown landing site and
 Marconi Transmitter station,
 Derrigimlagh Bog   3 mi. (5 km)
 s of Clifden, Connemara (sign-
 posted)
Coole Park   Off N18, 2 mi. (3 km)
 NW of Gort
 Tel +353 91 631804
Thor Ballylee   3 mi. (5 km) NE of
 Gort
 Tel +353 91 631436

Co. LEITRIM

Glencar Waterfall   Off N16, 5 mi.
 (8 km) NE of Sligo (signposted)
Creevylea Abbey   Dromohair

Co. MAYO

Moore Hall   2 mi. (3 km) SW of
 Ballyglass on shores of Lough
 Carra
Rockfleet Castle   Off N59, 2 mi.
 (3 km) NW of Newport on N
 shore of Clew Bay
Grace Kelly's Cottage   Off R311,
 2 mi. (3 km) E of Newport by
 Leg o' Mutton Lake
Bellacorrick Musical Bridge   On
 N59 at Bellacorrick 8 mi. (13 km) E
 of Bangor
National Famine Monument,
 Murrisk   On R335, 3 mi. (5 km)
 SW of Westport
Ceide Fields Visitor Centre,
 Ballycastle
 Tel +353 96 43325
Ashford Castle (Hotel), Cong
 Tel +353 94 9546003

Co. ROSCOMMON

Famine Museum, Strokestown Park,
 Strokestown
 Tel +353 71 963 3013

Clonalis House, Castlerea
  Tel +353 94 9620014
Douglas Hyde Museum   1 mi.
  (2 km) w of Frenchpark on N5

Co. SLIGO

Lissadell House, Ballinfull   5 mi.
  (8 km) w of Drumcliff
  Tel +353 87 6296928
Markree Castle (Hotel), Collooney
  8 mi. (13 km) s of Sligo
  Tel +353 71 9167800
Classiebawn Castle, Mullaghmore
  12 mi. (19 km) N of Sligo

Leinster

DUBLIN CITY

Marsh's Library, St Patrick's Close
  Tel +353 1 454 3511
Guinness Brewery, St James's Gate,
  Dublin 8
  Tel +353 1 453 6700

Co. CARLOW

Browne's Hill Dolmen   Off R726,
  2 mi. (3 km) E of Carlow
Adelaide Memorial Church, Myshall
  On R724, 3 mi. (5 km) E of Muine
  Bheag (Bagenalstown)

Co. DUBLIN

Hell Fire Club, Mount Pelier
  Off R114, SE of Tallaght
Malahide Castle
  Tel +353 1 846 2184

Co. KILDARE

Castletown House, Celbridge
  Tel +353 1 6288252

Kilkea Castle (Hotel), Castledermot
  Tel +353 59 91 45156
Straffan Steam Museum, Straffan
  Tel +353 1 627 3155
Rath of Mullaghmast, Ballitore
  w of N9
Wolfe Tone's Grave, Bodenstown
  1 mile (2 km) s of Clane
National Stud and Japanese
  Gardens, Tully
  Tel +353 45 521617

Co. KILKENNY

Kilkenny Castle
  Tel +353 56 21450
Dunmore Cave   Off N78, 3 mi.
  (5 km) N of Kilkenny
  Tel +353 56 67726
Jerpoint Abbey, Thomastown
  Tel +353 56 24623
Duiske Abbey, Graiguenamanagh
  15 mi. (24 km) sw of Kilkenny

Co. LAOIS

Killeshin and Timahoe Round
  Tower   On R426, 3 mi. (5 km)
  SE of Portlaoise
Emo Court   4 mi. (7 km) SE of
  Portarlington
  Tel +353 502 26573
Rock of Dunamase   3 mi. (5 km)
  E of Portlaoise

Co. LONGFORD

Michael Casey's Bogwood
  Workshop, Barley Harbour
  3 miles (5 km) w of
  Newtowncashel (signposted)
Corlea Iron Age Trackway Visitor
  Centre   Off R397 at Kenagh, 8
  mi. (13 km) s of Longford
Carriglas Manor   Off R194, 2 mi.

(3 km) NE of Longford
Tel +353 43 45165

Co. LOUTH

Monasterboice   Off N1, 5 mi.
(8 km) N of Drogheda
Mellifont Abbey, Cullen   6 mi.
(10 km) w of Drogheda
Tel +353 41 26459
Faughart   Off N1, 3 mi. (5 km) N of
Dundalk

Co. MEATH

Newgrange and Knowth   5 mi.
(8 km) E of Slane
Tel +353 41 24488
Hill of Slane   N of Slane (signpost-
ed)
Hill of Tara, Kilmessan   5 mi.
(8 km) E of Trim
Tel +353 46 25903
Trim Castle
Tel +353 46 37111
Battle of the Boyne centre, Oldbridge
3 mi. (5 km) w of Drogheda
Loughcrew House, Gardens and
Cairns   Off R154, 2 mi. (3 km) E
of Oldcastle
Tel +353 49 85 41356

Co. OFFALY

Charleville Forest, Tullamore
Tel +353 506 21279
Birr Castle, Birr
Tel +353 509 20056
Clonmacnoise   4 mi. (7 km) N of
Shannonbridge
Tel +353 905 74165
Rahan   6 mi. (11 km) w of
Tullamore
Clonony Castle   2 mi. (3 km) w of
Cloghan on R357

Co. WESTMEATH

Belvedere House (Jealous Wall)
Off N52, 4 mi. (7 km) s of
Mullingar
Tel +353 44 48650
Hill of Uisneach, nr Ballymore
Off R390, 10 mi. (16 km) w of
Mullingar
Fore Abbey, Fore   3 mi. (5 km) w
of Castlepollard
Tullynally Castle   2 mi. (3 km) NW
of Castlepollard
Tel +353 44 61159
Locke's Distillery, Kilbeggan
Tel +353 506 32134

Co. WEXFORD

Enniscorthy Castle
Tel +353 54 35926
Father Murphy's Home, Boolavogue,
Nr Ferns
Tel +353 54 66898
Kennedy Homestead,
Dunganstown, New Ross
Tel +353 51 388761
Hook Head Lighthouse
Tel +353 51 397055
Tintern Abbey, Saltmills, New Ross

Co. WICKLOW

Russborough House, Blessington
Tel +353 45 865239
Glendalough, Laragh
Tel +353 404 45325
Killruddery House, Bray
Tel +353 1 2867128
Powerscourt, Enniskerry
Tel +353 12046000
Tinakilly House (Hotel), Rathnew
2 mi. (3 km) N of Wicklow
Avondale House, Rathdrum
Tel +353 404 46111

Munster

Co. CLARE

Burren Perfumery, Carron
Tel +353 65 7089102
The Burren Centre, Kilfenora
Tel +353 65 7088030
Colleen Bawn's grave, Burrane
cemetery, Killimer   3 mi. (5 km)
SE of Kilrush
Spectacle Bridge   On N67, 1 mile
(2 km) S of Lisdoonvarna

Co. CORK

Blarney Castle, Blarney
Tel +353 21 385252
Jameson Heritage Centre,
Midleton
Tel +353 21 613594
Bantry House, Bantry
Tel +353 27 50047
Mizen Vision Visitor Centre,
Mizen Head
Tel +353 28 35115
Ballycrovane Ogham Stone. Beara
Peninsula   Off R571, 2 mi. (3 km)
N of Eyeries

Co. KERRY

Derrynane House, Caherdaniel
Off N70, 2 mi. (3 km) W of
Caherdaniel
Tel +353 66 9475113
Gallarus Observatory   Off R559,
5 mi. (8 km) NW of Dingle
Blennerville Windmill, Tralee
Tel +353 66 21064
Staigue Fort, Beara Peninsula
Off N70, 5 mi. (8 km) NE of
Caherdaniel

Co. LIMERICK

Foynes Flying Boat Museum
Tel +353 69 65416
Glin Castle, Glin
Tel +353 68 34173
De Valera's Cottage   1 mile (2 km)
N of Bruree

Co. TIPPERARY

Rock of Cashel, Cashel
Tel +353 62 61437
Mitchelstown Caves, Burncourt
Off N8, 8 mi. (13 km) NE of
Mitchelstown
Tel +353 52 67246
Cahir Castle, Cahir
Tel +353 52 41011
Swiss Cottage, Cahir
Tel +353 52 41144

Co. WATERFORD

Reginald's Tower, Waterford
Tel +353 51 873501
Waterford Crystal
Tel +353 373311
Ballysaggartmore Towers   Off R666,
2 mi. (3 km) W of Lismore
Lismore Castle, Lismore
Tel +353 58 54424

Ulster

BELFAST

Crown Liquor Saloon, 46 Great
Victoria Street   NT
Tel +44 28 9024 9476
Belfast City Hall, Donegal Square
Tel +44 28 9032 0202
Grand Opera House, Great Victoria
Street
Tel +44 28 9024 1919

Co. ANTRIM

Ballywillan Churchyard 1 mile
(2 km) s of Portrush on
Ballywillan Road
Old Bushmills Distillery, Bushmills
Tel +44 28 2073 3224
Carrickfergus Castle
Tel +44 28 9335 1273
Andrew Jackson Centre,
Boneybefore, Carrickfergus
Tel +44 28 9338 4927
Chester Arthur Ancestral Home,
Culleybackey 3 mi. (5 km) NW of
Ballymena
Tel +44 28 2563 8494
DeLorean Factory, Dunmurry
Industrial Estate, Dunmurry
3 mi. (5 km) sw of Belfast
Carrick-a-Rede Rope Bridge 1 mile
(2 km) E of Ballintoy on B 15

Co. ARMAGH

Armagh Observatory, College Hill,
Armagh.
Tel +44 28 3752 2928
Dan Winter's Cottage, The
Diamond, Loughgall
Tel +44 28 3885 2777
Kilnasaggart Stone 1 mile (2 km)
s of Jonesborough (signposted)
Gosford Castle, Markethill 5 mi.
(8 km) SE of Armagh
Tel +44 28 3755 1277
Derrymore House, Bessbrook, nr
Newry NT
Tel +44 28 8778 4753

Co. CAVAN

Shannon Pot Off R206 on western
slopes of Cuilcagh Mountain
15 mi. (24 km) sw of Enniskillen
(signposted)

Cloughoughter Castle On island in
Lough Oughter, 3 mi. (5 km) w of
Cavan (signposted)
Life Force Mill, Mill Road, Cavan
Town
Tel +353 49 436 2722
Cavan Crystal, Cavan Town
Tel +353 49 433 1800

Co. DERRY

Amelia Earhart Centre, Racecourse
Road, Ballyarnet Off B194 road
to Muff
Tel +44 28 7135 4040
Mussenden Temple, Castlerock
NT
Tel +44 28 7084 8728
Abhartach's Sepulchre, Slaughtaverty
In a field off B64 between
Garvagh and Dungiven 2 mi.
(3 km) w of Garvagh

Co. DONEGAL

Rathmullen Heritage Centre
Tel +353 74 915 8131
Station Island, Lough Derg
Tel +353 71 986 1518
Tory Island (Hotel)
Tel +353 74 913 5920
Glenveagh Castle On shores of
Lough Gortan at Churchill 15 mi.
(24 km) NW of Letterkenny
Tel +353 74 37088

Co. DOWN

Hillsborough Fort, The Square,
Hillsborough
Tel +44 28 9268 3285
Castle Ward, Strangford NT
Tel +44 28 4488 1204
Helen's Tower, Clandeboye Estate
On coast 3 mi. (5 km) w of Bangor

Co. FERMANAGH

Caldragh Cemetery, Boa Island, northern end of Lower Lough Erne   Off A47. Near east bridge connecting Boa island to the mainland

Crom Castle Estate, Upper Lough Erne, Newtownbutler   NT
Tel +44 28 6773 8118

Castle Coole, Enniskillen   NT
2 mi. (3 km) SE of Enniskillen
Tel +44 6632 2690

Florence Court   8 mi. (13 km) SW of Enniskillen, off A32
Tel +44 6634 8249

Marble Arch Caves   4 mi. (7 km) w of Florence Court
Tel +44 28 6634 8855

Belleek Pottery Visitor Centre, Belleek   5 mi. E of Ballyshannon
Tel +44 28 6865 9300

Co. MONAGHAN

Castle Leslie, Glaslough
Tel +44 870 050 3232

Co. TYRONE

Gray's Printing Press, 49 Main Street, Strabane   NT
Tel +44 28 718 80055

Ulysses S. Grant Ancestral Home, Dergina, Ballygawley
13 mi. (21 km) w of Dungannon
Tel +44 28 8776 7259

Wellbrook Beetling Mill   Off A505, 4 mi. (7 km) w of Cookstown (signposted)
Tel +44 28 8674 8210

Tyrone Crystal, Dungannon (signposted)
Tel +44 28 8772 5335

Ulster American Folk Park   Off A5, 3 mi. (5 km) N of Omagh
Tel +44 28 8224 3292

Index of People

Index of Places

Acknowledgments

I would like to thank Hugh Montgomery Massingberd for his guidance and wise counsel and my agent, Ros Edwards, for her patience, help and support.

Also Harry and Joan McDowell, Michael and Teresa Fewer and Patrick and Caroline Pilkington.

My special thanks to the home team at Ebury, Carey Smith, Natalie Hunt and Caroline Newbury, for their dedication, hard work and enthusiasm. Also Steve Cox for his sensitive editing, Peter Ward for his inspired design and David Eldridge at Two Associates for all his help.

And my love, admiration and gratitude to Mai Osawa.